UNPLUGGED

UNPLUGGED

ADVENTURES FROM MTV TO TIMBUKTU

TOM FRESTON

GALLERY BOOKS

New York Amsterdam/Antwerp London
Toronto Sydney/Melbourne New Delhi

G

Gallery Books
An Imprint of Simon & Schuster, LLC
1230 Avenue of the Americas
New York, NY 10020

First Gallery Books hardcover edition November 2025

Interior design by Hope Herr-Cardillo

Manufactured in the United States of America

10 9 8 7 6 5 4 3 2 1

Library of Congress Control Number: 2025932829

ISBN 978-1-6680-8979-8
ISBN 978-1-6680-8981-1 (ebook)

For my sons, Andrew and Gil,
and in memory of my brother, Bill

CONTENTS

PROLOGUE

HARPOONED

Sometime in the mid-nineties, the heavy metal band Anthrax sent me a small chain saw. They'd all autographed it. It was a more useful gift than a platinum album or tour jacket—I had a few closets' worth of those—and I proudly kept the signed chain saw on display in my New York office, on the fifty-second floor of 1515 Broadway. From that space, perched high above Times Square, I ran the entertainment giant Viacom, which included MTV Networks, BET, and Paramount Pictures.

My eyes focused on that chain saw on a hot Tuesday afternoon in 2006. I was trying to fill an empty banker's box with a few important or sentimental items before I left that office for the last time. I spotted a framed picture of Sumner Redstone, Chairman of Viacom, outside of UCLA's Pauley Pavilion before the 1993 MTV Video Music Awards. Sumner was covering up a smile as he stood under a large homemade banner that read "Repent MTV Scum," held aloft by two Holy Rollers, one in a "Jesus Saves" T-shirt.

It had been less than twenty-four hours since the now eighty-three-year-old Sumner had fired me in his Beverly Hills mansion, amid a battery of huge fish tanks that lined the walls of his living room. I felt like I was being taken out in an aquarium, harpooned by a mad Captain Ahab. I had not seen it coming.

I had entered the company in 1980 as the marketing guy at the start-up that would become MTV, rising to president in 1986. Then, for seventeen years, I held the position of CEO of MTV Networks, the sun in Viacom's solar system. In that role, I ran MTV, Nickelodeon, Comedy Central, VH1, and other cable TV networks. In 2004, I became co-president of Viacom and added Paramount Pictures and the publisher Simon & Schuster to my portfolio. Two years later, I was made the CEO of Viacom and Sumner's personally designated successor. But no more. Now I stood in our Manhattan office tower one last time, defeated, picking up a few pieces from what had been a euphoric, twenty-six-year run. The job, in all its incarnations, had been the center of my life.

I knew with 100 percent certainty when I took over as CEO of Viacom that I would eventually be fired. Redstone had fired both of my predecessors, good men, arguably more talented than I. But when I was offered the job, I had to go for it. Running a Fortune 500 company is the career gold ring.

I should have had a clue that the axe was coming. Sumner Redstone liked to fire people on holiday weekends. The last two took their bullets on a Fourth of July and a Memorial Day weekend; mine was on Labor Day.

I had only been fired once before. Back in 1970, I was a bartender on St. Thomas in the Virgin Islands. I made perfect daiquiris and other rum conconctions, but the owner wanted to give my job to a friend of his who had just gotten out of prison. "Ex-cons deserve a second chance," he told me. Who was I to argue? I hopped on my motorcycle and, as I rode into town, a bird shit on me. I've been told bird shit is good luck. Plenty of luck lay ahead.

This time around, it wasn't an ex-con taking my slot; it was Sumner's estate attorney, Philippe Dauman, a colorless, balding man with a mortician's demeanor and a penchant for gold cuff links, who liked to tell everyone that, as a teenager, he had gotten perfect scores on the SATs. A few years later, after Dauman had hollowed out the company, Sumner dusted him, too. But that was in the future. For now, my goal was to sneak out of the building with my dignity intact. No bad-mouthing or whining, just me, my cardboard box, and a chain saw.

There was no getting around that I was deeply embarrassed. On Redstone's CEO firing scoreboard, I'd set a new speed record: eight months on the job. I had solid plans for the company and was just getting warmed up. The part of me that suffered from impostor syndrome and wondered if I had really earned my success whispered that I was being unmasked at last. Now I just hoped that none of my people would see me go.

I took a last look around, said goodbye to my long-serving assistant, Diane, and got into an elevator. But when the doors opened on the first floor, I couldn't get out. The cavernous 1515 Broadway lobby was jammed wall-to-wall with people. I thought it must be a fire drill. Instead, it was a flash mob of employees gathering spontaneously—for me.

Later, CNBC said there were over a thousand people. They were chanting, "Tom! Tom! Tom!" and the occasional "Fuck Sumner!" It was a rolling, thunderous ovation. You'd think I had just won the Super Bowl. My people were giving me a hero's send-off. Hands were extending to touch me as I tried to work my way through the crowd. A couple of people had tears in their eyes. Everything seemed to be in slow motion.

In a quarter of a century, I had built a multibillion-dollar company with this cast of clever, crazy, and creative characters. Ours was an eccentrically organized operation full of life, fun, and hard work. We helped shape popular culture around the world and brought joy to hundreds of millions of people. Looking into the faces that I had worked with, traveled with, and sometimes fought with, now pressed shoulder to shoulder, it started to sink in: They didn't just respect me as a boss. They actually loved me. And I loved them. And I was leaving forever.

The ovation went on and on, making me self-conscious about all the affection coming my way. I fought back tears, telling myself not to exit a crybaby. Slowly, I reached the escalator, and descended into Times Square. People followed me out the door onto Broadway. I flagged down a taxi, threw my stuff inside, and made my final escape. As I looked back at the group now gathered on the curb, waving and chanting my name, "Tom! Tom! Tom!" I considered how much nicer an exit this had been than other chapters of my life. I snuck out of Kabul, Afghanistan, on the cusp of a communist coup and smuggled tens of thousands of dollars of contraband from Canada into the US down the St. Lawrence River. I'd survived all that. I'd certainly survive this.

There would be new adventures ahead.

CHAPTER ONE

NEW FRONTIER

Decades don't start on time. I turned eighteen on the very day that President Kennedy was assassinated. At 1:30 p.m., when Kennedy was shot in Dallas, I was coming out of a college Western Civilization class. My birthday was forgotten. We rushed to the dorm in shock and turned on the lone television. Years later, historians and social critics would suggest that the real 1960s began with Kennedy's assassination. The Beatles arrived later that winter, and within a year, the World War II generation was prematurely superseded by their anxious, rebellious kids. My adult life and the true 1960s started arm in arm. I had no idea what was coming.

If the baby boom began with the first children born to the veterans returning from World War II, then I must be among the first boomers. My dad, Thomas Freston Jr., fought with the navy in the Pacific. He drove a landing craft used for amphibious assaults on Japanese-controlled islands. A ramp in the front would drop and the soldiers would charge out. These were grisly assaults—often as many as half of the men were cut down right away. Dad was a hero. He fought in Saipan and other epic battles, but, eventually, he went into what was euphemistically called "shell shock." He was sent to a hospital in Hawaii and spent the last year of the war as a ninety-pound ghost of his six-foot-two self. He was released, married my mom, settled into a house in the suburbs, and never went anywhere again. Looking back, it's clear he suffered from post-traumatic stress disorder, but we had no words for it then.

The one family trip we ever took was to the other end of Connecticut from our home in Rowayton. One hot August day, Dad drove my brother, my mom, and me up the coast to Mystic Seaport. We saw some smelly old whaling ships and were back home by 7 p.m., Dad's happy hour. He mixed a martini, went into his den, and cued up the soundtrack to *South Pacific.*

Dad kept it all inside. We never heard one word about his war experiences. We'd all watch the TV series *Victory at Sea* together on Sunday nights, and I'd ask him questions about combat, but I never got a peep out of him.

My father was a commuter, riding the New Haven Railroad in and out of New York City every day. He worked in public relations at a paper company. We got free paper bags for our school lunches. Dad had a quick wit and extraordinary social skills. He was a driven man and ambitious, but not obnoxiously so. Like many of his peers, he was satisfied to have a steady job. His real life was with us and with an eccentric group of creative friends right out of *Mad Men*—art directors, cartoonists, and copywriters. My younger brother, Bill, and I spent many Saturday nights in our bedroom trying to watch *Sea Hunt* over the din of laughter and conversation from a living room filled with noise, cigarette smoke, and cocktails.

Underneath his cheerful demeanor, Dad would go through unexplained dark periods. Some nights when he came home, Mom would tell us to leave him alone, just say a quick hello and disappear. He'd sit quietly with his martini.

My father was not much of a ball thrower or source of life advice. Three valuable exceptions were imbuing me early on with the virtues of good manners, proper dress, and earning my own money. I bought a used lawn mower for $40 when I was fourteen and made a small fortune mowing lawns in the neighborhood. I started a local newspaper that I printed on a toy printing press. I painted houses and shoveled snow. At sixteen, I stocked shelves at the Grand Union after school, and in the summer, I got a job for $1 per hour as an umbrella boy at the nearby Wee Burn Beach Club. There, I met actual rich kids. It was a world where parents bought their children brand-new cars. That seemed incredible to me. As for school, I never put in much effort. Grades came easily, and I coasted.

My mother, Winifred, or Winny, was sweet and cheerful, the classic 1950s stay-at-home mom. She was by nature a caretaker and especially protective of my father. Before they married, she had worked as a secretary and a model. Both my parents came from once well-to-do families who were financially devastated by the Great Depression. My folks had grown up with disappointment and accepted hard work and sacrifice as the price of living.

Dad had paid $16,000 for our two-bedroom house that backed up on a creek. He thought it was heaven. Rowayton was forty miles east of New York City on Long Island Sound; on a clear day, you could see the Empire State Building from the beach. But I hardly ever visited Manhattan. Rowayton was a mostly blue-collar community next to the fancier towns of Darien and New Canaan. There were no Black people, and no Jews or Italians, either, as far as I knew. My consciousness was low enough that I did not think it odd.

Bill and I shared a bedroom. We lived a mostly *Leave It to Beaver* childhood. There were woods to explore, a pebbly beach where we'd cover ourselves with Coppertone and flirt with girls, and ponds and rivers that froze in the winter where I passed entire days skating in the cold air. I loved to read. Dad would bring home six New York City newspapers every day and would explain the editorial differences between them. I read the Hardy Boys mystery books and built an extensive stamp collection, specializing on ones from exotic faraway lands: the Belgian Congo, French Morocco, Zanzibar.

Dad and Mom were hardcore Catholics: confession, Latin Mass, Sunday school, and catechism class, holy days of obligation, and no meat on Fridays. I had the strictest curfew in town. Sometimes, I had to be home earlier than the girls I dated, which was humiliating.

My high school buddies applied to Colgate and Yale, but Dad insisted I go to a Catholic college—he didn't care which one. I was a high school hockey player, and I figured if I went to college in northern New England, I could be on the hockey team. Turned out my college, St. Michael's, had no indoor hockey rink. I was seventeen and details were not yet my strong suit. When I waved goodbye to my folks and got on the Greyhound bus from Norwalk, Connecticut, to Burlington, Vermont, it was the first trip I had ever taken by myself. I would never really come home again. I was escaping the conformity of suburban life and my parents' tight restrictions.

As soon as I arrived at college, I needed to find a job. My father had agreed to pay my tuition, but I had to cover my room and board and living expenses. I started as a dishwasher in the college cafeteria, rose to headwaiter, and ran the entire operation in my junior and senior years. But the most fun I had was when I befriended guys in local rock bands and began booking their gigs. In Burlington, there were always plenty of fraternity parties eager for bands to belt out "Louie, Louie" and hits from the British Invasion into the wee hours.

I started hosting parties. I would rent an empty hall, hire a band, and buy some beer. Once, I booked Tom Rush, a popular folk singer from Cambridge, Massachusetts, and the first professional musician I would ever meet. He walked in wearing a buckskin jacket and boots. Frye boots, he told me. I bought a pair on Monday.

I also sold "college cards" to new freshmen every year. The cards entitled them to discounts at movies and local shops. These cards made me thousands of dollars over my college career. When I graduated, I took a big pay cut.

The sixties before Kennedy was killed were pretty much an extension of the fifties. The underground literary rumblings of the Beats, the folk music revival, and the new pop art movement were distant. Bob Dylan had just blown into Greenwich Village, but I had no idea. Folk music to me was the tidy Kingston Trio singing, "Hang down your head, Tom Dooley."

My main connection to the bigger New York City culture was through Top 40 radio. From sixth grade on, I was addicted to the fast-talking deejays like Murray the K (who my father called Murray Decay) and the crazy collision of music from doo-wop and Duane Eddy to "My Boyfriend's Back." Music animated almost every aspect of my teenage years, and I had an encyclopedic knowledge of the singers and their hits. I never would have believed that this sort of knowledge would be useful in my adult career.

CHAPTER TWO

LAKE GEORGE

"Coming through! Coming through!" I heard the voice shouting above the rumble of a motorcycle. I turned around to see Tom Malone, a classmate at St. Mike's, atop a brand-new Triumph Bonneville. It was early September 1964, the start of our sophomore year.

"Hey, Freston! How was your summer?"

"So-so," I said. "I was back in Connecticut. What about you?"

"Best summer ever! I worked in Lake George, an hour north of Albany. It was wild. Motorcycle gangs, rich girls in speedboats, lots of musicians, and other cool folks. First, always spend your summers in resort towns. Tourists are in a good mood and spend a lot of cash; you can make plenty for yourself. And Tom, there are so many girls."

Now he really had my attention.

Lake George is a slender thirty-two-mile body of clear water that snakes its way through the wilds of the Adirondack Mountains. Lake George Village sits on its southern shore. In the spring of 1965, before the season started, I wrangled an introduction to a Mr. Greenberg, the owner of the Georgian Inn, the most expensive establishment in town, where the high rollers stayed, the colorful crowd of gamblers that came in August for the horse races at Saratoga. Mr. Greenberg offered me a coveted job as a bell-hop. I spent my days driving a Vespa around the property, taking people to their rooms, and getting them whatever they needed. I made $300 to $400 a week in tips, a fortune then. Every guest seemed to carry big wads of cash. You just had to say hello, and they'd peel off a fiver. Overtipping was part of their ethos. Bring them a *Wall Street Journal* that cost a dime, they'd tip five bucks. There was a rumor that one of them, after throwing back a few drinks, started tipping his fellow guests.

Mr. Greenberg was a showman and a bigot. His costume was a patterned short-sleeved shirt, always untucked to allow his belly to drape over his baggy tweed pants. His stage was the reception desk. His role was to fill the hotel with what he considered the ideal clientele, Civil Rights Act be damned. Watching him work was an ongoing lesson in racism, insult, ripping off, and swindling. He was a rich man on a rampage, with no regard for others, a type new to me, but one that I would encounter again and again in life.

I rented a run-down wooden Victorian home on the lake's rural east side, between two loud roadhouse bars, smack-dab in the vortex of the action. It was on the shores of Lake George that I got my first eye-opener into the protocols of the rapidly advancing sexual revolution, which was indeed in full swing at the lake. The sex could not have been more casual. When a bar was closing, a woman that I might not have even talked to would slide up and invite herself over. There were no parents keeping track of me, no priests doling out penance.

Those summer seasons at Lake George also could not have had a better soundtrack—folk, rock, and soul music. An overlooked effect of the Beatles and the British Invasion was the rise of many excellent regional bands. A few of these bands wrote their own material and left their garages and church halls to play in new venues popping up across the country. Like the Asbury Park, New Jersey, or the Virginia Beach scene, Lake George became a mecca for the best of them. They held down the stages in the tourist clubs. Two bands would play alternating sets until 3 a.m. After that, they would head to parties at someone's lake house or order the $1.29 breakfast at the twenty-four-hour Tad's Steak House.

The hottest band in the summer of '65 was the Show Stoppers. I'd cough up the dollar cover charge and two-drink minimum and stay late into the evening. These musicians had skills, but I was struck by all the fun they had, riffing back and forth, cracking jokes, generally ecstatic to get paid for making music.

We had sex and we had rock and roll. What about drugs, the third leg of the sixties stool? I was introduced to marijuana that summer by Gimpy, part of the high-flying Aspen crowd that migrated to Lake George every summer. Gimpy was the town's first pot dealer. His sales pitch was simple: He'd pull out a small brown bag and hold it up. "This is a nickel bag, Tom. That's marijuana in here. Dealers would charge you five dollars for it; a 'nickel,' get it?"

I had heard about "grass," and now here it was. It looked like oregano. This was the old-fashioned, mild Mexican marijuana of yesteryear. In 1965, I knew no one who had smoked weed. Even the Beatles had only lit up for the first time months earlier when Bob Dylan introduced it to them.

Gimpy licked two Zig-Zag cigarette papers together. He sprinkled in the grass and carefully rolled it up, explaining, "This here is a joint. Some call it a reefer." Gimpy lit it up and showed me how to inhale.

It took some time, but a subtle calm came over me. I had heard that pot made music sound better. When I got in my car, the first song on the radio was "I'm Henry the VIII, I Am" by Herman's Hermits, a terrible song. But even Peter Noone sounded better on marijuana. I found it subtle, pleasant, and innocent. I know it's not for everyone, but it sure seemed to make a lot of things more fun.

My education really began at Lake George. Those summers taught me more about my possibilities than I ever picked up at school. Lake George was where I got my first whiff that life could be a lot more interesting off the main track, forging a less conformist path. I picked up hints of that from musicians I hung with along with an up-and-coming magician named Ricky Jay. Ricky, a roommate for a while, was a sweet, elf-like twenty-two-year-old with a beard and hair halfway down his back, a dead ringer for Rasputin. He would go on to be the greatest sleight-of-hand artist in the world. He was the first person I knew who possessed true greatness, one of the precious few who soared above the rest of us.

The highest level of the free-spirited social class at the lake were the Aspen guys. They were older, more handsome, and funnier. They drove motorcycles and seemed to have a monopoly on the best-looking women. They were ski bums or bartenders or clever schemers. They were the first bohemian wanderers I ever met. Their career path was not to have one.

One group would drive back and forth to Colorado to fill up a big truck with Coors beer, which was unavailable in the East. They made it sound like some exotic new brew and would charge triple the price and sell out. People drank it up. Marketing, it's always marketing.

By the 1967 season, I had moved on to bartending, a trade that can serve you well in a rambling life. If you know your stuff, you can always get work. It keeps you off the streets at night, saves you money, and is a nice way to meet girls. I worked at a place called the Station, a former railroad station. The owner, my friend Bill Dow, hired a house band, the Oz & Ends from Ithaca, and what looked like a full football team as bouncers. They'd stand on picnic tables and scan the crowd looking for trouble. When a fight erupted, they'd break it up and carry the fighters away in headlocks, throwing them out the front door like in a Western. The crowd would cheer. The band played on. The show never stopped. I once helped book Chuck Berry to play for a big weekend. He pulled up in a rent-a-car by himself and demanded cash in a bag before he'd take the stage.

Every good scene seems to contain the seeds of its own destruction. The bubble around Lake George was punctured by the dark events of 1968: the assassinations, the riots, the Vietnam War protests, the nasty Nixon campaign. Undesirable types began to appear, with nicknames like "Animal" and "Swine." Wannabe Hells Angels roared in, bringing harder drugs, especially speed, and real violence. A woman I knew was brutally raped and killed in the woods behind the house I had lived in.

The time had come to switch locations, but I also had a bigger issue to face: I was of prime draft age and there was a war raging on the other side of the world.

CHAPTER THREE

DEFERRED

Most Americans couldn't show you Vietnam on a map in 1960, but by 1967 Vietnam had colonized our imaginations. For most young men, the war itself was not the central obsession. Our obsession was the draft. The draft was personal. It followed you everywhere, closing off options and influencing all your plans and choices. The draft could swoop in and snatch you away for at best two years of forced servitude. The worst possibility was death. Because of the draft, I made choices I would not have made if I had been free to coast through my twenties.

I got my first draft card in 1963. I was proud and laminated it right away. A draft card was a badge of honor, a sign of the end of adolescence. A year later, watching college kids set fire to their draft cards on TV, I thought, *Why the hell would anyone burn their draft card? How do they expect to get into bars?*

At the time, my father and much of the population thought those draft resisters were cowards or communists. But in early 1966, I watched Muhammad Ali, the heavyweight boxing champion of the world, tell America he wasn't going: "I ain't got no quarrel with them Viet Cong," he said. I nodded. No quarrels from me, either. And I considered myself a patriotic American. I came to college a fan of the conservative columnist William F. Buckley. For American Catholics of the World War II generation, Buckley was the flip side of JFK, the wealthy Irish Catholic who could outtalk the snobby Protestants. I even had a subscription to Buckley's magazine, the *National Review*.

My politics came out of the libertarian corner. What I wanted from the government was to be left alone. I read Ayn Rand and Milton Friedman, who said the draft was akin to slavery. I was all in with Milton. His ideas on the sanctity of personal freedom were a siren call to me. The Beats, my new literary heroes Ginsberg, Kerouac, and Ferlinghetti—the apostles of exploration and freedom—sided with the libertarians. While you'd never see Rand and Friedman at San Francisco's beatnik City Lights Bookstore, this odd cohort was unanimous about one thing: conscription was abhorrent.

Libertarianism (and let's be honest, self-preservation) brought me into the anti-war movement. Most of my college classmates supported the war, if the subject came up at all. The Johnson administration had framed it in black and white: a democratic ally of the US, South Vietnam was being invaded by a communist army backed by the Red Chinese. It took a lot of reading to figure out that South Vietnam was a Western construct, a jury-rigged government propped up to stop the people of Vietnam from electing as their leader the war hero Ho Chi Minh, who was a communist.

By 1967, I was on a collision course with my draft board. My last student deferment would expire when I graduated college. I could be picked off by the end of that summer. Draft calls were reaching forty thousand a month. That's a small city's worth of cannon fodder every thirty days. By the time I picked up my diploma, fifteen thousand Americans had been killed, including two of my hometown friends. Other kids I knew had been drafted and were already fighting.

I didn't have the guts to burn my draft card. I figured I'd have to serve eventually. The goal was to postpone it as long as possible. The government kept telling us the war would be won any day. My ambition was to stay out of the army until peacetime returned.

Of course, one could sign up for an officer training program and hope to be posted to some warehouse in Germany. Or pull some strings to get into the National Guard, like George W. Bush. You could always defect to Canada like the folk singer Jesse Winchester. Or take the conscientious objector route like Ali.

The draft dodger's tool kit had many options. You could claim to be a homosexual like Lou Reed. You could become a missionary like Mitt

Romney. Get married and crank out a couple of children like Dick Cheney. Get a psychiatrist to say you were crazy like James Taylor. Others complained they suffered mightily from hard-to-detect medical ailments. Donald Trump had bone spurs. Joe Biden claimed asthma. Bill Clinton wrote his senator an impassioned letter saying he hated the war as much as he hated racism. But the most popular choice in the mid-sixties for young men wishing to postpone their military obligations was simple: just keep going to school.

Vietnam was a boon for graduate schools and the well-to-do who could afford them. But I was not about to become a doctor or dentist or lawyer. One day someone I worked with in the college cafeteria suggested, "How about graduate business school, Freston? Go get an MBA."

"MBA?" Never heard the word. I was amazed that you could actually go to graduate school for business. MBAs were uncommon in those days.

Business school it would be. New York University had an impressive program, an interesting faculty, and it was in the Big Apple. But it couldn't offer me a much-needed scholarship. "If you want to be a 'professional student,' that's on your dime," my dad told me. I figured I'd hustle the money somehow.

New York in 1967 might have been filthy and crime-ridden with dog shit scattered all over the sidewalks, but to me it was glorious. It was also cheap. I found a friend from college who had a fourth-floor rent-controlled apartment on East 58th Street. Two bedrooms, $90 a month. We called it, with good reason, the Roach Motel. There was a Ray's Pizza around the corner—twenty-five cents a slice and a dime for a Coke. A delicious dinner set you back sixty cents. The subway: twenty cents. A big night out had begun, and you had not broken a dollar.

In those last days of the "Summer of Love," it seemed like I had entered some new, weird America, centered around Greenwich Village, the town square of the ascendant counterculture. The scuzzy three-block stretch around 8th Street and Sixth Avenue was a delight. First came a man who looked like Jesus, who sat on a towel and sold elaborate hash pipes, lining them up on the fender of a parked car. Then came my first Hare Krishna unit, commanding a piece of sidewalk to jump up and down and chant, shaking tambourines. *Who thought that up?* I wondered. Beyond the Hare Krishnas was a custom leather shop and an army-navy store selling peacoats and bandoliers. Around the corner was a gay Howard Johnson's. Some weekends there were "Psychedelic Block Parties." They'd close off a three-block stretch of St. Mark's Place to traffic. People in full hippie regalia would mill in the streets and hang out on the tenement fire escapes dropping daisies and blowing up helium balloons. I absorbed my NYU business and marketing classes through the filter of the bohemian culture in which I was living. I was interested in how entrepreneurs were catching these cultural changes to start new kinds of businesses. Here we had, in marketing parlance, a new demographic—one interested in new clothing styles, music, sexual liberation, civil rights, independent cinema, drugs, and left-of-center politics. I wondered who would be the visionaries to start businesses for this crowd.

On East 9th Street was "the Head Shop," not yet a generic term. The Head Shop and its imitators sold anything a pothead needed: rolling papers, bongs, roach clips, everything but the pot. What they were really selling was the whole hippie lifestyle. Want a poster or Day-Glo paint or black lights? Cheap hoop earrings, Indian scarves, or tunics called kurtas? Flavored condoms or edible underwear? This was your spot. You could also buy underground newspapers. Most were sloppy and amateurish, but perfect for the time. By the end of 1967, a young San Francisco entrepreneur, Jann Wenner, would consolidate all these bits and pieces about music, politics, and social philosophy into one professional publication: *Rolling Stone*.

As for nightspots, the leading players were the Dom and the Electric Circus located on St. Mark's Place. The Dom was the downstairs of a former Polish social hall. Andy Warhol and Paul Morrissey ran it and hired the Velvet Underground as the house band in 1966. Drinks were fifty cents. A mash-up of Warhol's films was projected onto the stage and onto the Velvets. Their dark, droning sound and their lyrics about heroin and sadomasochism, with the overlay of Warhol films, personified the New York avant-garde of the era.

The Electric Circus tried to capture the wilder, more experimental spirit of the moment. This was where you went to smoke pot or drop acid. The inside was like entering a big Moroccan tent. Trapeze artists, jugglers, and face painters mixed it up with the customers. Strobe lights pulsated, and home movies and experimental videos were projected all over the walls. The first time I maneuvered myself inside, the Chambers Brothers were singing, and a guy in a gorilla suit handed me a joint and said, "Welcome to New York."

The Village didn't just have counterculture, it was heavily politicized—the epicenter for Vietnam War resistance. The American Communist Party ran a recruitment table in the middle of Washington Square Park. This stunned me. I thought commies were illegal. But here they were, sitting down like respectable people behind piles of pamphlets. There were a couple of cute young women manning the table, including one in a Che Guevara outfit. I kept walking by trying to get her attention. She smiled back at me, so I plopped down.

"How's business? Signing up any interesting new comrades?" I began, like a jerk. She said there was a good deal of interest and went on and on about it, and I sensed some interest in me. She was a political science major. I asked if there were many communists on the faculty. "Is it infiltrated?" She smiled again. "Well, there are a few communists, yes, good ones, too. But I would categorize them more as 'tenured' than 'infiltrators.' Their classes are popular. A revolution is coming, you know."

"Yeah, I'm on the lookout for that. I don't want my few assets to be nationalized."

"What school are you in?" she asked. Innocently, I said, "I am about to begin at the graduate business school." I thought she was going to barf.

"You're serious? Right now, in Greenwich Village, you're learning how to become a capitalist?"

I realized then that I better be delicate in talking about business school. I was evolving. Going forward, I would know when to bite my tongue. For the next two years, I would straddle a dual existence—the bustling, creative life I enjoyed at nightclubs and galleries and the business life I was preparing for in grad school. I would straddle those two worlds for my entire career.

NYU's graduate business school was in Nichols Hall, located a block from the American Stock Exchange on Trinity Place. What looked like the largest hole in history was being dug behind my ten-story campus. I spent my time there watching the World Trade Center rise.

Until graduate school, I had never really applied myself as a student. But at NYU, the work was much more challenging, my peers were smarter, and if I flunked out, I'd be in the army.

Tuition was my major worry. I was able to hustle a student loan for $500 from the Knights Templar Educational Foundation. I got a job bartending at Your Father's Mustache, a grim franchise place on Seventh Avenue and 10th Street where mostly drunken people from Boston sang along with a Dixieland band. I wore a red-and-white-striped shirt. I'd get out of work close to 3 a.m. some nights. I studied my ass off. I got straight A's that first semester, six for six. I reapplied for a scholarship, and my last three semesters were on the house.

Something profound changed in me along the way. I loved the classes. My professors were the best I'd ever had. One was Peter Drucker, the preeminent management guru of the time. Drucker whittled the purpose of a business down to its simplest goal: to create a customer. He felt America needed a more entrepreneurial society where innovation was steady and continuous.

Entrepreneurs, he taught, do not so much create change as exploit changes that have already happened. A successful entrepreneur would look and listen for these opportunities. Drucker felt innovation and creative marketing were the key functions of a business. I have watched those lessons play out ever since.

At NYU, I was aware that I did not have the skills of artists; I was not a painter or a musician. But I could think creatively and cleverly. I deduced I could prosper and be happy as an entrepreneur working around creative people on something I loved.

But as soon as I had come to this realization, the rug was pulled out from under me. One morning I learned that the Selective Service System announced there would be no more draft deferments for graduate students. In May, I'd be back in the draft pool. My classmates were shocked, but I was not defeated. There had to be a way to let me finish my second year. There were the various reserve options, Army Reserve, National Guard, Coast Guard, but a person needed exceptional connections to get into any of these outfits. If you were lucky enough to get a reserve spot, you had six months of boot camp. Then years and years of meetings. So, even if I got in, my studies would be interrupted. Only the Naval Reserve had a slower start:

a year of meetings to start, then two years of active duty. The Naval Reserve would allow me to graduate. I knew only one person who'd been a military officer, Bill Dow up in Lake George, an officer in the Naval Reserve's Glens Falls, New York, unit. Every Naval Reserve unit needs a ship to train on. Bill had the unusual distinction of owning that ship—the MV *Ticonderoga*, his sleek 168-foot-long motor vessel, which ferried tourists up and down Lake George. It had sailed with the Pacific fleet in the last year of World War II.

Bill pulled a string, and I got inducted into the navy in 1968, Seaman Third Class Thomas Freston. I cut my hair, got the uniform, and twice a month made the trek—six hours each way by Greyhound bus—from New York City to Glens Falls for meetings. I'd go up on the morning bus and come back late the same night. I would study for my classes on the ride.

I was not popular with the enlisted men in my unit. I had cut the line, and they knew it. The chief petty officer, our leader, detested me. My name tag clearly said "Freston," but he continually called me "Frunston." I'd be kept after meetings to clean out the bathrooms.

As the end of business school drew near, I'd become increasingly alienated about the war and the political situation and wondered if I had examined every option for avoiding boot camp and a sailor's life. I did not know a doctor, but I knew a medical student. Mike was the fiancé of my next-door neighbor's sister. I called him, and we met at the NYU medical school cafeteria.

"Mike," I said, "I'm in the navy now, finishing school, and will be off to active duty in the summer. But I have some family medical history that might keep me from active duty."

"Like what?" he asked.

"Well, my mother has a bad case of colitis, and it really bothers her periodically. And my father had severe shell shock in World War Two. I might have inherited either colitis or some nasty nervous condition."

"You never seemed that nervous to me. But colitis can be serious. Let me get you the name of a good gastroenterologist."

I went to see a doctor on East 68th Street. We talked and he examined me and was concerned. He did some unpleasant tests and came back with a diagnosis: irritable colitis. "You can get over this. It may not be with you for your entire life, but I am going to recommend you go immediately on a strict diet and ask you to take it easy."

"How long will this diet last, Doctor?"

"Could be six months. Maybe years. Let's not take any chances."

Then I let it out. "It's going to be hard to follow this as I go on active duty in the navy in three months."

"Oh, no way can you go in the military. Impossible," he said. "I'll write you a note for that." Those were the magic words. I turned the note in to my chief petty officer up in Glens Falls. He thought it was bullshit (it had that smell), but he had to hand it in. I was suspended from further meetings. No more Greyhound trips.

On a sunny April day, I was summoned to the St. Albans Naval Hospital in Queens for an examination by a navy doctor. I was led through a ward of wall-to-wall Vietnam casualties, many in terrible condition and missing limbs. The doctor, a crew-cut marine, was not sympathetic at all. "If you think you have problems, take another look around the ward you just walked through, son," he barked. "Look at these poor bastards." It was my first direct experience of the waste this terrible war was visiting on my generation.

After preliminary tests and yet another unpleasant examination, he said someone somewhere would get back to me. No one ever did. I returned to my student life and finished my last classes in May 1969. I graduated with a near-perfect record: twenty-three A's and one B. I was first in my class of 250.

On graduation morning, I left my fourth-floor walk-up and stopped by my mailbox. There were two envelopes. One confirmed details of my NYU grades. The other was from the navy notifying me of an honorary discharge for medical reasons.

I was a free man.

My dad, a decorated naval officer, was also happy. By 1969, my parents had moved to the anti-war camp. They were thrilled about my performance at NYU. Son Tom, they hoped, would now be getting a grown-up job. The realization hit me like a brick. A job! Expecting two years of forced naval labor, I hadn't bothered looking for a job. Maybe some of that was subconscious as well. To the free-floating men on the circuit, the Kerouac nomads I had encountered at Lake George and around Greenwich Village, the grown-up career was a trap to be avoided at all costs.

Bastions of alienated long-haired young men and their free-spirited girlfriends quit the cities and migrated to communes in Vermont and Northern California. They embraced a kind of intentional poverty. They would grow their own food, have no-commitment sex, and make furniture. More free-spirited souls hopped cheap Icelandic Airlines flights to Europe, where they strapped on backpacks and dispersed in all directions. America was held in such low esteem that some young travelers put Canadian flags on their packs to avoid being lectured about Vietnam.

In 1969, we didn't have "gap years"—that sabbatical thing that kids do before or after college hadn't been invented yet. In 1969, it was called "dropping out." Dropping out meant no one would hear from you. It meant leaving everything behind.

There was still some summer left. My old roommate in the city had purchased a set of three-day tickets to the "Woodstock Aquarian Exposition" for $18. We were to meet there. I bought a 1960 Nash Rambler for $100 and headed south toward tiny Bethel, New York. I was barely into my journey when I ran into a girl at a bar in Saratoga, a cheerfully flirtatious brunette. She convinced me to bag Woodstock and hang with her for the weekend. "It's just going to be a mess," she told me with great confidence and her hand on my leg. "No one will remember it in a year. Besides, there'll be others." This would not be the last time I'd accept terrible advice from an attractive woman. By Sunday, the romance was over, the New York Thruway was closed, and I wanted to shoot myself.

After Labor Day, I returned to New York City to make some traveling money. I got a job at a singles bar called the Tittle Tattle on First Avenue and 63rd Street. I made $300 or more in cash a week peddling drinks to thirsty young New Yorkers clustered four or five deep at the bar.

After Thanksgiving, I bought some traveler's checks and embarked on a mythic journey: to California. I planned to drive eight hours a day. I'd take Route 70 to Denver, then head to Aspen. After Aspen, I figured I'd freestyle it, working my way to San Francisco, LA, and finally San Diego, where I had a pal who lived on Mission Beach. I planned to then head to Mexico.

I pulled out of New York City days after turning twenty-four. I thought I would have my year on the road and then settle into a straight job, like my father. Halfway across Colorado, mountains appeared on the horizon. As I approached Denver, the snow-covered Rockies rose in my windshield. It was a magnificent sight. The Continental Divide and Aspen lay ahead. I shivered a bit; I was finally getting somewhere. This exact feeling would recur throughout my life and travels. It reaffirmed what I had hoped: dropping out was the perfect move.

CHAPTER FOUR

A YEAR ON THE CIRCUIT

In 1969, most Americans had not heard of Aspen, Colorado. Unless you were a serious skier, it was off the map. Sitting at 7,950 feet in the Rockies, Aspen was the "Island in the Sky," a pirate hideout where skiing and hedonism were the prime pursuits. When I arrived, the "Battle of Aspen" was underway. Hunter S. Thompson had started the "Freak Power" party to take over the town in a mayoral election. His constituency was "longhairs, heads, fun hogs, and weird night people of every description." This was to be my new home. Freak Power lost by only five votes.

None of my Lake George pals who had migrated to Aspen knew I was coming, but I knew some of them worked at the Aspen Inn. The Inn was a low-rise affair, a collection of buildings spread out at the foot of Ajax Mountain. The restaurant was also a nightclub with a heavy-duty sound system and a stage where bands performed. The restaurant's manager, Gary Plum, was part of the Lake George summer mafia. He hired me as a dishwasher and gave me the name of the one place I might find cheap housing: the Independence Lodge, an 1874 landmark from the silver-mining boom. The lodge's last available room was the size of a small jail cell. The bathroom was way down the hall, past a lineup of doors to other cells. There was no window.

"You have nothing with a window?" I asked calmly, not wanting to seem too pushy.

"Windows are in short supply. Let me tell you, though, if you are working with Gary and that crew at the Aspen Inn, you don't really need a window. You'll work till late at night, then they'll have you at one party or another up on Red Mountain or somewhere till dawn. You'll sleep all day. You'll thank me for not having a window."

In the years to come, I would stay in some dismal hovels and fleabaggers, but the Independence would hold the crown for the darkest accommodation.

Aspen was brimming with drugs, copious quantities of everything, all freely consumed. People snorted, smoked, tripped, or popped pills for every occasion. Folks skied on mescaline and torched up joints on the chairlifts. They took quaaludes and reveled in group sex in piles of naked bodies. For dinner, your server might bring not only your entrée, but, if you asked, a gram of cocaine for dessert. It was an easy place to get drugs and a beautiful place to take them.

The band in residency at the Aspen Inn for part of that winter mostly played their own material. They were a bit like the "narcocorrido" bands popular today in Mexico who sing songs about the dudes from the drug cartels. They had worked up their own Smuggler's Songbook celebrating our brave American marijuana importers and the important work they do. Some of my Lake George pals there were doing just that: flying weed in from Mexico in small planes.

"Here's one about a VW bus running weed over the Mexico line," the furry lead singer would announce, kicking off a set with a nod to the smugglers in the crowd. You did not need to be Columbo to figure out what was greasing Aspen's underground economy. I was not a big drug guy. I smoked some weed, which relaxed me, enhanced my sense of humor, and gave me a certain clarity. I could smoke and get great ideas and be quite productive. But with both booze and pot, I knew my limits. The last time I was falling-down drunk, I was fifteen. Aspen, however, became the site of my psychedelic introduction. I fell in with the twenty-four-hour party people, who started at 2 or 3 a.m. Many nights we'd roll up Red Mountain for soirees at the sort of cavernous homes you see in *Architectural Digest*. There would be an open bar and a lively crowd. Wandering around would be a Johnny Appleseed character, a psychedelic wrangler in full cowboy attire with a gallon-sized plastic bag filled with hundreds of light green tabs of mescaline, handing them out like they were M&M's.

This was my first experience with psychedelics. Sitting outside in a chair by a fire under the starry mountain night sky, I felt supremely happy, spiritual even, connected to everything. I'd listen to the Moody Blues and Neil Young and be transported. Then, like Count Dracula, I'd come home at dawn and collapse into the peaceful, dark vibes of my little mausoleum, waking in the dark late in the afternoon. I'd slowly get ready for work, stick my immersion coil into a cup to make tea, and be off. Few have gone to Aspen and skied less than I.

I succeeded at my meager job. Gary promoted me to busboy, then waiter. Bartender would be next, at the top of the heap. But I didn't stick around long enough. And I'm very glad I knew when to leave the party. I learned a lot about my limits in Aspen.

Almost every year now I go back to Aspen for one conference or another. The airport seems to have the largest assemblage of private jets on the planet, wingtip to wingtip. If Hunter Thompson could see all this "corporate vermin" in one place, his place, he'd turn over in his grave. It's a good thing his ashes were shot up into space.

On these visits, invariably, I stroll by the Independence building, pause, and tell whoever I am with, "Hey, I lived there fifty years ago." If they ask me to point out my window, I'll admit proudly that I didn't have one. It's now a huge Ralph Lauren store.

I drove out of Aspen bound for San Francisco and on March 17, 1970, woke up in a cheap motel in northern Lake Tahoe. My $100 car had gotten me to the California border. I was surrounded by the stunning Sierra Nevada mountains, the setting for Jack Kerouac's *The Dharma Bums*. That night, I would go to sleep in San Francisco. The city felt smaller than I had expected, but it was beautiful. Flowers were coming up in Market Square. After months of only seeing snow, I was stunned that there were palm trees. For the first time in my life, I saw the Pacific Ocean.

My brother, Bill, had a friend from Rowayton named Denny Ladrigan, who had moved to San Francisco. Denny caught the Summer of Love fever in 1967. He headed west, flowers in his hair, and settled into the tenements of Haight-Ashbury. I figured, what better guy to see? Maybe he could show me the ropes, let me stay a night or two.

Denny was thrilled to see a face from home. He was about to hang up his San Francisco life and return to Connecticut. He told me he had tickets for the Jefferson Airplane at the Fillmore that night. He'd seen them the night before, too, but he was treating himself to a last San Francisco binge. "Have you ever done mescaline?" he asked. Trying to be cooler than I was, I said, "Oh yeah, last week in Aspen actually."

"Mescaline and the Airplane, you know, it's the full-on San Francisco treatment," he said. "I've got some if you want to join me." I had resolved to put an end to my psychedelic phase back in Aspen. But maybe one more time would not hurt.

Of all the sixties San Francisco bands, the Airplane was my favorite. I loved their 1967 album *Surrealistic Pillow*. I thought it defined the San Francisco "peace and love" vibe with tracks like "How Do You Feel" and "White Rabbit."

The Fillmore was the original psychedelic Garden of Eden, a wellspring of hippiedom. The mescaline kicked in as soon as I entered the Fillmore's auditorium. I was a little jittery at first, a dazzled first-timer, a new kid in town in a navy peacoat. My only contribution to this heavily costumed psychedelic soiree was a small "Pot Is Fun" button.

As soon as I stabilized, I felt as if I had walked into a *Life* magazine photo exposé on the San Francisco hippie scene. Before me swirled a couple thousand bodies, decked out in every imaginable form of hippie regalia. A bearded man in a fringed buckskin jacket and a red cape with brightly colored striped pants had painted half his face in Day-Glo. He danced ecstatically, hands thrown high in the air, with a blond girl in a loose dashiki. She was braless, draped in strands of turquoise beads like a Navajo priestess, and an embroidered headband hovered like a halo above her parted, pigtailed hair.

I slowly turned myself around, watching people give each other those beatific half smiles and knowing nods, the stoner signal that they, too, were bombed out of their minds. The tempo picked up on the PA system, and to great applause, the heroes took to the stage.

Denny was a frequent Fillmore flyer. As the Airplane hit full throttle with "Volunteers," he grabbed my hand and led me through the crowd to an area behind the stage—you did not need a pass. We sat and watched the eight Joshua Light Show (the now-legendary signature art form of the Fillmore East and West) guys in action as they produced a psychedelic rendering of the music using a flat screen and an overhead projector and slide tray. In the age before computer graphics and light boards, they would overlay hardware and craft store materials—hair dryers fanning scraps of Mylar—to create a multidimensional, hallucinatory experience. As we gazed at colored liquids swimming in shape-shifting globs, Denny and I were watching the creation of the quintessential images of "psychedelica." Seeing the flow of random imagery—distant galaxies, coral reefs, farmlands, and erotic shapes—was like swimming in a volcano of creation and light, all magnified by the mescaline. Was I watching a hallucination or having one?

I'd seen light shows before in the Village, but now I was in the engine room. That night made an indelible impression on me. When great music was combined with a flow of engaging visuals, the power of the song was multiplied. That sounds obvious now, but this was a new idea to me then, a kind of alchemy.

When I started at MTV, ten years to the day after St. Patrick's Day 1970, I could draw a line back to the Fillmore, when the Joshua Light Show and the Jefferson Airplane merged into one.

Having made my San Francisco stations of the cross—the Fillmore and visits to the iconic locations of the Beats—I hopped in my Rambler and headed south to try my luck in Mexico. My plan was to drive to San Blas and Puerto Vallarta, a land of beautiful beaches, a chill vibe, and warm sun, where I had learned the captains of the surfer/hippie marijuana-smuggling industry relaxed between drug runs. I imagined a sun-soaked beach town for friendly criminals. This was way before the cartels started hanging severed heads from Mexican highway bridges.

In San Diego, I sold my Rambler for $100, exactly what I had paid for it.

When I watched it be driven away, I realized that ugly little car was the best I'd ever owned. With my cash, I bought a cheap plane ticket to Puerto Vallarta, then took a broken-down local bus to San Blas. This bus, with chickens on board and passengers carrying bulging burlap sacks as luggage, kicked off a lifetime of my traveling the developing world on rickety transportation.

At first glance, San Blas seemed a paradise. An old fort sat on top of a bluff behind the town and a thick green jungle descended to the beaches and the blue tropical water. The Sierra Madre mountains spanned the coastline. The Doors' Jim Morrison had hunkered down in San Blas and written "L.A. Woman" at the Playa Hermosa Hotel. I rented a $2 room in a beachfront house made from broken concrete blocks.

The beaches were gorgeous: flat and broad and lined with cafés and palapas, VW buses parked haphazardly all around, housing surfers who had traveled down the coast for some cheap living and great waves.

But I needed money and had to find a warm place where I could legally work. That was not going to happen in Mexico. The US Virgin Islands, America's sun-kissed colony in the Caribbean, seemed perfect. In 1970, the scourge of mass tourism—all-inclusive resorts and fleets of cruise ships—were a decade away. The Caribbean islands still had simple one-story homes with slotted jalousie windows and small independent stores with handwritten signs. Rum was $1 a bottle.

On St. Thomas, I got lucky and scored a bartending job at Indies House, an upscale hotel "overlooking one of the most beautiful beaches in the world, Magens Bay." I developed a mixologist's tropical repertoire: piña coladas, daiquiris, and mojitos. I moved into a flophouse called UpChucks; the Mamas & the Papas once lived there. Think of a Bowery Hotel in the Caribbean. The daytime hot spot was Morningstar Beach, a gay beach, which was the best spot to meet interesting people. There were skinny models from New York, girls crewing on the sailboats and motor yachts, and folks on the run from one thing or another.

I was living my perfect beach life, putting money away, and then about three months in, it came crashing down. For the first time in my life, I got fired. The owner pulled me aside to tell me his best friend had just been released from prison in Atlanta and needed a gig. I packed my bag and headed north to another island, Martha's Vineyard, because I had friends from Lake George who had migrated there.

That year, 1970, was one of the last peaceful small-town summers for Martha's Vineyard. This enchanted ninety-five square miles of open farmlands, gingerbread cottages, shingled estates, and beautiful beaches was slowly morphing from a sleepy farming and fishing community to a famous destination resort. Cars sported "No Jets" bumper stickers, in opposition to extending the small airport so that jets could land. It was a noble cause, but, as with Aspen, Martha's Vineyard's days of remoteness were doomed.

The seeds of change were already there—the previous July 1969, Senator Ted Kennedy gave the island a jolt when he drove off the Dyke Bridge, which connected the Vineyard to the tiny island of Chappaquiddick, and his companion, Mary Jo Kopechne, drowned. The national scandal vaulted Martha's Vineyard into the media spotlight. Hotels had signs on their front desks saying "Please Do Not Inquire About the Kennedy Incident."

Everyone, however, was more than happy to talk about James Taylor. His *Sweet Baby James* album had just been released—its soft confessional style kicked off a new singer-songwriter genre. The single "Fire and Rain" would break through in the autumn and land him on the cover of *Time* magazine. That summer on the Vineyard, his music was everywhere. His two albums were in the window of Stop Look & Listen Records, and his songs poured into the street via outdoor speakers. Alex Taylor—James's burly older brother—owned the store.

I got a plum job bartending at the Lampost in Oak Bluffs, ground zero for the Vineyard's colorful summer mix. Every sailor, carpenter, artist, fisherman, shopkeeper, chambermaid, trust-funder, musician, waitress, hippie farmer, and derelict on the island passed through the Lampost. The Post was the type of place where Tom Rush and James Taylor would come for happy hour and sit at the bar unbothered.

I moved into an abandoned chicken coop on a farm on the outskirts of Oak Bluffs. There was no running water or electricity. I kept my clothes on the shelves inside an old stove. I had candles and a mosquito net. For transportation, I'd mostly hitchhike—bands of hippies in VW buses were plentiful.

Early on, I met Susanne, a captivating young woman from Stamford, Connecticut, near my hometown. She had just graduated from Boston University and was part preppy and part bohemian. We met on a nude beach. One reason Susanne had migrated to the Vineyard that summer was to try to meet James Taylor—"Fire and Rain" featured a "Susanne." *Whatever*, I thought. This Susanne and her roommate lived behind the small Edgartown jail. I would often stay at their place, taking a break from the chicken coop.

The mainland USA was being roiled by the war, Cambodia, Kent State, and Nixon, but that was blissfully far away for the summer island escapists. College kids and commune-dwellers from the island's wealthier families were embracing back-to-the-land, walking down country roads, and sleeping in tepees and geodesic domes.

The Vineyard stayed with me long after I left. The people I met there kept popping up in my life. Susanne and I were an on-and-off item for years. She would be the one who encouraged me to quit my advertising job to join her on a quest to the Sahara Desert in 1972. The waitress at the Lampost, a stunning blonde named Jill Lumpkin (who may have had a romance with James Taylor; to this day if I run into James and mention her name, he'll break out in a big smile), and I would spend years together in Afghanistan and India.

Joe Potter, who had worked with me in Lake George, improbably became an Oak Bluffs policeman and lived next door to me at the chicken coop. In 1973, Joe would become my business partner in my import company.

But summers don't last forever, even on the Vineyard. A few days after Labor Day, I manned up, took the ferry to the Cape, and headed to New York to try my hand, finally, at a straight job. "Put the MBA to work," my dad told me. My parents and their friends said, "Well, it's great that you finally got that out of your system. Now you can dig in and settle down." I smiled and nodded, but if my rambling year had taught me anything, it was that the free life was in my system to stay.

CHAPTER FIVE

ESCAPE FROM MADISON AVENUE

When I rolled back into New York City, everything felt a little darker. The optimism, idealism, and naivete of the sixties' counterculture were colliding head-on with the institutional realities of the Nixon administration. The expansion of the Vietnam War into Cambodia meant that almost everyone who once believed that Nixon had a plan to end the war had given up on that illusion. But capitalism was proving itself more than capable of absorbing the patina of progress. Wall Street traders grew shag haircuts and put on flared pants and went right on as before.

On Madison Avenue, the martini-soaked Mad Men were loosening up, growing sideburns, and smoking doobies. Psychedelic imagery and notions about feminism, anti-materialism, and peace crept into advertising. Woodstock, *Hair*, and *Easy Rider* proved there was a market among the flower children, and there would be big rewards for those who figured out how to tap into their consumer power, an exploding market that *Ad Age* labeled the "youthquake." The gurus had decided that successful ad campaigns were now less about a product's particular virtues than about making emotional connections. Fake doctors endorsing cigarettes were gone. Women as possessions ("My wife, I think I'll keep her") began to disappear. Volkswagen told us to "Think Small." Coca-Cola became "the Real Thing," a drink about peace and harmony, while Pepsi tried to lay claim to the new generation.

In 1970, the *New York Times* plastered an ad campaign all over the subway walls: "I Got My Job Through the *New York Times*." Smiling people looked up from their desks holding a copy of the paper. It worked on me. I saw that ad on the 59th and Lexington Avenue platform and immediately started thumbing through the classifieds. Before I got off at 34th Street, I had spotted: "Junior Executives Wanted. MBA Required" from one of the top-ten ad agencies, Benton & Bowles. A week later I was working there, at a hefty $13,500 annual salary.

Benton & Bowles had invented the radio soap opera in 1929, then created *As the World Turns*, the first network soap for television in the fifties, which ran for fifty-four years. Procter & Gamble put the soap in the soap operas; the serials they underwrote were sponsored by P&G's Tide, Ivory Snow, and other brands. These companies were the backbone of B&B's client roster, along with Crest, Scope, and Pampers.

Working at an ad agency sounded like fun and mobility could be quick. It was a launching pad to other jobs in the media world at one of the three broadcast networks, or radio, or print. Or that hot new media darling, FM radio. Benton & Bowles alums from my era included Howard Stern, *Law & Order* creator Dick Wolf, and Dick Gershon, a media planning guru who would go on to partner with the legendary George Lois at Lois Pitts Gershon, the agency that would help create the "I Want My MTV" campaign.

Benton & Bowles' offices were on 53rd and Third (also the title of a Ramones song about a gay prostitute, but I think that was coincidence), blocks from my roach-ridden East 58th Street walk-up. Some days I'd wander home for lunch to save money. B&B's offices sparkled; they were mid-century modern and minimal in design. The all-white spaces were softly lit and filled with sleek furniture by Eileen Gray, Mies van der Rohe, and Eames. The walls were covered with lithographs by artists like Rauschenberg. They had comfortable 35mm screening rooms with cushy gray velvet chairs that had gray Princess phones on consoles next to them. It looked like a Hollywood set. In fact, Hollywood would periodically shoot film sequences there.

B&B wanted clients to feel as if they had entered a magic temple of creativity. There was a dress code, tailored to make a perfect impression. We account men wore suits and ties. There was no casual Friday, no casual any day. Things were purposely looser for the "creatives," the art directors, copywriters, and producers. Those free spirits could look like English country dandies in ascots, or like long-haired British bass players. Clients were expected to think that these oddballs must be creative and interesting.

B&B exuded coolness, but we did not have sexy car, beer, or soft drink accounts. The bulk of the roster were boring package-goods brands like toilet paper. The coolest part of the roster included Canoe, the French men's fragrance, and the Puerto Rico tourism business.

My first assignment was Hasbro toys. It sounded fun until I learned I would be working solely on G.I. Joe, the world's first action figure and the biggest war toy in history. Both G.I. Joe and the Beatles hit the US in February 1964—and American kids went crazy for both. But by 1970, the Beatles had disbanded, and war toys were out of favor. Having beat one draft, I got conscripted into the toy division of the military-industrial complex—anti-war Tom was peddling "America's Movable Fighting Man." There was no room for conscientious objectors at B&B, I was told. Grin and bear it.

Everyone on the account called him "Joe," and Joe was a man in crisis. Our assignment was to magically reposition Joe as a less lethal and more lovable character. We pitched a new concept: What if Joe hung up his military uniform and became an international man of action? Let's give Joe an honorable discharge and a new job as an adventurer who goes all over the world looking to fix any trouble he finds in his way. Hasbro loved it. Before you knew it, G.I. Joe was off the battlefield and searching for a mummy's tomb or solving problems in outer space.

After Joe, I moved to Prell concentrate shampoo, an old-school package-goods account. Its advertising employed a "slice of life" approach: normal-looking people in corny situations where they discussed the product's benefits—these ads were all about lather and the unbreakable tube.

I was on the agency fast track; my boss was Mike Kammerer, a tough and deliberate taskmaster six years my senior. He projected great authority and confidence with everyone, especially clients. I got an inkling from Mike as to what good leadership could look like. He saw marketing as a bit of a science, and he loved problem-solving. A ruthless but patient editor, he'd line-edit every memo or recommendation I wrote, sending things back repeatedly until I got my wording perfect enough to mail to a client or send to a colleague at the agency. Mike taught me the skills necessary to handle clients, as well as the most productive ways to relate to creatives and media executives. He also gave me my first international business assignment. "I want you to take over the French part of the Prell concentrate business," he told me one morning.

"Wow, that is fantastic," I responded, getting up out of my chair. "I've never been to Europe. I will not let you down."

"Well, don't get too excited. I'm talking Canada, not France, the area in Quebec province that is French-speaking. They do a lot of shampooing up there." French Canada it was. I learned a lot, maybe most importantly how to make commercials for one-tenth of what we spent in the US.

My next promotion moved me to the Scope mouthwash account, one of the biggest in the company. I quickly figured out that the mouthwash business was based on fear. Maybe the reason you can't get a date, and your boss doesn't like you is because you have bad breath. Bad breath would cost you. It could derail your life, take your job, your friendships, your respect, and your shot at ever having sex.

The more I studied the subject, the clearer it became that mouthwash was a scam. Most causes of bad breath did not live in the mouth, but down the digestive tract, usually in the stomach. Sloshing Scope around in your mouth was not going to do much for fumes floating up from your guts. This fact was furtively referred to in soft-spoken tones as the "efficacy issue," like it was a UFO report or something. Scope was not "efficacious," it did not kill bad breath, you couldn't say that. It would never get by legal. You had to figure out something else to say, like "Scope makes your mouth feel fresher." A lot of work had gone into selling a product that did not really work without running afoul of FDA regulation. This troubled me.

My last days at Benton & Bowles began when Steve Kolker, a pal who toiled on Charmin toilet paper, a huge piece of business, told me there was going to be a vacancy on that team. "With some luck, Tom, you could move over here. It could be a big step for you. They want you, but you'd have to pitch my boss."

Did I, Tom Freston, look like a toilet paper man?

In fact, Benton & Bowles had been broadcasting the Mr. Whipple "Please don't squeeze the Charmin" ads into our heads since 1964, with incredible success. Not only was Charmin the market leader, but Mr. Whipple had become a revered national figure. His job involved lurking around the corner of the supermarket paper aisle, suddenly appearing to bust groups of housewives who were sneaking in some unauthorized squeezes of the toilet paper.

At one point in the seventies the Charmin campaign was cited as "America's most famous." One thing I learned in my short career in advertising was the power of saying the same thing over and over.

Steve told me Charmin would be a great career move, to which I countered, "How much fun can Mr. Whipple be, Steve?"

"You'd be surprised. I'll give you a stack of background research on Charmin to read over the weekend. You will be laughing out loud." On a cold January Saturday morning, I curled up on my couch and began reading. It would mark the end to my advertising career.

After going over a bunch of the basic stuff, pre-/post-ad campaign awareness studies and attitudinal analyses, I came to the report that Steve must have been referring to as "hilarious." It was a psychographic report that divided America, as only Procter & Gamble could, into three segments of toilet paper users: the rollers, the folders, and the crumplers. I saw myself as a crumpler. In my more meditative moments occasionally a roller.

The folders, it turns out, were neat, deliberate folks. They carefully folded layers of paper on top of each other. Rollers, as you might imagine, wound the paper more liberally around their hand. They had a good opinion of themselves, less so for others—one respondent thought that crumpling the paper was "for barbarians." But the prime target audience, the best customers, were the crumplers. They were the "devil-may-care impulsive individuals" who "liked the tough texture of the wad." These crumplers were more anxious, had things to do. They weren't sitting around reading the *Saturday Evening Post* on the can for a half hour.

And where did all this important ass-wiping information lead? It turned out that crumplers used 20 percent more toilet paper per "session." And they had more sessions. "Crumplers" were the coveted "heavy users," the advertiser's bull's-eye. But how could one find them within the general population? Turned out, they were heavily concentrated. They lived side by side in major urban areas where, I supposed, anxiety was higher, and people were more time-pressured. My neighbor was probably also a crumpler. Media planners could target these wasteful defecators very easily by skewing the advertising spending to cities. I put down the report and went to Central Park for a heart-to-heart with myself.

True, my experience had not been worthless. I had seen how a large organization operated and how some leaders could be more effective than others, down to little things like sending handwritten notes of congratulations to lower-level folks. I recognized that creative people were the heart of a company, and I saw how much I enjoyed being around them. I had toned up my interpersonal skills, navigated office politics, and saw that people with outsize personalities needed to be tolerated and protected. I was a much better, more concise communicator and certainly more appreciative of the power of solid strategy. I had also learned the ABCs of video production.

I was never a quitter. But regaining my freedom might be the right move. That afternoon, I went to a screening of a new movie called *Walkabout*, by the Australian director Nicolas Roeg. A "walkabout" is an Australian tradition where one separates from their tribe and goes out and sees the world. In this film, the protagonists try to escape the crushing forces of city life and return smarter and stronger. That rang a bell. Joni Mitchell's brilliant album *Blue* had also just come out, and I played it repeatedly, envious of her tales of freedom and intercontinental adventures: "I am on a lonely road and I am traveling, / Looking for the key to set me free." I saw a book called *Vagabonding* in a bookstore window and bought it. Every cultural experience I had seemed to focus on hitting the road and heading off without a map.

In early January 1972, I got a phone call, very long distance, from my old girlfriend Susanne in Paris. We went through some quick chatter, and then I let the Charmin opening rip.

"All those years of school, that fancy MBA degree, and you are selling toilet paper?" she chimed back in hysterics. "You are better than that, Tom. How about this: Quit that job and get on a plane. Meet me in Paris. I'm heading across the Sahara Desert. I'm hitchhiking down through France and Spain, and into Morocco, then the Sahara. Come with me."

Like a true crumpler, I made an impulsive decision right there. I was twenty-six, I had $5,000 saved; I would quit. The only people I'd be letting down were my ever-patient parents and Mike Kammerer, who had invested so much in me. I took Mike to lunch and explained about my misgivings. Lo and behold, not only did he understand, he agreed. Mike was simply waiting for an entrepreneurial strike of lightning before exiting himself. (He soon quit to start ITN Networks in his garage, selling it later for hundreds of millions.)

I headed to the passport office on Fifth Avenue at 53rd Street to apply for my first passport. Next door was the Icelandic Airlines office, where I bought a round-trip ticket to Luxembourg for $165 that was good for one year. I would return on the last eligible day.

As for Mr. Whipple, our paths finally crossed in April 1996, a quarter of a century later. His real name was Dick Wilson, and he was a vaudeville vet. He had had a wonderful run for twenty years, scolding toilet paper squeezers while raking in around $300,000 a year, along with a lifetime supply of very soft bathroom tissue. In 1996, my MTV Networks team and I were preparing to launch TV Land, a twenty-four-hour classic television network. I wanted to add in some old TV commercials to amplify the nostalgic presentation. We located and cleared rights for over one hundred classic ads, including some old Charmin spots.

I asked that we find Mr. Whipple and invite him to our launch party at Universal Studios in Hollywood. At one point, I walked up and said, "Dick, I'm Tom Freston. I'm the CEO of MTV Networks, and TV Land is our newest baby. We are so happy you could join us." I paused and added, "I want you to know something: you profoundly changed my life."

"Well, I've never heard that before," he replied.

"Not to offend you," I went on, "I have deep respect for your career and what you have done, but when I heard I would be moving to the Charmin toilet paper account at Benton and Bowles back in 1972, I couldn't face it, and I quit and ran off to cross the Sahara Desert. It turned out to be the single best thing I ever did. I owe you."

We both smiled and raised our glasses to toast our fortuitous lives.

CHAPTER SIX

TAKING FLIGHT

Just before I left New York, an American Express card magically appeared in my mailbox. I hadn't even applied, but early in the credit card era, they would just mail you one assuming you were a respectable job holder.

The American Express card offered a thin veneer of respectability, ranking me higher (in my own mind anyway) than the more ragged travelers I would meet in the months ahead. It was an insurance policy, a cash machine, and a post office rolled into one piece of plastic. They would hold mail for their "members" at all their offices. When I told my mom, "You can write me 'care of American Express' in Marrakesh. They are expecting me," it eased her worried mind.

I arrived in Luxembourg with no set plans and a pocket full of cash. I paused on the jetway stairs to gaze at the wintery airport, as free as I had ever been—or likely ever would be again. There was nothing on my calendar for an entire year.

Susanne was waiting at the Gare du Nord train station in Paris. Spotting me, she called out in a French accent, "Hey, stranger, looking for a good time?"

Susanne and I were not an obvious match. Three years younger than me, she was a considerably more empathetic person—which was both a challenge and an education. It was a time when a lot of young women were civilizing their boyfriends, helping us transition from the James Bond/playboy fantasies of the early sixties to the feminist, anti-macho seventies. We were both very independent, but we had good times together. We hoped our romance would flower on foreign soil.

One night over couscous I asked Susanne how exactly the Sahara trip would work. I had been studying a map of North and West Africa. "That's a big-ass desert," I said. "It's a long way to Timbuktu and there are no roads."

"Timbuktu?" she said. "Oh, no, we're not going to Timbuktu. I never said that. That's way, way south, down in Mali. It would take weeks to cross to there, and you can only do that in a camel caravan. Did you really think we were going to cross the entire Sahara?"

"Well, yeah, I thought that was the idea. I quit my job for it." I felt both dumb and disappointed. I tried to make a joke of it. "Don't tell me that you've ruined my life for nothing."

"No worries," Susanne said. "We're going to the Sahara all right, but to a smaller section of it. We are heading to the 'Spanish Sahara.' That's the one we're gonna cross."

"You mean Spain has their own separate Sahara?"

"Yes, it's right there on your map, 'Sahara Español,' see? Right below Morocco and just above Mauritania." It was a big empty space. "It's the last speck of the Spanish Empire, their last colony. It's nothing but desert. But it has a capital, so to speak, El Aaiún. We're heading there, not Timbuktu. But like Timbuktu, there's no road to it. The tricky part will be to figure our way through a few hundred kilometers of desert to the Spanish Sahara frontier. The border post there opens twice a week. Then it's more desert to El Aaiún. I got the whole plan from a guy I met in Sweden. He'd done it." She broke into a wide smile.

I was a bit deflated. I had imagined a Lawrence of Arabia moment, bobbing up and down on a camel over the crests of dunes that stretched out to the horizon and spending nights drinking wine with Susanne in lush oases. Spanish Sahara? I should have asked more questions before quitting my job. Susanne read my face. She said, "Don't look so sad. We'll get all the Sahara we need. The Spanish Sahara is for people like us—people who might not be prepared to spend sixty days on the back of a camel making our way to Timbuktu. Plus, no one goes there. El Aaiún is mostly just soldiers and prostitutes. The soldiers do some marching around and then drink beer in cafés with the hookers the rest of day."

"No one goes there" got my interest. As I traveled that year, "No one goes there" became a favorite recommendation. There were not a lot of European colonies left. Better see them now, I figured. I began reading up on this last small African outpost of what was once a worldwide empire. In 1884, Spain laid claim to a western corner of the Sahara. Before that, Spain had been too busy looting Latin America to focus much energy on pillaging Africa. After France gobbled up endless African desert spaces, Spain had to settle for a rump strip on the ocean. There was no port and only a few nomads wandering around. The Spanish didn't even bother to show up to govern it until the 1930s when someone discovered the world's biggest phosphate deposit under its sand. That led to the beginnings of El Aaiún, which grew into a low-rise, gloomy city of cafés and hotels and squat, rocky hillsides full of small, white-domed buildings twelve kilometers from the Atlantic Ocean.

On a windy and bitter January morning in 1972, Susanne and I took a bus to the edge of Paris, whipped out a handmade sign saying "*Espagne*," and started hitching south.

In Europe, hitchhiking was called "auto-stopping," although in France and Spain, sometimes hours passed before any autos stopped for us. I was lucky to be traveling with an attractive woman. On my own, I might be out there still. Instead, we averaged two hundred to three hundred kilometers a day. France was cold and rainy. We'd freeze all night in cheap hotels, then get up for an early start. Once we hit Spain our spirits lifted. We reveled in the warm sun, the great Catalan energy of Barcelona, and the amazing array of vivid Gaudí architecture, in stark contrast to the rifle-toting soldiers in German helmets and groups of stern-looking Guardia Civil policemen that stalked the streets. It was the last gasp of the authoritarian Francisco Franco years.

Susanne and I weren't the only ones bound for Morocco. In 1969, just thirteen years after Morocco's independence, Crosby, Stills & Nash released "Marrakesh Express," which set in motion a long caravan of tricked-out VW buses and other hippie transports rolling south through Spain and across the Strait of Gibraltar to Tangier and Marrakesh.

These were the early days of what became known as the "Hippie Trail," a human highway that traversed the 1970s, winding from Amsterdam and Athens to the islands of Ibiza and Crete, crossing through all kinds of inexpensive countries like Lebanon and India, before dead-ending at the Himalayas in Kathmandu, Nepal. Although we had a war in Vietnam, most of the rest of the world was at peace. You could drive right across Asia. Iran and Lebanon were party hot spots.

The Hippie Trail mixed nomadism with escapism and traces of spirituality, the European equivalent of America's back-to-nature movement. Instead of heading to the woods to create new Waldens, Europeans headed south and east. This was a whole new kind of tourism, and these nomads wanted to travel as long as possible.

Despite the name "Hippie Trail," few self-identified as a "hippie." Travelers ranged from long-haired goofballs, to upper-class English girls in fancy peasant clothes, to French junkies, to travelers with genuine curiosity, like me.

Local entrepreneurs tried to monetize this new flow of low-spending migrants. Budget restaurants opened, serving banana pancakes and Mexican food. There were pudding shops for exotic sweets, and a network of cheap hotels, cafés, and dope dens. Underground bus lines popped up. Small fleets of thirdhand, battered English double-deckers regularly cruised overland from London to New Delhi for fifty pounds. An amphetamine-fueled driver would race across desert spaces of Iran and Afghanistan to deposit new batches of windblown travelers who'd stagger off like zombies in Connaught Place, the carnival center of New Delhi, where they'd be met by a mob of beggars, peddlers, and predators.

In my travels, I encountered people who had been on the road for years. Travel was their life vocation. Some are still out there, I'm sure, like those Japanese soldiers who hid on Pacific Islands into the 1960s and '70s, refusing to surrender.

When Susanne and I reached Algeciras, the Spanish doorstep to Morocco, a full panic was underway. The Moroccan police had grown weary of the flood of hashish hunters and were instituting a hippie crackdown. If you were a boy with long hair, they'd refuse you entry. You had to ride the ferry back to Spain or get your hair cut right there. A row of barbers lined up behind piles of shorn hair, clippers in hand, waiting for new victims. It looked like arrivals day at the Fort Dix army base.

No self-respecting nonconformist wanted to wander around Marrakesh in a Moroccan crew cut. Anxious Samsons tried piling their locks under a hat or they took the night ferry over. My own hair was still short enough to pass muster. Thank you, Madison Avenue.

Susanne and I got on a late-afternoon ferry to Tangier. As soon as we disembarked, I was hit with a high I would chase the rest of my life: the peculiar joy of disorientation. Night was falling and there was a damp chill in the air when we entered the darkened city. I heard my first call to prayer, the captivating chant that boomed out of minarets from mosques across Tangier. On the street, a donkey was carrying a refrigerator. Veiled women drifted by like shadows. Men in pointy-toed slippers and ankle-length woolen djellabas appeared from all directions, their heads hidden under peaked hoods; outside of tourists, very few people wore Western clothes. A swarm of touts and beggars tugged at our sleeves. I was hit with a musky assortment of new smells. It was as if I had entered a time machine and rocketed back a century. I didn't know it yet, but this newness was exactly what I had been looking for.

That first evening was my initial face-to-face encounter with extreme poverty. It was a far cry from the luxe Morocco of today. These were not New York panhandlers. The beggars huddled at the quay in Tangier were struggling to stay alive. "Mistah, you want slippers? You want guide? You need hashish?"

We tried to push forward. I was glad I wasn't stoned. I was off-balance enough with the electricity of being in an alien land and feeling slightly in danger. Susanne tugged me closer, feeling the culture shock, and declared, "I don't want to stay in Tangier tonight. Just get me out of here." Tangier, I would later discover, was at the time the seediest and most decadent of Morocco's major cities, the Tijuana of North Africa. We headed to a line of old buses idling near the pier. We saw one with a sign for Rabat, a few hours away. "Let's go there," she said. "It's the capital. Has to be nicer."

Rabat, a government town, was a rare Moroccan city with a sense of calm. The streets were wide, lined with flowering citrus trees and administrative buildings. From Rabat, we took the train to Casablanca, and rather than hop on the Marrakesh Express, which we heard was slow and not that much of an express, we tried our luck at hitchhiking and got there in one ride. A smiling, jolly man in a new van stopped for us, and then picked up just about everyone else along the way. One guy got in with his bicycle, another with half a cord of wood.

Marrakesh is the jewel of Morocco, one of the most magical cities in the world. In the winter, it felt like spring. The city commands the southern part of the country and is surrounded by flat plains and palm groves, and in the distance, the snowcapped Atlas Mountains.

At dusk, throngs would fill the Djemaa el-Fna, the square that was the beating heart of the city. In would come acrobats, fortune tellers, dentists on blankets with pliers, storytellers, beggars, amputees, Berber drumbeaters, nut and spice venders, lunatics, juice sellers, and row after row of pop-up open-air restaurants that set up and broke down every night. The square could overwhelm and mesmerize. The high-pitched hypnotic drone from the multiple flutes of the snake charmers was constant, as was the darbouka drumming that stretched till dawn. The old city, known as the medina, was a maze of winding lanes and dark alleys where time seemed suspended. Even with all its over-stimulation, Marrakesh put out a peaceful, mystical feeling and had a hold on me.

Susanne and I settled into a clean six-dirhams-a-night hotel on a side lane, in a room with a view of a sunny, quiet courtyard. We went on long walking expeditions, exploring every corner of the medina. At night, we'd roam the square, pull up a seat at a favorite stall, where we could dine for a dime, and later grab a ride in a horse-and-buggy taxi, clip-clopping away.

Morocco would become one of my favorite countries, the nearest faraway place. It was there that I learned the ways of foreign travel: how to meet locals and pick up some conversational language, how to get things done and how to get from A to B. The confidence that grew with that early success led me to believe I could go anywhere. Developing cultural competence, curiosity, and fearlessness are essential tools on the road. Open-mindedness, building your empathy muscle, and developing the ability to step into another person's shoes are the gifts of travel. Later in my career, I'd look for these competencies in hiring people, particularly for jobs outside the US. At work, I'd find myself gravitating to those with whom I shared this sensibility.

Susanne and I couldn't stay in Marrakesh too long. The Sahara was calling us. We set out, first to hitch to the coast, then farther south, winding our way through the Anti-Atlas mountains to the end of the line, a place called Tan-Tan. On the coast, we found Essaouira, a beautiful small, whitewashed town. The big talk about town, among both Moroccans and travelers, seemed to center around Jimi Hendrix. He had stayed in Essaouira just before he died eighteen months earlier. Just about every hotel claimed that he had slept there. Jimi Hendrix was the George Washington of Essaouira. A side street restaurant named Café Hippy played "Purple Haze" and "Hey Joe" all day long, along with some Cat Stevens, another musician who had wandered through.

On our final run south to the Sahara, we stopped in at Taghazout, a small Berber fishing village about as far south as most young Western travelers would wander. A sea of camper vans, tents, and lean-tos stretched out on a broad beach as far as we could see, a 1970s Nomadland. Hundreds of grizzled travelers lay around or sat in the sand leaning against their VW buses. We were passing through, only stopping for food. Then I heard "Hey, Tom! Hey, Freston, over here!"

Waving his hands amid the crowd on the beach was my former Martha's Vineyard chicken coop neighbor and Oak Bluffs policeman Joe Potter—who was accompanied by his pal Mike, a joyful bear of a man with a voracious appetite, who always said his goal in life was to work as little as possible. They were both tan, dressed in T-shirts and bathing suits, just as they had been the last time that I saw them, on the Vineyard. Although they were smiling ear to ear, they looked a bit haggard. Joe had been the most disciplined guy I ever met, a double black belt in karate. Now it was as if Dean Martin and Jerry Lewis had turned into Cheech and Chong.

I had no idea Joe and Mike were in Morocco. This was a wonderful surprise. They hustled us off to their tent. It wasn't huge, but it had a nice red Moroccan kilim laid out over the sand.

"We just wanted to hang on a warm beach for the winter," began Mike.

"But after Tangier, we went up into the Rif mountains to Katama. That's where they grow the best hashish. Crazy up there. Very cold and total outlaw country . . . But look." Mike reached into his shoulder bag and produced a brick of brown hashish about a foot long and a half-inch thick. It was wrapped in cellophane. "Check it out," he said proudly, holding it up like a fish. "It's a kilo and it's primo."

I had never seen so much dope. "That should hold you a while. Let me get a whiff."

"We're working on it, Tom. Keep chipping away at it every day. And we're living in paradise on zero dirhams a day."

"Well, it looks to me like you two have a lot of smoking to do before you head home."

"Actually, most of this is coming home. It's going to pay for this trip and then some. My valuable Moroccan souvenir."

"That's ambitious," I said, trying to be supportive. "God bless you for risking your freedom for us smokers."

"Let's smoke a couple of bowls. Try a little, man. Then we catch up."

We sat out on the sand, got high, and laid back on our bags. A kid came by selling chicken sandwiches and Coca-Cola. I could have been in Malibu.

We told them that we were continuing south to Tan-Tan and across the desert to the Spanish Sahara. Then we were going to try and catch a freighter to the Canary Islands, a couple of hundred kilometers off in the Atlantic.

Mike perked up and raised his eyebrows. And I heard the words that put a chill down my spine. "The Canary Islands! Hell, I've always wanted to go there. Hey, I'm in. We'll come with you."

Susanne tensed up. I had not intended to extend an invitation. Mike, however, sure took it that way. But the idea of traveling with him, worrying every second about the kilo of hashish he was lugging, gave both Susanne and me the Midnight Express jitters. Hash was officially illegal in Morocco, but no one seemed to care. However, a kilo of it was another story. And we would be passing through Spain's Sahara. The conservative authoritarian Francisco Franco was still in charge, and the Spanish *policia* weren't messing around. If a person was caught with hash or marijuana, even a couple of joints, the penalty was six years and one day in prison. Spanish prisons were full of half-assed, long-haired amateur smugglers who had made the mistake of looking to make a quick peseta coming out of Morocco.

I hoped this was a fleeting hashish moment. Being a polite stoned guy, I told them how we planned to finagle our way to the southern border from Tan-Tan. Then Susanne gave me a look, and we rushed out. "Got to hit the road, guys. Darkness is approaching. Maybe see you down the line!"

Our next stop was Goulimine, the "Gateway to the Sahara," a drab and featureless town where camels roamed the roads. A sign with a painted camel pointed south: "Timbuktu 60 days." Susanne loaded up on psychedelic glass Goulimine beads, which fetched princely sums in Europe. These colorful little glass tubes were originally made in Venice and used in the Sahara as currency to buy slaves. Now they had become the sought-after bead for the Aquarian age, trippy and hippie-dippie. Goulimine beads were my first inkling of the possibilities of using exotic imports to fund an adventurous lifestyle.

Goulimine was also where we began to meet the Blue Men, tall, slender Tuareg nomads who populate the Sahara from Libya to Mali. The bluish tint to their bronze-colored skin comes from the indigo dye of their clothing. One friendly Tuareg immediately took a liking to Susanne. He was a dyed-in-the-wool Blue Man, who drove a blue convertible and had three wives, all dressed in blue and sitting in the back seat. The man insisted that we join them, so we piled in and headed to "El Biano," the local hot springs. We took a swim, reveling in real hot water for a change. Then he took us to his house for a couscous feast meticulously served by his son. He told us tales of the Sahara. The next day, he ushered us off, dropping us at the bus to Tan-Tan. He gave us the name of a person who could take us to the frontier. "Be careful out there," he warned. "You are really going to be out on your own."

Was I scared? A little, but mostly I was excited. Tan-Tan was the end of the line, where the bumpy road became a single lane. Unscrupulous-looking characters walked around shouting, "*Sahara Español! Sahara Español!*" The signs on stores said "Duty Free" in English, like this was Heathrow Airport. I saw clothes dryers for sale. *Who needs a clothes dryer in the Sahara?* I wondered.

In Tan-Tan, my Lawrence of Arabia fantasy began to unwind. I sadly learned that there would be no camels on this trek. The only thing going our way were trucks running goods to the border. We had to ride in the back of a dump truck, an old, rickety, dented-up red Ford. The front bumper was hanging off. I negotiated a price of ten dirhams for each of us. The driver, a turbaned Blue Man with leathery skin, advised us to buy turbans and some water in the bazaar before we left. He showed us how to wrap them.

We met Adrian, a Dutch bicyclist, who was pedaling from London to Dakar. He lifted his bicycle and pack into the back of the truck and joined us. The three of us squatted down on our bags. Two Tuaregs jumped in. Then the driver reappeared, put in some more boxes and, once we were comfortably settled, said that he had to double the price. "Sorry about that." He had us cold.

We stood up and waved to the locals as we were carted away. They waved back like we were celebrities, me in my navy peacoat, Susanne in a yellow parka, and both of us in perfectly wrapped indigo-blue turbans.

In my conquest of the Sahara, I had not pictured being thrown around in the back of a filthy dump truck. Susanne and I tightly wrapped ourselves around each other. We tried hanging on to the edge of the truck, then to the ropes securing the cargo, anything that could stabilize us. For the first few hours, it was constant banging and bruising, no smooth stretches. Then the wind picked up. Swirling sand stung our skin. We were covered with grit. My tongue stuck to the roof of my mouth like a bad hangover. The wisdom of the turban became clear as we wrapped our faces.

There was no change in the landscape. The truck followed a series of sand tracks that wove up and down the dunes. We'd bounce into the air when the truck crested as if we were riding a roller coaster. Occasionally, Adrian or I would pound on the roof of the cab to get the driver to stop for a pee break and to stretch our legs. At one point, Adrian broke out a joint of Moroccan kif. If there was ever a time for cannabis, this was it. They say it's made for pain. The driver and his cohort eagerly joined in, all of us smoking and smiling at each other with no common language, just the shared knowledge that we would all soon feel better. But once this brief sense of community came to an end, we were ordered back into the dump truck bed.

A couple of hours after a quick, colorful sunset, it began to rain, the last thing we expected. It began as a drizzle, then became a downpour riding a strong wind. Already freezing, now we were soaked. Susanne pulled out a plastic tarp, and we struggled to huddle under it. It would be impossible to sleep. We just had to hang on for dear life.

Around 3 a.m., the truck abruptly came to a stop between a couple of dunes. It was still pouring. The driver had a problem seeing out the window. He motioned that he was going to take a nap. In the cab, of course. We should take shelter under the truck. We crawled under, laid out the plastic mat, opened our wet sleeping bags, and slipped in. Water and oil dripped on us.

At about 6 a.m., the engine roared to life, and we were off again. The rain had stopped, and the desert gave off a fresh earthy scent. Susanne, Adrian, and I watched the sun climb, illuminating the desert. It was magnificent. The desert had become smoother, the sand packed down from the rain. We crashed through puddles, wound our way between tracks, and made better time. In the early evening, we pulled up to a group of about eight dark, low-lying shacks. This was "La Frontier," our destination, the southernmost point in Morocco and the border with the Spanish Sahara. There were no dunes, no sand, just flat terrain scattered with rocks and puddles as far as I could see. A couple of trucks piled high with cargo were parked near a small group of camels. I spotted one decent-looking concrete building in the distance, the Spanish border post.

A man in a torn wool sport coat, stained pants, and sandals stood outside the door of a crumbling brick and tin structure identified as the "hotel." There were no rooms to speak of. We bargained in French for floor space for two dirhams and were warned to look out for scorpions. We claimed a spot and immediately fell asleep.

The building next door, covered in part with animal skins, was the "restaurant," a genuine pop-up. By the light of a kerosene lamp, a wrinkled old Tuareg woman was stirring a vegetable tagine, mostly carrots and potatoes, in what looked like a cauldron. She smiled and offered warm soft drinks. A man who spoke a smattering of English told us that it would be three days before the Spanish border would next open and we could cross. This way station for nomads would be our temporary desert home.

In the morning, we went for a walk. We were advised not to stray into Spanish territory, but to stay on the Moroccan side, although there was no border line in the sand. The desert was hard, more pebbly than sandy. The only vegetation was a bit of grass along with scattered acacia trees and a group of stunted date palms. The Spanish border post seemed empty.

"We appear to have reached nowhere," said Adrian.

Three mornings later, a small busload of soldiers arrived to open the border. Adrian, Susanne, and I, and a few Moroccans, were told to start walking to the Spanish side, where a one-lane dirt road connected the border with El Aaiún. The small band of uniformed Spanish soldiers, each armed with a machine gun, stood outside the building and gestured for us to form a line. They were not smilers, and we looked our worst. A soldier asked us to fill out some forms. We declared ourselves as "*turistas*." For "destination" Susanne and I wrote, "*Islas Canarias*." We still had no clue how we would get there.

The three of us put the forms in our passports, and a soldier gave them a good going-over. He stamped the passports and handed them back. Another soldier asked if we were carrying weapons. Negative, we said. Then he gestured for us to put our bags onto a low platform for customs inspection. The soldiers took almost everything out and examined it very closely. They gave Adrian's bike a good going-over and were intrigued. He told them in Spanish that he planned to bicycle all the way down to Mauritania. This got a laugh and a shaking of hands and heads. Then they told us to get on the bus, the express to El Aaiún. We paid about $7 in pesetas, and a soldier meticulously made out our tickets.

There were checkpoints all along the way. No one seemed happy to see us.

El Aaiún was a town devoid of any character. There were drab military installations and barracks, a few stores and cafés. A *supermercado* sold wine and liquor, withered fruit, and stale biscuits. Adrian got on his bike and headed south. Susanne and I found a dirty pension. We asked around and located the office for the freighter that plied the Spanish Sahara–Las Palmas route. It would depart in three days. There were no cabins available. We would have to sleep on the deck.

Three days was just enough time to fully investigate the dustbin of El Aaiún. Each day, around dusk, a parade of goose-stepping troops stomped down the sandy streets. This sad outpost of Franco's Spain may have been the last repository of actual goose-stepping.

We cleaned up and tried to look presentable—presentable enough that we were able to pass muster to hold down a table in the outdoor café at the hotel El Aaiún Parador, allowing us to use its bathrooms, swipe the toilet paper, and drink cerveza in comfort. The other tables were largely filled by Arab and Spanish hookers, waiting for their regular soldier boys. For prostitutes, El Aaiún was like shooting fish in a barrel. There were no spouses. They had a monopoly over these lonely, bored soldiers.

Late in the morning, the day before we were to leave, an American voice rang out in our pension lobby: "I was hoping you would still be here."

Oh my God, it was Mike. Susanne was not amused. "Nice dump truck ride on the way over," he shouted.

"Jesus, this is a surprise. Where is Joe?"

"I think Morocco got to him. He was feeling sick, homesick, too. He headed back . . . to New York. But you got me." Mike followed us to our room. Grinning ear to ear. I whispered, "Whatever happened to the kilo of hash, Mike?" I was hoping he had given up on the idea of smuggling it home.

"Oh, I've still got it," he said, tapping his belly. "Right here under my belt, wrapped tight."

I was mortified. "Spain is a tough place to start a smuggling career," I said. "The penalty, even for an ounce, is six years and a day in jail. We'd be your co-conspirators."

"Well, I've got it this far. Don't worry."

"How the hell did you get it over the border?" I asked.

Along with his unbridled hedonism, Mike was a clever man. "Well, I cased the Spanish border post the night before it opened. Walked over from that dump we stayed in. There was a water tank in the back. I buried the hash in the sand there, at the base."

"Go on."

"After they stamped my passport and searched my baggage, I asked if I could go out back and fill my canteen. I knelt at the spigot, then dug up the hash and stuck it into my pants. Then I got on the bus."

Susanne and I were stunned. I told Mike he better leave it wrapped until we got to the Canary Islands. "If you get busted, we're all going to have our asses thrown in prison. I have better plans for the next six years, Mike."

"Don't forget that extra day," piped in Susanne.

We waited in the sand for a boat to take us to the freighter. There was no dock. An Austrian longhair in filthy clothes with no shoes was handcuffed and being shuttled around by three guards with machine guns. They allowed him to talk with us. He said he'd been busted for a bag of hash cookies at the same border crossing we had just passed through. He'd been in the El Aaiún prison for three months and now was being transferred to a nicer prison, he hoped, in Las Palmas. Susanne and I gave him some books. We slept on the deck that night. It was warm and there was a full moon.

After the boat docked, Susanne and I went to Lanzarote, where we camped in an abandoned bunker on a gorgeous empty beach on the south end of the island called Papagayo.

Mike ran off with a blond Norwegian woman, who took him to Oslo. His prized hashish made it across countless borders undetected. Five years later, I hired Mike to run my import company's operations in India. His optimism, can-do attitude under any circumstance, and manic jubilance made him perfect for the job.

After a couple of sun-kissed weeks in the Canary Islands, Susanne girded herself for her return to the States. We had been dreading this moment. Our relationship had deepened, and we were happy to be there together. We had talked about how she might be able to stay longer, but her plane ticket was nonrefundable, and she was slated to begin a job as a teacher in New Hampshire.

It was a tough goodbye. She waved to me until her boat slipped out of sight. I had a bit of a cry. Susanne's departure meant that my apprenticeship was over. For the next ten months, I'd travel alone. My real adventures were just getting started.

CHAPTER SEVEN

EUREKA

By the summer of 1972, at the age of twenty-seven, I had stopped thinking about my future. While my peers from home were marrying and mortgaging, turning into commuters, capitalists, and conformists, my attention was consumed by my new vagabond life. Six months of travel had quieted my impatience and anxiety.

Baba Ram Dass's seminal counterculture book, *Be Here Now*, had just been released. Once known as Richard Alpert, he was the Robin to Timothy Leary's Batman for the now-legendary early sixties LSD experiments at Harvard. But after leaving the acid behind, Dass argued that the secret of life could be distilled down to living vividly in the present. Someone slipped me a dog-eared copy, and I felt like Ram Dass had been reading my mind. The nagging question that tormented me—*Dear God, what am I going to do now?*—was shaken off like a stone from my shoe. Relax, Dass advised. The "aha" or eureka moment would just suddenly come to me. "Eureka" is a Greek word.

I wound my way to Greece after hitchhiking all around North Africa. In Tunis, I jumped on an overnight boat of migrants to Sicily. Days later, I was on another boat to the Greek island of Corfu. For veterans of Western Civ classes, Greece has the wonderful quality of being familiar and exotic at the same time. The Greek people, kind and welcoming, slid between labor and leisure like it was all one activity.

The Greek Islands were spellbinding. That summer, I was insatiable, a madcap sailor cruising the Ionian and Aegean, lying carefree on the decks of ferries with a beer bottle and a tomato sandwich. I explored Corfu, Hydra, Spetses, Santorini, and Crete. The stark, pure Greek sunlight intensifies every color, but especially blue, a hundred shades of it, the color of tranquility and calm. The azure sky, the deep water, the aquamarine flag, even the teal trim on almost every building refracts into a bouquet of blue hues.

In June 1972, just as five Republican operatives were breaking into the Watergate Hotel in Washington, DC, I stepped onto Mykonos, the crown jewel of the Cycladic islands. It felt like I was walking into a postcard. The jumble of spotless whitewashed buildings in the port, the lineup of seaside cafés that encircled the quiet harbor, and the hill behind it dotted with windmills all made a stunning first impression. It was a perfect place to start the summer.

Sitting by the port, nursing an espresso, I met interesting people from all over. I bought some new polo shirts and a pair of shorts. I got a haircut. Next thing I knew, I was getting invited to house parties. I met the well-heeled summer community who came to the island every year. I'd seen the same vibe on Martha's Vineyard: delighted people reuniting in their happy place after a cold winter out in the world. One afternoon at the port, an English girl sat down at the table next to me. We started talking. She asked if I'd been to Paradise Beach. "No," I answered.

"Come with me tomorrow," she said. "A good time is guaranteed." Paradise Beach was in a hard-to-reach spot on the other side of the island. It was a "clothing optional" beach. Most people went fully naked. Greece had an ancient heritage of public nudity. They even had naked Olympics. Plus, it was the seventies. Nudity was au courant. Baby boomers were young and beautiful then. Outside of Burning Man, I don't notice much public nudity these days.

From one end of Paradise Beach to the other, bronzed gods and goddesses spread out on towels, a mix of the well-heeled and the long-haired. At night I'd run into the sun worshippers with their clothes on in the bars in town. We'd give each other a knowing nod.

The unofficial mayors of Paradise Beach were two brothers, George and Freddy, who ran George's Taverna. The siblings had a total monopoly on this flawless strip of beachfront. Their taverna functioned as the town square of the naked city. No nudity at the tables, though. The brothers ran a respectable joint.

After a couple of weeks there, my eureka moment arrived. Sitting at a table under a bamboo roof nursing a beer, I spotted a young woman selling clothing to customers in the café. I had seen this woman in town, a wispy, dark-haired beauty with a beatific smile and a nose stud. That afternoon, she was the center of attention, selling summer clothing out of a trunk covered with paintings of Hindu deities.

A circle of tourists, mostly German, were listening to her pitch and were carefully inspecting her collection of sundresses, blouses, and cotton drawstring pants, all made in light, breezy Indian fabrics. A tourist would hold up a piece of clothing to show her friend for approval. The friend would nod and out would come the drachmas. Some shoppers put on their new outfit right there and marched off to the beach. A new group of tourists stopped for a drink and ended up buying stuff. The woman also sold colorful needlepoint purses from Afghanistan and silk scarves and sarongs from India. As the sun dropped lower and people began to leave the beach, a sort of frenzy developed. Folks were grabbing stuff, hoarding it, afraid that her supply would run out. It was like a final clearance at Bloomingdale's. When things calmed down, I went over and introduced myself: "Boy, that was something. I thought you might have been trampled. I'm Tom. From New York City."

"Thanks, Tom. I'm Susan, from Long Island. Bay Shore, to be precise. Yeah, sometimes it gets crazy doing this. It's my dream, though." Her accent was unmistakable. I sat down. She was a clothing designer by trade and, like me, had quit her New York job to hit the road. She'd been living in India and Nepal for four years. To support herself, she started designing and making these beautiful cotton garments. In the spring, she'd ferry them overland through Pakistan, Afghanistan, Iran, and Turkey to the Greek Islands so she could sell them directly to tourists. They were simple clothes, but stylish, perfect for the European summer hot spots. The secret, she said, was to bring beachwear right to the beach, where people were in the mood, and sell it directly, no middleman. She had invented her own vertically integrated, one-woman small cottage industry around her creativity.

We chatted further, and I asked her to dinner in town. She'd spend late spring and summer in Greece and Italy selling her wares, missing the South Asian monsoon season. When summer passed, she'd wander overland, back to India and Nepal. Beneath her calm aura, Susan was a determined woman. She loved having the means and freedom to travel, and travel well, and there was no shortage of places she wanted to see. I was enchanted. She made me believe I could accomplish anything if I went to Asia. "It's the greatest show on earth," she said. I could ride horses in Afghanistan, trek in the Himalayas, and surf the beaches of Hikkaduwa in Sri Lanka. Susan told me that she rented a house in Kathmandu with a beautiful garden and had servants. She threw parties and lived like a maharani.

A seed was planted. I'd seen the deluge of cheap Asian clothes and embroidered sheepskin Afghan coats back in New York. And I'd seen plenty of low-quality ethnic clothes for sale in Morocco. What if I could do better? Focus on higher-quality, more contemporary stuff like Susan did? And not sell them on the beach, but sell them wholesale to better stores and boutiques in the States? Boutiques were a hot new thing. I knew absolutely nothing about this, but I knew business. Susan gave me some contacts in New Delhi and Kathmandu. I began to imagine a new life as an entrepreneur on the margins, able to make enough money to finance further travels, utilize my abilities, and follow my desires. I imagined having a house in India.

Years later, at MTV Networks, I'd sometimes bring in consultants to meet with our top leaders and guide them in visualization exercises to break new creative ground and keep us on the cutting edge. I'd also ask, "What's the *New York Times* headline you'd like to see in three years?" Some people would snicker, but there's a lot to be said for visualizing goals as a means of articulating strategy. What you want to be has a lot to do with what you visualize, and what you visualize will affect what you can accomplish. It's not magic, it's mapmaking. And I know that it can work if you are open to it, because it had worked for me.

India was the travelers' holy grail in the early 1970s. People went to India for spiritual enlightenment and to seek the meaning of life. In 1968, the Beatles famously went to an ashram in Rishikesh to study meditation. I saw myself operating on a lower level. I would not be meditating in some cave above the Ganges with holy men. I saw my journey more as a feasibility study.

But I was not going to head to India until monsoon season passed. Instead, I said goodbye to sweet Greece and headed to communist Yugoslavia. I was shocked to find out that this shotgun marriage of a state formed at the end of World War II was less of a socialist utopia and more of a Nevada on the Adriatic. It had twenty-eight casinos. Karl Marx was not a high roller. Lenin did not shoot sevens. But its current ruler, Marshal Josip Broz Tito, had figured out that gambling could be a wonderful way to liberate people from their money, especially the many foreign tourists who flocked to the coast of what is now Croatia. Unlike other countries in the Eastern Bloc, Yugoslavia promoted tourism. Its Dalmatian Coast was a little Monaco.

The name "casinos" had too much of a capitalistic ring for the Yugoslav communists. Instead, their gambling dens were called "pavilions of games of chance." But three lemons would pay off just as well in a pavilion as at the Golden Nugget.

I needed money. I could dream big about India, but if I didn't make some dough fast, I was going to be sailing back to New York in steerage. I decided to enter a pavilion and test my luck. As I watched some Germans play roulette, I thought, *I could be a gambler*. Up to now, my entire gambling experience consisted of a few hands of blackjack in Reno and a few quarters pumped into slot machines in Lake Tahoe.

I calculated how much money I would need to survive for the next few months and decided I would bet the balance—$800, or about $5,000 in today's money—on a single color for one spin of the roulette wheel, fifty-fifty odds. If I won, I'd be a flush vagabond off to India, a man with a spring in his step and a boot full of cash. If I lost, I'd keep going just above the poverty line. Win or lose, it would be one spin.

"Remember, win or lose, drag yourself out of here by the hair after that one spin," I told myself as I walked in the door the next night. A couple of roulette wheel tables were three deep with Slavic gamblers. I observed, then walked to the cashier, and handed over $800 in traveler's checks. I approached the rail, found a spot, and placed my $800 in chips on red, like a man who did this every day. All eyes were on me. The croupier dropped the ball. It spun and spun, gradually descending onto the wheel itself, then it bounced about, finally landing in a red slot. The wheel spun a couple more times. But the ball did not come loose. I won.

I'd doubled my money. There was zero urge to try again. I tucked the cash inside my boots and skipped out of the casino, not knowing how far that spin of the wheel would take me or that I would never be the same.

CHAPTER EIGHT

WELCOME TO AFGHANISTAN

A barren ten-mile-long stretch of no-man's-land separated Iran from Afghanistan. When I passed through the Iranian border post, I looked back and saw large signs hanging over black garbage cans, greeting travelers arriving from Afghanistan: "Deposit All Heroin, Opium, and Hashish Here." Sort of like being told to toss your plastic bottles at a TSA checkpoint. These instructions, however, were more along the lines of "Do This . . . or Be Executed." The shah's Iran viewed its poorer, anarchic neighbor more like a crack house. The smooth new Iranian highway with its yellow reflectors, part of the shah's ambitious infrastructure program, stopped cold at the border. Approaching the Afghan side, it became a broken-down gravel track.

That day, I struck hitchhiking gold. The vehicle that stopped was a brand-new VW bus driven by two cool, bearded musicians I had met on Mykonos—Peter and Dennis, who were originally from Indiana. They played guitar and serenaded guests at George's on Paradise Beach. Now having made it to Mashhad in Eastern Iran, they were strumming their way to Kathmandu with their girlfriends. This was no filthy, dented, hippie transport. Peter's dad had gifted him a brand-new Volkswagen van, a custom order right off the assembly line, which they had taken delivery of in Germany. Peter and Dennis had turned it into a mini recording studio with a reel-to-reel tape deck, microphones, and a bunch of speakers, to play seventy-five hours of recorded folk, blues, and rock music. Mounted above the windshield were water buffalo horns.

As we exited the Iranian border post, Dennis pressed play, and Neil Young's "Everybody Knows This Is Nowhere" began, appropriate for a trip through any no-man's-land. At 5 p.m. we pulled up in a swirl of yellow dust to the sanctuary of the Afghan border post. A smiling man with a three-day growth of beard and wearing a peaked policeman's hat approached. He had on a blue uniform with gold trim. Then I saw that the jacket said "Akron High School Band" on the sleeve.

"Border closed, sir. Closed for hour or more," he said in halting English.

"How much longer than an hour?" I asked as politely as possible.

"This, sir, we don't know. But darkness coming." He paused. "You be safer to stay the night here. We would welcome you at our government tourist hotel, sir. Nice hotel. You can do immigration in the morning." He pointed just behind him. I smelled a scam. The low light of the late-afternoon sun draped the hotel in an eerie haze. It was brown like the desert and looked to be made of dirt. Beggars in rags sat in the dust outside the entrance.

The hotel was a flophouse. As we entered, we heard the light switches turn on and a fan started to spin. A man in a karakul lamb hat, wearing another tattered high school band uniform, stood up. "*Salaam alaikum*," he said, making a slight bow. "Welcome to Afghanistan. May I please see passports? I give back in the morning," he added, placing them all in a little stack. The formal business over, he turned to the real business. "You need change money, good sir? Best rate here, seventy-eight afghanis for US dollar."

"Is that the official rate?" I asked.

"No, sir. The best rate. Black-market rate."

I pushed $100 in cash across the counter. He slowly counted out the equivalent of what seemed to be a shoebox worth of currency as an old fan wobbled overhead. The faded, wrinkled afghanis were the filthiest bills I'd ever seen. Many were tattered or ripped or looked as if they had been buried in dirty shoes. In Asia, I learned to carefully go through every bill and reject any that had the slightest tear. Currency could be threadbare, stained with betel juice, or moth-eaten, but if a corner was missing, forget it. No one would accept it.

"How much for a room?"

"One hundred afghanis, sir. Good rate." He was holding the key, smiling now. I agreed. He waited a second, then dropped the bomb. "You want hashish, sir?" He held up a few small black, shiny disks about three inches wide. "Good quality. We have the best hashish. This is widely known."

I guess he knew his clientele. "The government hotel sells hashish?"

"Oh yes, best quality. Hashish no problem, sir. Police no problem. It is very good. And duty-free. Best price." Indeed, "Afghan Black," as I came to learn, was the Dom Pérignon of hashish, considered by the cannabis cognoscenti to be the best in the world. "What else do you have in your duty-free shop?" I asked. "Have any whiskey?"

"No whiskey, sir. Only hashish selling." The clerk held back a giggle. He appeared to be high on his own supply. Looking around in the shadows at the edges of the lobby, I saw slouching figures gazing back at me, nodding with the same laid-back, happy expression. I had entered the Wild East. I bought a disk. It was soft and pliable and smelled sweet and earthy. I slipped the little pancake into my bag, then headed down a dark corridor to my room, hoping for a hot shower to rinse off the layers of dust. The room was bare. A single light hung down from the ceiling attached by a long cord that was covered with black flies, thousands of them. The cord was like a super flypaper strip.

At daybreak, the flies awoke en masse, formed a black cloud, and attacked me, buzzing and screeching like kamikazes trying to enter my nostrils. I rose, batted them away, and rinsed out my mouth and dirt-clogged throat with Coca-Cola (drinking the water was about as high-risk as it got). Escaping the flies, I made a beeline to the restaurant for breakfast—chai and delicious Afghan naan. The border crossing had miraculously reopened, and we officially entered Afghanistan. There were virtually no cars on the road, just horses and buggies, like it was Amish country. The buggies were covered in red pom-poms and the horses were outfitted with bells.

Before long, a stream of colorfully painted "jingle trucks" passed us. Chains hung off their bumpers to jingle-jangle when they collided with the ground below. Dark exhaust poured from their tailpipes. These vehicles were old, sturdy Bedford trucks, with metal cabs and wooden frames. Generally, they were overloaded with burlap sacks of melons or lord-knows-what.

Almost always a group of smiling, spirited Afghans sat on top, the loose part of their turbans blowing in the wind. Sometimes the passengers would hang off the truck's sides with one hand like daredevils.

Afghan caravan drivers used to cover their camels with tassels, ribbons, and small carpets for good luck. In the automotive era, commercial semi-trailer drivers, who sat atop the transportation hierarchy, decorated the sides of their long-haulers with elaborately hand-painted, flashy psychedelic designs: calligraphy, montages of flowers, or dreamy fantasies of paradise. The motifs included sensual, buxom women, a rare sight in Islamic Afghanistan, or sacred imagery, such as the Taj Mahal or the Black Stone of Kaaba in Mecca. They were a traveling oasis, art galleries amid the arid, austere landscape. Truck drivers were Afghanistan's rock stars. They'd often have that ripped-on-amphetamine look with piercing eyes, tight smiles, and a dangerous machismo. They traveled with teams of apprentices and gofers to change tires and cook.

We passed women encased in blue and green burkas that billowed in the hot wind behind them like small parachutes. Their view, when outside their home, was bracketed by a small, embroidered screen, their eyesight-limiting window to the world. We also passed camps of nomads called Kuchis, whose dark tents were made of animal skins. Kuchi women were free from burkas. They were draped with jewelry and had little silver chains that connected their earrings to their nose rings. Their dresses were fantastically colorful combinations of embroidery, velvet, and soft floral-patterned cottons.

The first stop for travelers like us coming overland from the West was Herat, a city in a fertile valley on the eastern end of the Iran-Afghan plateau. Marco Polo had stopped there. This was the old Silk Road, which turned Herat into a prosperous trading center, the most civilized city in the Islamic world, the "Pearl of Khorasan," and "the pleasantest of cities," according to the poet Rumi. It became the artistic and cultural capital of Afghanistan.

By 1972, hard times had befallen Herat. The architectural centerpiece of the city, the famed Citadel, a sandcastle of a fortress from the time of Alexander the Great, was collapsing. A severe drought and famine were underway, and the once-lush city had devolved into a dusty metropolis of flattened earth and crumbling buildings surrounded by a rugged landscape of stark brown mountains. Herat had been dry for so long that the locals paved roads across its empty riverbeds.

My relationship with Afghanistan began in Herat and turned into an unexpected five-decade love affair. It was easy to fall in love with Afghanistan back then. The country was exotic, a living glimpse of an old world, an Orientalist's fantasyland. There were breathtaking vistas that led to snow-covered mountains and patchworks of small farms in lush green valleys. The men had pride and dressed with great individual style. They were honorable, independent, welcoming, and carried themselves with dignity and a certain sophistication. The land had never been conquered or successfully colonized. Afghans had their own rules. They were trying to move forward by fusing a conservative Islamic society with some level of modernity, particularly in the cities.

I arrived during the tail end of Afghanistan's "golden age." That's what the old-timers now call it. Today, Afghanistan is portrayed as a barbaric place, a nation that eats itself and is continually at war. It has been locked in a constant series of conflicts since 1978. But for fifty years before that, Afghanistan was at peace. It was one of the poorest nations on the planet, but there was an optimism for the future. The tourist posters in the flyblown lobby of my first Afghan hotel said it all: Afghanistan was "Your Passport to Peace," the home of "The World's Friendliest People."

Arriving in Herat, I saw a group of policemen marching in their heavy woolen uniforms with antique single-shot British Enfield rifles on their shoulders. They were hauling five men, who I assumed were bad guys of some kind, dragging them down the center of the street. A single rope was tied around the prisoners to keep them together. Dressed in rags, they marched slowly with their heads bowed. Behind them came an angry mob chanting for blood. I flashed on *Frankenstein*.

I got a room at the Shark Hotel, a dusty hot spot for the overlander set. Grimy longhairs in skullcaps sat out front drinking chai. The sign behind them said "Very Modern and a Lot of Fun." What more to ask? After checking in, I went out to roam the old city and its labyrinth of unpaved lanes. I could have been walking in any of the last three centuries.

I soon learned exactly how to put my hand over my chest, bow a bit, and go through the litany of greetings in Dari that Afghans give back and forth to each other. "How are you?" "How is your family?" And so on. The one that gave me a good laugh was "How are 'your motions'?" Your intestinal business was everyone's business. There seemed to be constant concern about each other's bowel movements—with good reason, I'd soon discover. Hepatitis and dysentery were like the common colds of Afghanistan. It was the pre–bottled water era. Aluminum strips of Lomotil pills, the morphine-laced anti-diarrhea medicine, were hawked to cars at intersections by smiling street urchins.

Walking around Herat was immediately liberating. Afghans had a devil-may-care self-confidence. Robert Byron, the classic British travel writer, described Afghans as "the only Asians without an inferiority complex." They could be hilarious with a country humor that they mixed with a trace of Persian elegance, which they frequently used to deftly navigate the underlying chaos: hence, the sight of smiling men selling toilet seats moving about with their wares draped around their necks.

Deep in the alleys of what was known as "the chirping bazaar" with all its elaborate birdcages, the thought that came to me was: *No one could ever find me here*. Afghanistan was a place invisible to the world. If a prophet had announced that forty to fifty years on, the US would spend $2 trillion there and get nothing in return, he'd be dragged off to a rubber room.

It was Ramadan when I arrived in Herat. People fasted all day and stuffed themselves after sunset. There would be sumptuous, overflowing piles of *pilau* with raisins and carrots and lamb and pumpkin dishes from all over the region. My first night at the Shark, two other travelers asked me if I wanted to join them to hear some live music. We jumped into a horse-and-buggy taxi and skirted through the darkened streets. I sat in the rear, facing backward. It was pitch-black—no moon, no streetlights, and very few lights on in the homes we passed. Periodically, the driver would slow down and carefully maneuver around trenches and holes in the dirt road.

The club, more a teahouse, was a stand-alone one-story building. In the back, it was open to the sky and filled with men, not a woman in sight. The night was cold, and the patrons huddled close together, sitting on the ground, monochromatic in their brown woolen shawls and turbans and beards. As we entered, the crowd parted, and we were shown to one of the few tables, near the front. As the only three foreigners there, we got special treatment, the legendary Afghan hospitality. I would have preferred a quieter entrance. We did nothing to warrant these prime seats. A pot of chai and three teacups were put on our table.

Three musicians then came out with their instruments—a rubab (an ancient stringed instrument that resembled a lute), a tabla, and a harmonium—and sat on a carpet on a low platform. They started to play ghazals—love songs—to periodic applause. Ghazals' lyrics are soft, a form of poetry, which was the highest art form in Afghanistan. The music had a dreamy, hypnotic sound like the modes of Indian ragas. Men held up microphones to tape the performance using Panasonic tape decks. Batteries and audiocassettes had recently democratized the music scene here. A bootleg business was off and running.

The men listened intently for hours, swaying, nodding, sipping chai, and passing hash joints. They politely invited us to partake. These guys could smoke. The air was thick, and the secondhand smoke was enough to make me drift away. It was as if I were back at the Fillmore East. About 2 a.m., we called it quits and headed back. It seemed even darker when we got outside. We picked a buggy out of the lineup, got in, and utilizing my first Dari sentence, I blurted, "Hotel Shark, *lotfan*."

The driver nodded, snapped his whip, and we were off, barreling along as if riding in a trotter at the Yonkers Raceway. "Jesus Christ, I don't believe this," said my companion next to me with a mix of fear and stoned enthusiasm. "I can hardly see my hand in front of my face."

"I hope this guy knows where those ditches are, or at least the horse does," piped up the guy in front. The one next to me said, "Don't worry, man, these drivers must know every inch of this town. There are not that many roads. There cannot be that many ditches. The driver's not crazy. And horses can see in the dark."

"Who the hell told you that?" I asked. "Horses have bad eyesight."

"Come to think of it, he did look a little crazy, our driver." Suddenly, crash, boom, bam. The high-flying horse stumbled into a deep ditch, and the buggy, with us in it, followed at a forty-five-degree angle. The driver and my new pal in front flew out, landing in the dirt. The two of us in the back rammed against the seat, shaken but not shattered. The horse was wailing in pain. Before I could climb out of the buggy, there was a single gunshot. *BANG!* The driver had shot the horse in the head. The driver had acted quickly to put the horse out of its misery, but he had killed his moneymaker. Scared straight, we pooled some money and paid the poor driver a good sum. I made the *I'm sorry, man* gesture, and we headed back to town, having absolutely no idea where we were going, but happy to be walking down the unlit streets. I was tingling.

"Welcome to Afghanistan," said my new friend.

CHAPTER NINE

DOWN AT THE END OF CHICKEN STREET

Afghanistan was almost entirely rural in 1972. Even the provincial capitals were small. Towns barely had signs of any kind; the people who lived there already knew where everything was. In Afghanistan, time's arrow was pointing backward, and I loved the feeling.

When I finally rolled into Kabul, the country's capital perched high on a plateau, I felt like I had entered a different Afghanistan. Today, Kabul is a metropolis of 5 or 6 million. When I arrived, the population was just 400,000. It had clear skies, sweeping views of the snowcapped Hindu Kush mountains, and the crisp mountain air of a ski resort. Colorfully painted slums crept up the sides of the rugged hills that intersected the city, and throughout the day, the Islamic call to prayer echoed between the peaks of the hills and the buildings, summoning citizens to worship.

Kabul was home to Afghanistan's small, powerful, and educated elite. Progressive ideas and innovation came from Kabul. I saw schoolgirls in short skirts and headscarves. I saw movie theaters, outdoor cafés, sidewalks, and broad tree-lined avenues bursting with activity, as well as bustling bazaars teeming with tribesmen in colorful, flowing turbans. Kabul had cars, spacious Russian Volgas that looked suspiciously like 1954 Fords. There were lush parks filled with cedar and pine trees and children at play. In the new city section, Share-Nau, I found curio and rug shops, modern restaurants, well-kept homes with gardens, and quasi-supermarkets with cases of beer out front.

The old part of Kabul gave me a feeling that I'd been transported onto a movie set where I was cast as the lone Westerner. The streets, often just mazes or long, coiling lanes, were noisy and crowded. In the bazaars, women shrouded under burkas squatted and extended their begging hands from beneath the voluminous blue cloth. I never felt as if I were in danger. Even the men walking around with old rifles seemed benign. I was only afraid of one thing: catching the dreaded hepatitis.

I immediately understood why Kabul was not on Susan's list of cool, chilled-out Asian garden spots. It would have been hard for a single woman to settle here. But it was entirely different for me. That Kabul was landlocked with barely a telephone added to its appeal. Maybe I could learn how to function in this strange place and pick up some of the language. Maybe I really could all but disappear, reinvent myself, and live an improvised life.

My first morning in Kabul I woke with "sulfur burps." Many things could keep you bound to a primitive bathroom back then, and I thought I'd had them all, but here I was burping little bursts of fetid air in rapid succession. "What could cause this?" I asked the man in the office of the Bost Hotel, which a fellow traveler had recommended to me.

"Mr. Tom, you have likely eaten something with a man's feces."

"You mean I've eaten shit?"

"Sadly, yes. But it will pass." He smiled in sympathy. Shit was the coin of the realm in Afghanistan. The stench was never far away. Shit lay in open gutters. You'd stumble by a vacant lot and see feces piled in leaning towers. I guess that a sampling had migrated onto my vegetables. Not the brightest way to start the morning. My damp hotel room had a worn, wooden rope bed and a cracked concrete floor. The green walls were stained with brown drippings. Scrawls of psychedelic graffiti supplied the evidence of earlier cosmic travelers. A small, round wood-burning stove called a bukhari stood in the corner. Its fire had died hours earlier, but its smoke had permeated my hair and clothes.

In the daylight, I learned I was living on the far end of the famed Chicken Street, a name with the ring of a blues song. Chicken Street was a shabby two-story strip of pastry, rug, curio, and clothing shops along with restaurants and cheap hotels. The Bost Hotel had a gated courtyard, which served as both a lobby and a communal bathroom. When I came out to take a shower, a bearded, gnomelike Westerner was sitting on the ground meticulously polishing a silver pistol.

You didn't so much take a shower at the Bost as make one. First, you had to start a wood fire under the water tank outside the bathroom. Then, for thirty minutes or so, you had to protect your place in line while your water heated up. That half hour allowed me the luxury of observing my fellow residents. After a few minutes, it was clear that this could have been the courtyard of an insane asylum. The gun polisher, a very focused Spaniard in grimy pajama pants and sandals, had the gaunt, strung-out look of someone who had been on the trail too long. Guns were common in Afghanistan, but I'd never seen a foreigner with one. "What's with the pistol, my friend? You travel with that?" I asked.

"Yeah, never, never without it. It protects me from the cannibals."

"Cannibals? Around here?" I asked.

"Oh, yeah. I just came from Nepal. Trust me, man, that country's full of cannibals. I was there for over a year. There's a whole tribe of them roaming around. People were always disappearing, you know. They're here, too. Watch out."

"I'll be on the lookout."

In another corner of the courtyard, a bearded New Yorker, dressed in soiled, white guru attire, was leaning against a wall—picture a Jesus look-alike with a Brooklyn accent. He shouted to the early-morning lobby squatters that he was a prophet. Then he held up a picture and waved it around. He said it was his mother, and he called her the "Rag Woman." He had spent three years in India, he said, mostly in Kashmir. "Where Jesus went, man," he said with great certainty. "You know, J.C. He escaped off the cross and split to Kashmir. This is documented. People know."

I showered and went upstairs to the Steak House, the second-floor restaurant, which would become my first Kabul hangout. They had a menu on a large chalkboard, with lettering that looked like a concert poster from the Fillmore.

Many marketing gurus will tell you that restaurants should create marketing slogans that forge emotional connections with their customers—think of McDonald's and "I'm Lovin' It." The Steak House went right to the point:

"NO HEPATITIS!" It was printed in red, the color of emergency, at the very top of the menu. That was reassuring. Not only did it not have hepatitis, this Steak House also didn't have steak. It was more like "the Stoner House of Pancakes," with endless munchable pancake and French toast variations. Say what you want about hippies, but they sure knew how to assemble a tasty breakfast menu. I had some eggs and naan and chai and then burped my way out the door to begin my reconnaissance mission in the city.

As I roamed Kabul's neighborhoods, I confirmed my impression that Afghans were extraordinarily hospitable people, with a keen sense of humor, which they used to make light of the many absurdities surrounding them.

The Hippie Trail passed right through Kabul. To me, it was more like a river. Wave after wave, the flotilla of seekers and freaks never stopped—long-haired flotsam and jetsam, brigades of zoned-out young travelers in skullcaps, embroidered vests, and peasant dresses, all drifting off to India to seek nirvana or adventure. A few overlanders would stay on and burrow into Kabul a bit, sometimes getting stuck for months. Many of those were dead-enders, junkies, or petty criminals. A part of the city—unfortunately, the part where I had temporarily settled—was their turf, Kabul's Desolation Row. I had no idea that along with its many charms, Kabul was also a mile-high resort for drug addicts. Afghanistan was a "source country" in DEA parlance. Drugs were plentiful, almost free. Junkies could pay less than a dollar a day for the chance to lie horizontal in a local drug den. There was a joint called Sigis with a giant chessboard where the chess pieces were four feet high. People didn't play so much as nod out on the board or against the rooks, knights, and pawns. You could get all the opium or heroin you might ever want to ingest. It was an opium den with a Doors' soundtrack.

While I was staying at the Bost, I learned a French girl had overdosed in the shooting gallery across the street. Not uncommon, they said, but no worries. Her remains would be dumped into a cheap pine box and shuttled off to the nearby "Christian graveyard," where, at best, a few of her fellow junkies might assemble to give their comrade a salute, kick a bit of dirt into her grave, shake their heads, and maybe tip the ragged gravedigger. Then it was back to business.

This special graveyard was located not far from the Bost, well away from any Muslim cemeteries. It was established after the Second Anglo-Afghan War in the 1880s. Inside, there were rows of marble headstones for the English soldiers who died in Kabul in the nineteenth century. Behind their headstones was a line of freshly dug graves for the new casualties of the heroin trade, plots marked by small, crude, white wooden crosses on which someone wrote names, nationalities, and dates of death. No remembrances, no flowers. I wondered how many of the dead had parents who were still waiting for them. (I visited when I returned to Afghanistan in 2007. The wooden crosses were gone. The watchman told me they had been burned for fuel during the worst years of the country's civil war.)

Robert Neumann, then US ambassador, was particularly annoyed at the early 1970s hard-drug scene in Kabul. He spoke in the press about the "scandalous activities of the international hippie community." He thought having rich young Westerners come to live in squalor and then die in one of the world's poorest countries set a bad example. "There is so much else they could be doing," he said, stating the obvious. "They are destroying themselves in Afghanistan. There is suicide, horrible sanitation, disease. They live in hovels." He wasn't kidding.

The Afghan officials, however, barely registered any concern. To them, the owners of these drug dens were job creators, key players in the growing tourist industry. "We have great tolerance," said one. "We've had dervishes addicted to hashish for thousands of years." But it wasn't the hashish that was drawing addicts to Afghanistan. It was the cheap, ever-available opium and heroin. Fifty years on, Afghanistan would produce 90 percent of the world's heroin and host over 3 million domestic addicts. Everyone from the Soviets to the Americans to the Taliban has tried to crack down on the opium trade, but the fruit of the poppy has proven to be stronger than any army.

I moved my ass out of the drug ghetto as quickly as I could and found the semi-upscale Mustafa Hotel, near the Indian embassy. Five stories high, the Mustafa was relatively new and clean and offered large windows and private bathrooms with hot water. Each room had a little balcony with a chair where you could relax and watch the nonstop action below for $2 a night.

Just as I was putting down roots in my comfortable new home, a busload of the worst people imaginable moved in and took over. I was told that my new neighbors were a contingent of convicts from the overflowing city prison. The authorities had decided to temporarily relocate the *ferengi* (foreign) inmates to the Mustafa until their trials, placing these prisoners under a special kind of Afghan house arrest. The Kabul authorities ringed the hotel with a gang of hapless-looking prison guards in fraying uniforms armed with antique single-shot rifles. Inside, the criminals commandeered the restaurant to drink and smoke dope nonstop.

These convicts were not hippies busted for having a couple of joints. They were hardened, don't-give-a-shit criminals. The prisoner next door to me was a German. He'd been arrested for bank robbery. I tried to imagine how bad a criminal you'd have to be to come to Afghanistan to rob banks. He explained to me he had not been "thinking straight" at the time.

I was bouncing around the bottom of the Kabul barrel and needed an upgrade. I couldn't afford to stay at the new Intercontinental Hotel on the edge of town, although I would periodically attend their poolside happy hour, where it was theoretically possible to meet a Lufthansa air hostess. I ended up moving to a place in a quieter and cleaner part of Share-Nau, the Seasons Hotel. Not the "Four Seasons," just the "Seasons." It had four rooms and one extremely clean shared bathroom with a bidet and a shower. Large, curtained south-facing windows looked over rooftops and poplar trees to the Hindu Kush mountains. The rooms were freshly painted, each had a wood-burning bukhari, and a basket of sweet-smelling firewood. There was a bar and a restaurant downstairs that served excellent chicken Kiev. The Seasons would be my Kabul headquarters for years to come.

Most days, I would head out to explore. I'd enter a bazaar and drift along. I would say *salaam* and bow slightly to a man carrying live chickens. He would respond by raising a hand full of birds in my direction. Rug sellers spread their carpets on the street so the car and donkey traffic would accelerate the aging process. Hazaras, the lowest ethnicity on the Afghan totem pole, passed by dressed in rags and bent under huge wooden boxes strapped to their backs, reduced to being human beasts of burden.

My medium-term plan remained unchanged, hightailing it through the Khyber Pass and heading across Pakistan for India, leaving Afghanistan in my rearview mirror. That changed on the morning of November 8, 1972, the day after the American presidential election while the votes were still being counted at home. Richard Nixon was running for reelection against the liberal Democratic peace candidate George McGovern. The famous baby doctor turned anti-war (and anti-spanking) activist Benjamin Spock was also on the ballot as a third-party candidate.

The US embassy had arranged for an elaborate election presentation in the auditorium of the US Information Center, which kept old *Herald Tribune*s and *Time* magazines in its library. Anyone could walk in; there were no security checks. I saw a crowd waiting outside and joined them.

This was in an era when our government did useful things to promote American ideals. The center had displays on the virtues of free speech and the Bill of Rights, screenings of Hollywood films, things that projected our beloved soft power. Over the next couple of decades, the US government would gradually turn foreign relations over almost entirely to the military-industrial complex and outsource other activities to nongovernmental organizations. Combat and affiliated NGO boots-on-the-ground replaced freedom and justice as our way of reaching out to vast swaths of the world.

That day, however, the diplomats had organized a vote-tally board and an announcer on the stage. Young American women hurried back and forth with election returns. Groups of Afghans, members of the local diplomatic corps, reps from the small Kabul business community, Peace Corps volunteers, and a mix of other locals and foreigners gathered for the grown-up equivalent of a high school assembly.

Sensing an opportunity, I headed for the men's room, tidied up my hair, dusted myself off, and launched into my "Tom Freston, respectable businessman" networking mode. I introduced myself to several American diplomats, smiling, clean-cut types in pinstripes and prep school ties. Many were my age. They were friendly and invited me to the embassy for a visit. In my nine months on the road, I hadn't dared to go near a US embassy, but I scheduled an appointment for the next day.

I also met a young American rug trader in the auditorium. He introduced himself as Mr. Don. It was common in Asia to be addressed with the honorific "Mr.," then your given name. I was always "Mr. Tom." Mr. Don was not just a learned picker of Central Asian rugs and old textiles, he was a great salesman, too. He'd been coming to Afghanistan to do business for years, spending months at a time combing the countryside for antiquities, which were still numerous, inexpensive, and beautiful. This was the seeker/explorer era. Business was out of style. Capitalism was unhip—until that moment, I didn't know anyone who had come to Afghanistan to do business. But Mr. Don opened the door for me. He was effusive about the great life he led. I still intended to see India, but I wondered if Afghanistan could become a serious long-term option, too. As I left the building, I noticed a "Nixon reelected" sign in the lobby.

The next day, I arrived at the US embassy, a small, welcoming two-story building on the road to the airport. It was a far cry from the multibillion-dollar walled fortress that the US would construct during the 2000s, only to eventually abandon it to the Taliban. In the 1970s, I could take a taxi to the embassy's front door. A handful of sharply dressed marines greeted me inside.

I met with the second secretary. He was a very nice man, smart about the country to which he was posted, and very encouraging about the emerging export business possibilities in Kabul, particularly with the new airfreight opportunities. Iran Air had begun twice-weekly service to Kabul. He gave me tips on restaurants and people to meet.

The international community in Kabul was small, tightly knit, and extremely happy to be there. The diplomats had wonderful homes with rose gardens and a coterie of servants. Some kept horses they'd ride in the countryside. Everyone admitted they lived better in Kabul than they could back home, and no one seemed eager for their tour of duty to end.

There were rumblings of trouble in the university and elsewhere, but few thought it would amount to much. The expats hosted tennis tournaments, ran a basketball league, and staged theatrical productions. One play cast an American and a Soviet diplomat in leading roles. It was like a small town lifted out of Ohio or Pennsylvania and set down in the Hindu Kush.

I looked to the biweekly English-language newspaper and government propaganda mouthpiece, the *Kabul Times*, for more clues and information about the country. Like the British *Hello!* magazine with England's queen and her offspring, the *Kabul Times* faithfully tracked and photographed the Afghan royal family, right down to watching the king at the opening of a matchstick factory. Basking in the camera's fawning gaze, the monarchy saw nothing but blue skies ahead. One night, Mr. Don took me to the 25 Hour Club, Kabul's first and only Western-style nightclub, the Kabul equivalent of Rick's Café in *Casablanca*. It had a white quartz dance floor lit from below and a mish-mash of beautiful people boogying to Led Zeppelin. Spies, dope dealers, government ministers, businessmen, and adventurers all came to the 25 Hour Club, which was operated by Prince Ali Seraj, a colorful long-haired royal who our DEA suspected was a drug-trade middleman. After the 1978 communist coup, the prince fled the country disguised as a hippie and eventually settled in Connecticut. He would return in the 2000s and unsuccessfully run for president.

But in the early 1970s, the talk was of new movie theater openings, new phone lines in the countryside, and novel land distribution programs for nomads. The Afghan Tourist Organization touted the country's huge potential as a vacation destination. They announced a study that projected 28 million annual tourist visitors by 1980. Never mind that the country only had two international standard hotels and just sixty-five thousand visitors in 1972, most of whom were day-tripping Pakistani bargain hunters who'd drive across the border to buy duty-free microwaves, stereos, and washing machines stacked on sidewalks by the Kabul River, and then split.

In Share-Nau, the shops were jammed with handicrafts, sheepskin coats, and embroideries. I collected samples of the embroideries and fabrics to take home . . . just in case. Were there ever to be a market for contemporary fashions made in Afghanistan, I felt confident I could find reliable partners to make quality clothes and ship them to the West. I'd have that market almost to myself.

I went up to Paghman, a summer resort in the mountains for the Afghan elite with large walled estates. King Amanullah, chased out of Kabul in the 1920s for attempting to modernize the country too quickly, had built a replica of the Arc de Triomphe there. Nearby, the current King Zahir Shah owned vast farmlands that included his royal vineyards, where the Muslim ruler produced Afghanistan's only wine, "Castellano, the Wine of Kings," a red cabernet. The label said "Made with Italian Collaboration," a term some might associate with World War II and Mussolini. You'd have to let the wine breathe for a day, but it could do the job. It's long gone now, another victim of Taliban abstemiousness. I hope there is a case or two hidden away somewhere deep in the bowels of Kabul.

My preliminary research over, I said goodbye and set off for India, hoping it would live up to its promise.

CHAPTER TEN

INDIA THE MINDBLOWER

I'm no name-dropper, but Mark Twain and I had a lot in common when it came to India. "Overwhelming!" he cried. "Holy shit!" said I. Twain had sailed into Bombay in 1895 to begin a three-month visit and paid speaking tour. India knocked him sideways. He called India the "most interesting country on the planet, the most extraordinary." Almost everything Western writers have said about India since, Twain had already eloquently captured—the dreams and romance, the riches and pestilence, the immensity and diversity, the optimism and despair.

"Bombay had a stupendous population," Twain exclaimed upon his arrival, feeling a touch of "delirium." It had "a MILLION people. . . . It was bewildering!" Mr. Clemens would be blown out of his sedan chair today. Bombay, now Mumbai, has *twenty-five* MILLION people! Citizens ride four deep on motorcycles, fingers affixed to the horn button, as they snake in and out of endless traffic snarls. Throngs hang on to the sides of moving commuter trains because all the seats inside are taken. Like my fellow countryman, the first thing to smack me was the sheer mass of humanity. India was 550 million strong at the end of 1972, while Afghanistan had just 11 million people. Everywhere else I had been was just a warm-up for India.

I had done my best to prepare for India. I watched Louis Malle's six-hour documentary *Phantom India* in London and read Ved Mehta's wonderful *Portrait of India*. I had picked up a phrase book in a street stall in Kabul, *Hindi Made Easy*. It was full of head-scratching phrases like "How do I load my musket?" and "I want to shoot a tiger." But after filling out endless forms at the customs office, I was marooned for hours in a throbbing crowd trying to squeeze over the Indian border from Pakistan. In the West, people move in lines, like cattle. In India, people tend to move like amoebae, shape-shifting into any available space, wagging their heads like bobble figures. Eventually, I would learn the systems, but the lessons took years.

When I arrived in 1972, India was a brand-new nation, just twenty-five years old and finding its way. Imagine America in 1800. India's mantra was "self-reliance." No imports. "We'll make everything ourselves." The reality was that the Indian people were led by a stifling socialist regime extremely wary of the rest of the world. After generations of constrictive colonialism and war, the government was suspicious of foreign influence and foreigners themselves. Tourism barely existed; the government would not even unveil its first tourist policy until 1982. The India I encountered was a country mired in paperwork, bureaucracy, and corruption, reluctant to embrace innovation, and burdened with an exploding population. Finally independent, India would not win its economic freedom until the 1990s, when the government rolled out game-changing economic reforms that would liberate the long-frustrated entrepreneurial class and lift millions out of poverty.

The country I squeezed into had few telephones, no television, and pretty much only one kind of car: the thirty-six-horsepower Ambassador, approximately the engine power of two American riding lawn mowers. Indians in Western dress were rare. Sixty percent of the population lived below the poverty line. (Today that number is 4 percent.) At night, sidewalks and train platforms were a mass of sleeping forms wrapped in cloth, heads covered but feet sticking out, surrounded by trash. Colonies of beggars lived under bridges. The idea of people sleeping in the street was shocking to me then.

I entered this human whirlpool on the back of a scooter taxi, which wove through the roadway traffic of cows, bicycles, and bullock carts into the crowded border city of Amritsar. The legendary mysticism of the East was well hidden by chaos and exhaust. It was humbling. Fortunately, India had English signs, often amusing. Shop signs unexpectedly paired products like "Birth Control Devices and Fishing Hooks." On Chandni Chowk in

Delhi, a store advertised "Toys and Toilets." Billboards hawked "Venereal Disease Specialists."

Newsstands were stuffed with English-language newspapers and periodicals. India, I discovered, was a reader's paradise. There were six or seven English dailies, and bookstores galore. I'd read three or four papers every morning. I clipped and saved some of the headlines, which were worthy of the best Western supermarket tabloids.

"COBRA RECEIVED IN REGISTERED PARCEL"
"SEVERED HEAD PRODUCED IN COURT"
"SINGING EUNUCHS ASSAULT COP"
"PRIME MINISTER RECOMMENDS DRINKING URINE"

Initially, I traversed much of northern India by bus and train: the beginnings of the Tibetan community in Dharamsala, where the Dalai Lama had fled after the Chinese communist forces invaded his homeland; Le Corbusier's impressive newly planned city of Chandigarh in Himachal Pradesh; the Taj Mahal, which did not disappoint; and the erotic temples of Khajuraho where, I was told, jet-setters went for orgies. I saw Varanasi, the holiest of India's holy cities. Mark Twain called it "a religious hive, older than history." It was a place where death was on full display. For Hindus, Varanasi offered a get-out-of-jail-free card. If you died or were cremated there, you could get off the reincarnation wheel, escape rebirth, and achieve "moksha." The streets were filled with old, sickly, and feeble people, a bit like South Miami Beach in the 1960s.

One fall moonlit evening in Kashmir, I stood on the back deck of a houseboat on Nigeen Lake, transfixed by the beauty of the landscape. The snow-covered Himalayas were reflected in the still waters of the lake. Suddenly, I experienced a moment of *satori*, a revelation of the future I'd been trying so hard to figure out. Almost a year had passed since I quit my job and hit the road. I was still tormented by that existential question: *What would I love to do?* I wasn't eager to go back to an America that had reelected Nixon in a landslide.

But I wasn't a hippie, a mystic, a vegetarian, a druggie, a protester, or a tree hugger. I wasn't a socialist. I was a capitalist by training and philosophy, an aspiring entrepreneur, although I did not believe that the free market was a license to bully. I never bought the bullshit lines that greed is good or that any abuse of employees, shortchanging of the customer, or ruthless tactic is excused by the obligation to deliver maximum profits for a faceless shareholder. I never thought that winning meant crushing the competition. I held on to the corny old idea that a rising tide should lift all boats. On Nigeen Lake, at age twenty-seven, I realized I should never again compromise my time or sell myself for someone else's idea of security.

I knew I was just a visitor to this part of the world, only skimming the surface, but I felt a deep connection. Susan from Mykonos's idea of producing clothes here and selling them in the West could be fun and creative and would let me set up a home base in India while continuing to explore Asia. I headed to New Delhi to find out how I might enter the clothing import-export business. I knew nothing about it, so I researched the bazaars to familiarize myself with what was available. I was also looking for someone who could be a reliable and honest partner, someone capable of producing high-quality clothing. But initially, I met with a variety of Indian shopkeepers and businessmen who treated me like a mark to rip off.

One afternoon, after combing through the Janpath Market, a series of handicraft and textile stalls near Connaught Place, I reached the last stall. A group of exquisitely embroidered woolen Kashmiri shawls caught my eye. Their quality was exceptional. Leaning back cross-legged against a pile of shawls under a ceiling fan was Khub Chand Sawhney, the man who would become my partner and, more importantly, my guide to India.

Khub Chand, a slender, gentle man who spoke halting English and chain-smoked harsh Indian cigarettes, was the proprietor of this "emporium," as he called it. At fifty-three, he had a receding hairline, neatly combed gray hair, and a prominent nose under which sat a closely cropped mustache. He was a Hindu from Srinagar in Kashmir, who left the disputed region soon after the partition between Pakistan and India in 1947. When the government decided in 1950 to provide retail spaces for Hindu refugees, he secured his market spot, which was now a valuable piece of real estate. His shawls and scarves were more beautiful and more expensive than anything else on the strip. His clientele was mostly Indian. They liked his goods, but were reluctant to pay his prices, and he tirelessly bargained all day with customers. Deeply religious, he carried himself with easy grace and dignity, quite a contrast to his rival shopkeepers, who seemed intent on ripping off any outsider.

Khub Chand told me that Kashmir was where India's finest, most intricate work was done. They had the most skilled embroiderers, the best quality wool, and a long tradition of fine craftsmanship. He unwrapped a cloth bundle to show me some beautiful kurtas (tunics). They were beige with fine, multi-colored embroidery around the neck on a medium-weight, very soft fabric, which he called "art silk." Years later I would discover that "art silk" was in fact rayon, "artificial silk." I could buy these for $3 and, with the new 747s and lower airfreight rates, have them in New York in twenty-four hours, where I could sell them for many times that. Greater airfreight capacity at lower cost was about to revolutionize the import business. My timing was perfect. Luck had landed me on the far side of the world in the early days of globalization. I had enough money left to buy a load of samples and send them to New York. How could I not try?

I bought seventy-five kurtas and a few embroidered shawls for gifts and a few pairs of soft cotton drawstring pants. I told Khub Chand about my plans to start a company to design clothes, manufacture them in India, and sell them to high-end stores in the US, concentrating on new boutiques. High quality and great design would set us apart from the cheap ethnic clothing that was flooding the US. These kurtas would be my samples. If buyers were interested, I'd be back for more. The two of us hit it off. He saw something in my drive and determination. He had a large family and many educated relatives, and if I was serious about a bigger wholesale operation, he had family members who could run such a thing.

"Let's see what happens," he said.

CHAPTER ELEVEN

CHRISTMAS IN KATHMANDU

After fifty weeks on the road traversing dozens of countries, I needed a vacation. Nothing sounded better than Christmas in Kathmandu. Closed to the outside world until 1955, Nepal had long occupied a revered place in the countercultural imagination. Timothy Leary's wingman, Richard Alpert, transitioned into Baba Ram Dass there. Cat Stevens and Bob Seger both wrote songs titled "Kathmandu." The city remained a mystical faraway place that people talked about, but few visited.

"Hey, Mr. Tom . . . watch your step!" Someone was shouting my name over the din of the traffic mayhem near the Ganges in the holy city of Varanasi. In my pajama pants and flip-flops, I was very carefully watching my step. You could put your foot into anything in Varanasi. I looked through the jam of rickshaws, past the bullock carts carrying the deceased down to the ghats for cremation and recognized a tricked-out VW van. The Paradise Beach gang was inching along in their little bus, water buffalo horns mounted above the windshield. Peter and Amy and Dennis and Natalie, now well-dusted travel veterans, had magically reappeared.

"Wow," I shouted. "If it isn't the Furry Freak Brothers!"

"Get in, man!"

After some hugs and hellos, I told them I was headed to Nepal for my grand finale. I already had a "reserved" seat on the train to the Nepalese border.

"Kathmandu! That's where we're headed! Come with us."

Who was I to reject the hand of fate? After a year on the trail, you don't argue with good fortune. Periodically in my travels I would cross paths with someone I remembered from somewhere. But these folks, well, we had history. We were once nudists together in Greece.

Soon, we were powering through the crowded flatlands of Uttar Pradesh in a VW bus of white privilege to the sounds of the Grateful Dead's *American Beauty.*

"Sometimes the light's all shinin' on me," they sang. At 2 a.m. by a lake in the jungle just below the border, I curled up in the front seat. "Ripple in still water when there is no pebble tossed," the Dead were singing softly as I drifted into sleep.

We crossed the border at noon. The customs man gave me the peace sign. I had escaped the frenzy of India. We drove uphill to the small hilltop village of Daman. Salman Rushdie has described the Himalayas as "land's attempt to metamorphose into sky." Somehow, little Nepal boasted the lion's share of the world's tallest mountains.

In Daman the clearest view is at sunrise, before the clouds settle in. We cooked dinner over a clay stove in a redbrick house and hit the rack early. It was too cold to sleep outside, so we crashed on the floor.

As the sun rose, poking into the crystal clear, icy blue atmosphere was a 250-mile range of towering, jagged peaks, the money shot. Mount Everest was on the right, Dhaulagiri on the left.

It was eighty kilometers downhill to Kathmandu. I noticed most of the bus riders were traveling on the roofs. That was the placc to be, riding free, out in the open air, hair blowing, drinking in the world's supreme panorama.

I asked Peter to stop. I wanted to ride up top of the VW. My grand finale, my entrance into Kathmandu, would be even more triumphant. I borrowed a parka and took the microphone to provide a play-by-play. With my free hand, I gripped the water buffalo horns still fused to the top of the van. Floating down through forests of pine and poplar trees, bamboo groves, and mile after mile of terraced hillsides, I was going to end my walkabout entering Kathmandu as if I were on a magic carpet ride. It had been a year of good fortune. I was overflowing with gratitude.

Nepal's relaxed capital was tiny and exotic then—only 150,000 people and hardly any cars. Today 3 million people call it home. Low redbrick buildings with carved wooden balconies lined narrow flagstone streets. Tall wooden pagodas and scattered royal palaces dominated the skyline. The prevailing sounds were the tinkling of bells and the brisk flap of prayer flags. The medieval, landlocked Nepalese kingdom was ruled by a king who was a month younger than me.

Kathmandu was still very much the idyllic Shangri-la of popular myth. It was also very poor. Their sewerage system had a lot more sewage than system. Pigs roamed the streets to eat up excrement. By the river, a colony of untouchables patted piles of cow shit into small pies, then slapped them on walls to dry. People used them as cooking fuel. The smell of cow dung mixed with the scent of wood fires and incense from the small shrines on most every street gave the city a distinctive scent, not unpleasant once you got used to it.

The first Western travelers to Nepal were spiritual seekers, followed by the escapers and stoners, and then the more wholesome mountain-trekker crowd. To serve all these foreign invaders, a strip of budget hotels and cafés opened in Kathmandu's Jhochhen neighborhood with names like Pie & Chai, Rose's Mushroom, King Curd, and Hotel Pot. The main drag was known aptly as "Freak Street."

If one were caught up in the Aquarian spirit, sick of a dead-end job in Birmingham, Boston, or Barcelona and dreaming of a place to fall off the map and start over, you could've done a lot worse than Nepal in 1972. A communal hut in Shangri-la sure beat a freezing commune in Vermont. Remote little Nepal was not just beautiful and bountiful. It was peaceful. The people were kind. Visa extensions were easy. The produce was healthy and the parade of hippies passing through had introduced a tasty variety of pancakes and pastries to the local menus. For those searching for a spiritual journey, the options for enlightenment were plentiful.

The Nepalese were a mix of Hindus and Buddhists. Most all the men wore little patterned caps, tight pants, and rough-looking jackets. Everyone seemed welcoming and humble. If you gave a smile, you got one back immediately, especially from the little kids, who seemed to be everywhere, running around and screeching their heads off.

I booked a double room for two weeks at the single-story wooden

Kathmandu Guest House, an extremely clean place outside the hippie ghetto, for $2 a night. Two spirited Australian girls, Ellen and Judy, were next door. The guesthouse's restaurant advertised "Fresh Hamburgers." Both were encouraging signs. Looking to create an illusion of permanence, I bought some fresh flowers and hung a piece of Afghan embroidery on the wall.

For a simple tourist like me, there was plenty to do in Kathmandu and the surrounding valley. I rented a bicycle and, day after day, rode in vivid sunshine through groves of palm trees, past roadside gangs of rhesus monkeys, exploring the valley's villages and religious monuments. I came across Tibetan communities where Chinese refugees were building a new life, having made it over the border and away from the communist dictatorship. They had lost their homes, and yet somehow, they still beamed with happiness.

The hiking was superb. One day Judy and I headed out to the edge of the valley and I had a brainstorm. "Let's go all the way to China!" I said, "Right now! The border's just eighty kilometers north."

We hailed down a small Mercedes taxi, stopped to get a couple beers, then slowly began to ascend as we wound between the foothills. The Himalayas kept appearing and disappearing from both sides of the car as we passed small villages. I popped open two Star beers and Judy broke out some bread and cheese.

The town of Kodari was deep in a gorge next to a closed-off bridge spanning the narrow Trishuli River. This was a border no one crossed, the end of the line. On the other side was Chairman Mao and what communist nomenclature called the "Tibet Autonomous Region." Barricades blocked it off. We got out to stare across. There were some concrete Chinese buildings and a couple of stern looking border guards guarding a permanently closed border.

Tibet, the most mysterious place on earth, was going to maintain its mystery.

Riding back to Kathmandu, a wave of depression began to rise up. It was the feeling I got every year when Labor Day rolled around. The party was over. Summer would disappear by dusk. Kodari was my high-water mark. From there on, I'd be moving in reverse, retracing my steps back to New York.

But I was not empty-handed. I had a new mission. I was going to start my own company. I would return to Asia as soon as I could. And I was going to settle down there for a while.

I asked Judy out for Christmas dinner at the upscale Yak & Yeti, finally breaking out my American Express card. We exchanged simple presents. I gave her a big, beautiful, old yellow Tibetan banknote. Cash is always a welcome present.

After dinner I hailed a taxi. "Take us to the Eden Hashish Center," I commanded with a smile. Don't get to say that often. Ganja and hash were legal in Nepal. They weren't calling them dispensaries back then. More like "mariwana centers." Nepal was the only country on earth offering this convenience in 1972.

Earlier that afternoon I had heard footsteps outside my hotel room, then watched an envelope whisk under my door. The letter was addressed to me. Inside was a pink invitation to a "Cosmic Hashish Christmas Party," words I never imagined would be used together. It was being held at "the Heavenly Pleasure Room" at the Inn Eden, where "every type of hashish product will be available as always." How many types could there be? I wondered. I pictured a long narcotic buffet. It was signed by a guy named DD Sharma.

This was the same yuletide evening that Richard Nixon ordered the Christmas bombing of Hanoi. Kissinger had announced, "Peace is at hand," just before the election. Those guys had quite a sense of irony.

I flashed my invitation at the door. We entered "the Pleasure Room." It was like some imaginary world. Inside was an opulent, colorful Rajasthani tent held up with bamboo poles. It covered the walls and billowed under the ceiling. Low candlelit tables were full of smiling revelers lounging on thick cushions in gypsy finery—locals, expats, and travelers. The mellow yellow music of Donovan was coming through large speakers. DD Sharma, our unseen host, had flown in all the latest records from Europe.

"I Can See Clearly Now" by Johnny Nash came on as we crossed the room to find a table. It was hard to see clearly in the Pleasure Room. Each table was its own smokestack of chillums and spliffs. The patrons were chatting away, drinking, coughing, and nodding. Some were up shaking themselves in a trancey Grateful Dead kind of way. I saw Peter and Dennis with their ladies in the back, and we joined them at their table.

Our waiter, a young stylish Nepali dude in a pink button-down shirt and a Seven Dwarfs hat with a bright purple scarf tied in a Windsor knot came up to our table and smiled. He set down a bowl full of hashish chunks, along with some cigarette papers. "Merry Christmas!"

It was like the free bowl of chips and guacamole you get in a Mexican restaurant so that you'll drink more beer. Here hash was the loss leader, not nachos. In the Pleasure Room the dope was free, but a scotch and soda cost an arm and a leg.

"What would you like to drink?" he asked.

I ordered two Star beers. Peter asked for a coffee.

"Would you be wanting hash cake or hash bread with that?"

"No, but I could go for a good joint."

The waiter pointed to the bowl on the table. "Help yourself, sahib. It is there for your smoking."

Judy, laughing, pinched me. "That's just to let you know you are really here," she whispered.

Dennis poured a round of beers, and we raised our glasses and toasted each other. Kathmandu Christmas was the perfect finale. Peter and Amy were off to Burma in the morning. Dennis and Natalie were headed to western Nepal, to Pokhara. This was our last hurrah. I realized I'd probably never see these cool folks again.

The maître d', a rotund, happy German man in a turquoise Nepali hat, came through handing out 1973 Eden Hashish Center calendars. New Year's Day was but a week away. They had colorful drawings of Hindu deities on them. I took a Christian one . . . Jesus, Mary, and Joseph huddling around the manger above three words in bold caps: "EDEN HASHISH CENTER" and their grammatically challenged mission statement: "Let Us Take Higher."

I copied the calendar idea when I started my company, Hindu Kush. We created calendars for our clients every year. I'd pick five or six colorful deity drawings like, say, with Hanuman, the monkey god . . . or others. Just "Hindu Kush" with our phone number and showroom location. We sent them out in tubes. Clients loved them, hung them up, and people remembered our name.

Leaving the Pleasure Room, we were feeling buzzy and carrying our calendars. The doorman handed each of us an Eden-embossed plastic bag of hashish for the road. He giggled out a final "Merry Christmas!"

Stepping out into the real Kathmandu, we were immediately mobbed by a circle of begging children. I passed out some rupees and we walked on, covering our eyes against the dirt that was blowing off Durbar Square. No one was around. It was late, dark, and silent. There was no moon, no streetlights. The Nepalis were sleeping.

As we moved on, we were startled by werewolf-level howls. We both knew what it meant. Late at night, packs of wild dogs terrorized Kathmandu. They huddled in groups at dark intersections, like now, snarling silhouettes lit from the back. As we got closer, they barked louder and louder. Judy tightened her grip on my arm, but I was the one trembling inside.

I was bitten by a big dog as a child, and I'd been secretly terrified of them ever since. The German shepherd–sized strays in Kathmandu were notorious. You could mistake them for wolves, always furious, plus a bunch of them had rabies, another scourge of Nepal. Any monkey or dog, any animal you encountered, could be rabid. I was haunted by thoughts of injections with foot-long hypodermic needles at the Kathmandu hospital.

As the dogs moved toward us, I remembered the local wisdom. I whispered to Judy, "Bend down and pretend you're picking up a rock." It worked like Pavlov's bell. These dogs had been bombarded with many a stone. The beasts ran off, we sighed and smiled, and resumed our stroll home.

That Christmas was the last tango for the Eden Hashish Center. President Nixon, opponent of dope smokers wherever he could find them, pressured the young king to close the cannabis shops in 1973.

Pot shops would open near Nixon's home in San Clemente, California, in the mid-nineties. I wish he had lived to see it.

CHAPTER TWELVE

GETTING STARTED

I had been totally gone for a year. I had not spoken to my parents, my brother, or my friends. Not a single phone call. In my year of nomadism, I had wandered mostly alone with two changes of clothes—and from the vantage point of almost half a century later, it remains the defining year of my life. My world grew bigger. I grew freer. I would take a new path. It became perfectly clear how I should live my life. Other travelers have had more dramatic trips. Perhaps mine wasn't all that remarkable, but it set my course. I had developed a confidence that would never leave me. I felt I could go anywhere and accomplish whatever I set my mind on doing. I had developed a new empathy and a much more sophisticated and nuanced view of the world. The year 1972 began a never-ending curiosity about other cultures, especially those in Asia and Africa.

My greatest discovery was myself. I vowed never to lead an uninteresting life or give myself to work that I did not love. There was no more guilt about that. And the wilder and odder, the better.

That winter of 1973, I felt like a sailor returning to port after a voyage around the globe. To my parents' astonishment, their prodigal son had reappeared with a plan to make a living. The seventy-five kurtas and other samples I'd found in Kabul and selected from Khub Chand were waiting at their house. When my parents saw I was serious, they were supportive rather than skeptical. Later, when I became successful, they were deeply proud of what I had accomplished.

The early 1970s was a profoundly conflicted time. It very much seemed as if America was heading into the toilet—Vietnam, the gas crisis, a recession, Watergate, etc. But, little noted at the time, that period also became a golden age for entrepreneurs. Not the kind we see these days, brash twentysomethings lionized in the press and showered with venture capital. Back then, it was about bright, independent-thinking young people dropping out of college, quitting traditional corporations, and quietly innovating new kinds of businesses, often on shoestrings. The first Starbucks opened in Seattle in 1971, the same year that a young sneaker importer named Phil Knight christened his company Nike and paid $35 for an art student to design the "Swoosh" logo. Patagonia, Billabong, and the UK's Monsoon, three powerhouse clothing import companies, all started in 1973. In 1975, Bill Gates quit Harvard to start Microsoft with Paul Allen. In 1976, another India pilgrim, Steve Jobs, joined forces with fellow college dropout Steve Wozniak to start Apple Computer, Inc.

I'm in no way comparing myself to these business giants; I'm just saying that unconventional thinking and a disinterest in a corporate cookie-cutter life was in the air. These guys (and they were all guys) bet on themselves against conventional wisdom. They intuited something about the future that few others saw. Building a company with the ultimate goal of selling it was not in their game plans. Money was not yet the motivation. These entrepreneurs had different, more personal agendas.

Back in the US, I realized I needed a partner. Someone who was capable and simpatico, and, most of all, someone who was flush with cash. I was dead-broke. Joe Potter came to mind, my old friend from Lake George, NYU, and Martha's Vineyard, whom I had last run into in southern Morocco, where he was sleeping on a straw mat on a beach. Joe, never a stoner, had been uncharacteristically out of sorts there—pale, dissipated, blown out. He fled back to New York, and when he got there, he discovered that he had inherited a bunch of money. Joe and I had been on parallel journeys, except for the inheriting-money bit. Like me, Joe wanted no part of the conventional life. He was looking for something unusual. I told him I had just the proposition.

I explained my scheme and why the stars were particularly aligned. The fashion trends were there, there was an explosion of boutique stores, a huge drop in airfreight costs, I had Asian connections, and hardly any other

Westerners were doing this. Plus, it sure could be a lot of fun. I showed Joe my samples. We shook hands and became fifty-fifty partners. He happily carved out $70,000 of his inheritance to put into our venture.

Joe went to work settling all the legal requirements, trademarking, registering the company, opening bank accounts, and tending to the many complexities of setting up a multinational business. We named the company Hindu Kush, after the Himalayan range in Afghanistan. I asked Pat Nagle, a pal from business school, to design a multicolored logo that would project a stylish, upscale image and make us appear legitimate. Brown and red, it had "Hindu Kush" written in a modern font below three angular mountains. We made labels in Manhattan's garment district to take back to Asia.

I would be Hindu Kush's president and cheerleader, the front man who would handle most of the Asian duties. Before I bought my return plane ticket, I figured I had better test my thesis. Was there a market for what I wanted to sell? I rented a friend's VW bug for $5 a day and cruised the New York area for weeks with my bag of samples.

The sixties had set off a flowering of thousands of small boutiques across Europe and the US, an alternative to mass-market department stores. They first appeared in London to outfit rock stars and stylish young people. These shops rejected mainstream fashion trends and focused on handmade items and crafts, and they had a cool aura about them. Earth shoes, bell-bottoms, and Birkenstocks exploded in small boutiques. Much of their clothing was a continuation of the loose, flowing hippie style that developed in the sixties and came from India, Mexico, or Guatemala. I sought out boutiques from eastern Long Island, to deep into Westchester, New Jersey, and Connecticut, walking in and cold-calling.

The owners were enthusiastic about the finely embroidered kurtas, Afghan purses, and very soft, light pajama pants that I presented from my little suitcase. Even better, they were anxious to see more. I took orders and they agreed to pay me COD (cash on delivery). My key stop was Bloomingdale's, where I had a good friend from Martha's Vineyard, Sydney Bachman. Sydney worked in the Fashion Office, a very influential spot at the most influential store of the era. She ordered some of everything and was very encouraging. She especially liked the drawstring pants. We'd do tons of business in the future.

Flush with that initial encouragement—and orders—I sent telegrams to my prospective partners, Khub Chand Sawhney in New Delhi and a Mr. Loynab in Kabul. (It might have been crazy to try to start a production business in two countries at the same time, but I figured I was doubling my shot at success.) I wanted my local partners to not just be suppliers. I wanted partners—honest, reliable businessmen skilled enough to produce clothing of a high standard. Mr. Loynab was an Afghan merchant whom I had encountered in a shop in Kabul. He talked a good game. He would turn out to be a two-timing fraud, unlike Khub Chand, with whom I hit the jackpot.

In late March, I bought a $430 round-trip ticket to Kabul on Pan Am. The travel agent told me it was the lowest cost "per air mile" price in the world. I flew first to Tehran, then changed onto Ariana Afghan Airlines to Kabul. It was a twenty-four-hour ordeal. I sat way back, near the toilets, crunched up in a fog of cigarette smoke. But I was ecstatic.

Mr. Loynab met me at the Kabul airport. He was a handsome man in his late fifties with an aristocrat's bearing spoiled only by his gray Hitler-style mustache. He had soft, uncalloused hands, a sure sign of membership in the Kabul elite. Always sharply dressed in woolen tweed coats and colorful shirt and tie combinations, Loynab kept a dark lambskin karakul hat permanently perched rakishly on his head. He spoke perfect English, picked up at an Indian boarding school, and he projected total confidence. His pitch always reverted to "With my connections, I can get things done." I would soon come to realize that it was a bluff—he had no experience making or selling clothes. Being a rookie, I was seduced by his apparent sophistication.

My guard was down partially because I was hypnotized by his daughter, the kind of upper-class Afghan woman with Western affectations you don't see anymore. Stylish and sexy, she had coiffed hair and carefully plucked brows that arched perfectly over doe-like eyes. She flirted with me, smiling behind her father's back. She would accompany us to the bazaar sporting oversized sunglasses, a miniskirt, and high leather boots. Picture a fashion model in an eighteenth-century bazaar crowded with ancient tribesmen. Her knowledge of the West came exclusively from the few glossy European magazines that made it to the city. I learned soon thereafter that consorting in any way with any Afghan woman was taboo, a justification for a nice, old-fashioned honor killing, happily meted out by family members.

I asked Mr. Loynab to copy a couple of simple shirts and dresses in various sizes using soft patterned fabrics from Uzbekistan, Afghanistan's northern neighbor, and at that time, part of the Soviet Union. It produced about two-thirds of the USSR's cotton, which the Afghans bartered for with raisins. You'd see these fabrics on the colorfully dressed Kuchi women, the nomads whose faces went uncovered. I would go to the bazaar, haggle over prices, then clean out entire inventories of fabric bolts from shopkeepers and load them into Russian Volgas. I wanted the fabrics to be as soft as possible, so I insisted they be washed before the tailors got to work. I asked Mr. Loynab to rent a house with a large garden to wash and dry the fabric.

My first clue that something was amiss should have been that Mr. Loynab did not seem to have any "factory." He was farming out the projects to tailors around Kabul. There were few ready-to-wear clothes available in Afghanistan, so tailors were plentiful, but not necessarily uniformly skilled. I inspected the early work myself, piece by piece, sending many back for adjustments. After the clothes were bagged and labeled, we prepared to ship them by air to America. To pay for that first shipment I went to the Da Afghanistan Bank with a small suitcase and, like a gangster, left with the bag bulging with dirty Afghan currency.

"There's a problem, Mr. Tom," one of Loynab's helpers told me as we were preparing our initial shipment. "We have to make some boxes for shipping."

"Can't we just buy some cardboard?"

"There is no cardboard in Afghanistan."

"Afghanistan has no cardboard?"

"We are still a backwards nation, sir," he said. "We need to make special tin trunks for the shipping."

Next thing I knew, I was in the old city in an entire bazaar full of tin-box makers hammering away.

Along with the clothing, I threw in piles of purses and embroideries and a couple of Afghan carpets, including a carefully chosen rug for my mother, and headed with the trunks to the Kabul airport. This was my introduction to the Afghan "baksheesh" economy. They didn't see a lot of Americans sending out airfreight from Kabul in those days. The biggest business any Americans were doing then seemed to be smuggling drugs. I was trying to export legal goods, a new idea, and it wasn't easy. Many palms needed greasing. Half of Kabul seemed to be hanging around the customs shed.

There were export-tax collectors. There were airfreight handlers and *bachas*, the poor men who did the lugging. Then there was a whole phalanx of supervisors from the airlines to be tipped. Then came the actual customs people, the top of the supply chain, who sat around in rumpled uniforms drinking tea until a shipper showed up. I was told they were very prone to delay the movement of goods unless there was some "consideration." Without it, my trunks could sit on the tarmac forever. I did what I had to and waved bon voyage to my tin containers. I rewarded myself with a road trip to Bamiyan, in central Afghanistan, a tough ten hours by bus.

Bamiyan was one of the most beautiful places I'd ever seen. Some locals said that it was the site of the original Garden of Eden. On the northern edge of the valley were Afghanistan's greatest showpieces, from the days of the Silk Road, the towering, iconic twin Buddha statues that had been carved out of a huge stone massif in the sixth century, before Islam was born. I walked on the head of one of the Buddhas. They cast a spell of peace and serenity over the entire valley, where the only sound was birdsong. (In 1998, the Taliban massacred thousands of local Hazara people who were Shia, not Sunni, Muslims. Then the Taliban leader, Mullah Omar, with the encouragement of Osama bin Laden, ordered the destruction of the giant twin Buddhas. In early 2001, six months before bin Laden brought down the Twin Towers, he blew up Afghanistan's top tourist attraction for practice.)

After that first shipment, Mr. Loynab stiffed me. I wired him money for another order, but he didn't answer me and just kept the money. Probably he figured I wasn't coming back. Furious, I jumped on a plane to Kabul and made a beeline to the US embassy to see my friend Mark. He told me I had little legal recourse, since I had not set up a letter of credit. It was a tough way to learn the ropes. Then he smiled and said, "We could try and shake the old weasel down, though."

"How?"

"I cannot guarantee anything, but we could have my driver take us for a little spin in a big embassy car with an American flag on the front fender. We roll up to his home and keep it idling loudly outside while you go in and try to recover what is rightfully yours." This seemed an unlikely gangster move from the Foreign Service. But maybe this was how American foreign policy worked: unspoken intimidation.

"You don't show the gun," Mark said, "but pretend that you have one. You go to the door, you introduce me, he sees the car, then show him the bank wire details, and ask for your money back. Tell him there must be a misunderstanding. No one would want to risk his reputation and get on any kind of blacklist over something as petty as this. I'll be quiet and just stand behind you, like a big brother." This plan seemed badass.

Mr. Loynab was startled. He saw the big American car and was impressed with my flag-flying strike force. After some bumbling, he relented and returned the money the next day, handing me $10,000 worth of afghanis in a bulging cloth bag.

With Loynab gone, I needed a new Afghan partner. A British guy introduced me to a handsome, ambitious, young shopkeeper on Chicken Street named Aquil Mohammad. He and his two brothers, Lol and Khial, sat all day in low wooden chairs outside their shop shooting the shit and drinking tea. But their main business was garment production. Aquil had assembled an all-male workforce of tailors working away on pedal-operated sewing machines. This Chicken Street trio was roughly my age. They had left their impoverished village in Paktia, a southern province deep in Pashtun territory; Lol and Khial still wore their native Pashtun dress: oversized turbans, baggy, gray salwar kameez, sandals, and a touch of kohl below the eyes. Aquil, the oldest, had a great sense of humor and opted for a more modern look with an open shirt, Levi's, a trucker jacket, and shiny black cowboy boots, like the Marlboro Man. These guys were hungry, and they worked hard. They seemed to have good instincts and were up for a long-term relationship.

I had stumbled into a safe harbor. Afghanistan was still largely a trader culture rife with swindlers, but with Aquil and his brothers, I built a solid business over the years in a very complicated environment. Trust and humor can go a long way.

CHAPTER THIRTEEN

SKETCHES OF INDIA

Going from Kabul to Delhi by plane in 1973 was its own culture shock. It was tomorrow-land compared to Kabul.

The city of New Delhi had been beautifully laid out by Edwin Lutyens, the British architect who led its construction in the 1920s and '30s. The British had visions of it becoming the capital of their entire empire. They finished it just in time to hand it over to the Indians at their independence in 1947. By 1973, the paint was peeling, but New Delhi was still full of majesty, with magnificent architecture, grand monuments, wide tree-lined boulevards connected by roundabouts, public gardens, classic British bungalows, and nice hotels and shops. Old Delhi, a mile or two away, was more like the India of our Western imaginations, full of hustle and bustle and teeming tiny lanes.

I trudged down to see Khub Chand Sawhney in his shop. It was already clear to me that most of my business would be in India. I loved Afghanistan, but India, as constipated as it was in its socialist incarnation, was ever fascinating, plus an infinitely easier place to do work. And they had cardboard.

Khub Chand beckoned me to join him on the two chairs in his small back room. It was closing time, and he broke out his hidden bottle of Johnnie Walker Red. Illicit Western liquor could be purchased clandestinely at the Philippine embassy. He poured three fingers' worth straight up, Indian style.

After we had toasted each other, Khub Chand seemed elated to hear all my ideas. He had plans for a new company—Sawhney Exports. His dream had been to employ and engage his family. Sawhney Exports would be run by his two able nephews, Krishna and Chander, with an assist from their father, Rohan, who spoke perfect English, wore a tie, and sported a gray British-style brush mustache. The Sawhneys quickly bid on two industrial sites in the nearby Okhla area by the Yamuna River, a former slum being converted into an industrial zone. The Sawhneys wanted to build two multistory factories for garment production.

I rented a modern home in a new suburb, Greater Kailash Part 2. Most lots there then were still empty. My house, named "A2," was a walled-in compound with a garden full of young palm, banana, and mango trees. There was a gate at the driveway and three bedrooms, plus one over the garage. There was space for a separate design studio, an office for me, a fully equipped kitchen, outdoor patios, and air coolers. Rent was $650 a month. I asked about a telephone. There was a three-year wait for that.

Phone communication from India was poor and expensive. If you managed to get a phone in your home and wanted to call New York, besides it costing a small fortune, you'd have to shout until you were hoarse, along with banging the heavy receiver against the wall when you were disconnected. The alternative was to go to the Foreigner's Registration Office downtown and wait your turn to enter their malodorous phone booth and shout into its receiver. No matter, Khub Chand said, we would get a telex machine. He had one in his home. Telexes were the future, the high-tech must-have. You could type your message onto a perforated tape and let it rip. In New York, we installed a terminal next to our new computer. Afghanistan was a different story. The entire country only had ten thousand phone lines. There was no telex capability. We sent letters and telegrams.

I hired a watchman, a gardener, a cook, housekeepers, and a toilet wallah, the "untouchable" women tasked with cleaning bathrooms, a sad staple of the complex Indian caste system. Khub Chand lent me an Ambassador car and his Sikh driver, Joginder. I also borrowed a Royal Enfield motorcycle, which I used to tool around South Delhi.

Khub Chand would become my guru on the practicalities of how to best survive in India. He was full of practical wisdom, important to know in a poor, overcrowded country. Like how to take a shower in a dirty place:

"Never step off your flip-flops." Or how to sit more comfortably in the back of a taxi with no AC in 110-degree weather: "Be perfectly still. Do not even talk. Do not move a muscle." Want to find the perfect mango? He knew. Where were the most hygienic restaurants and healthiest juice spots in Old Delhi? Khub Chand was the man to ask.

Hindu Kush soared right out of the box and sales grew steadily for years. We hired an excellent and enthusiastic US staff, almost all women. Our culture was informal, collegial, and fun. Joe and I became millionaires in our late twenties. My parents were incredulous. Of course, that was just on paper. Our money was always tied up in inventory and receivables.

But while I lived well, dressed nicely, got a new apartment, and bought a new green BMW 2002 (which I still have), that was about it. I was just another cash-poor entrepreneur. I was working my ass off, but I kept telling myself I was beating the system.

Looking back, it feels like an invisible hand guided me. Friendships I had made at Lake George and on Martha's Vineyard turned out to be essential to Hindu Kush. Sydney, my tie to Bloomingdale's, was from the Vineyard. From my days at NYU and on Madison Avenue, I had built contacts at the Condé Nast powerhouse fashion trifecta—*Vogue*, *Glamour*, and *Mademoiselle*. They gave our designs plenty of editorial coverage that rendered us a hot, new, under-the-radar company.

Hindu Kush opened a showroom in the center of Manhattan's Garment District. I hired reps in Miami, Los Angeles, and San Francisco, and we began to sell to stores in Canada, England, and the Netherlands. Later, we started a second line, Company B, with industry insider Tomi Hager.

"Follow your bliss" was an old Joseph Campbell nugget. "Do that and doors would open for you that would not open for anyone else." Not the best advice for everyone—you also need the appropriate skills. I had the skills for this and great determination, so that nugget of wisdom worked for me.

Joe and I agreed that the best path for Hindu Kush was to remain a modestly sized, higher-end, niche operation—hovering on the sidelines, away from the more competitive, lower-margin world of larger importers. As Westerners, Joe and I were more relatable to buyers than our South Asian competitors. I was able to spend plenty of time rambling through the dizzying world of 1970s Asia. But just like bands need to write their own songs to really matter, we needed our own designer to create a fresh fashion point of view to make our mark. This most unusual job required a flexible, multitalented person. It was not enough to be creative and skilled. We needed someone happy to be immersed in India and Afghanistan, possibly for months at a time.

I quickly realized that moving to India and Afghanistan, as exciting as I thought it was, wasn't seen by most people as a plum opportunity. Especially by women. But Joe and I both knew one woman who might be willing to pull up stakes and join the ranks: Jill Lumpkin, the freest spirit I would ever know.

Our friendship was formed in that 1970 Vineyard summer when I was the bartender and Jill was the waitress at Oak Bluff's Lampost. Jill was the embodiment of the cool, unapologetic rock and roll girl. She was tall and blond with a model's silhouette and cheekbones. Men went crazy for Jill.

At the Lampost, Jill told me her life story. Her grandmother, a talented seamstress, began giving her sewing lessons when she was seven. Later, she made her own clothes, which had a sexy, breezy, and simple look. She went on to graduate from the Fashion Institute of Technology.

In New York, Jill had worked at Max's Kansas City in its heyday when Andy Warhol, Robert Mapplethorpe, and Brice Marden held court in the fabled back room. She had arrived on Martha's Vineyard on the arm of folk singer Tom Rush. That's her on the cover of his classic *The Circle Game* album, which includes "No Regrets," a song Rush wrote about Jill.

In July 1974, I returned to the States on a recruiting mission to find her. I asked around the Vineyard and was told Jill was often up at Zack's Cliffs, a secluded beach up on the Chilmark coast that sat under dramatic fifty-foot-high cliffs and had mud pits. There was a sandbar just offshore that created perfect waves for bodysurfing. It was also the best of the nude beaches. Jill was sitting in the sand with two girlfriends when I strolled by.

"Hey, Jill, good to see you. May I join you ladies?" I asked with a smile and squatted down on the sand.

"How's your import business going?" Jill asked. I had given her some of our drawstring pants, which she loved.

"It's a whole other world over there, Jill. You'd love it." Then I began my pitch: "I need a designer. I want to up our game. If you're looking for a little adventure, this could be fun for you."

"When would I have to start?" she asked, breaking into a smile.

"How about two weeks?" I took a beat. "Come with me to New Delhi, then Kabul. That's in Afghanistan."

"Are you buying me a ticket, Tommy?" Only Jill and my mother would ever call me Tommy.

"You'd better get a cholera shot."

She was in. There was no negotiation. We didn't even discuss salary. I had just hired a clothing designer who had no clothes on. It still stands as my quickest job interview, and the two of us would work together for seven years. Jill and I became close friends and partners in crime. We shared a house, traveled all over, becoming fellow explorers. At A2, we set up a well-equipped design studio, and she gave the compound a touch of glamour and warmth. She befriended the servants, treating them as equals. With our gardener, she'd cut flowers for the house. She played with the staff's children, made sure that we put them in school, and that they had the proper clothes. She would comb the bazaars, deep-diving for fabrics, and began to create the breezy, sensual, flowing boho look that became our signature.

Jill was a lively roommate. She had a soft spot for wild, unusual men, a breed that was plentiful in Asia. Through her, I got to meet an array of interesting gentlemen whom I wouldn't have met otherwise: smugglers, soldiers of fortune, antique hunters. You never knew who might show up for breakfast at A2.

Jill was invaluable in teaching the tailors new tricks and shortcuts. The tailors were all men, mostly Muslim, and they loved her. None had ever seen a woman like Jill, the archetype of the independent Western female. I can still picture her in the workshop with Shefi Mohammad, our master tailor. One of her feet would be up on a stool as she leaned over Shefi's table. She'd have on a sarong and a tight T-shirt with a brightly patterned scarf wrapped around her head. A lit bidi cigarette would droop out of the side of her mouth like a toothpick. She would demonstrate something to Shefi, and he'd be enthralled.

The manufacturing conditions were challenging even for someone as adaptable as Jill. India lacked modern machinery for garment production. The socialist-made domestic machines were shoddy and low quality, and the government made it nearly impossible to obtain import licenses to bring in state-of-the-art, foreign-built tools, which could have produced far more and better exports. We tried to upgrade the production process as best we could, including smuggling in machinery. I'd buy fabric-cutting machines in New York. We'd break them into smaller parts, hide them in our luggage, and cross our fingers that customs wouldn't open our bags. Shefi lit up when new machinery arrived. He'd carefully connect them to a voltage transformer and lock them away like precious jewels at the end of the day.

Like the entertainment business, the clothing business is very hit-driven. One success made up for a lot of sins. We had our hits—tight-fitting sundresses and patterned quilted jackets from Afghanistan. But our simplest item, soft cotton drawstring pants, was by far our most successful. They were sensual and inexpensive, and we made them in forty colors. Hindu Kush was the drawstring king of the 1970s. We sold a few hundred thousand pairs.

In 1975, *Women's Wear Daily*, the bible of the fashion industry, featured a big piece about our pants under the headline "Hitting thc Jackpot" about how "the simplest shapes became classic winners," which "move out of the stores as soon as they move in." Whenever I meet anyone who remembers Hindu Kush, it's always those pants. They bought them and loved them. Some still swear to have a pair or two.

Operations in the US gradually required more and more of my attention. I found myself spending a bit more time in New York dealing with important clients, especially the department stores, Bloomingdale's, Bonwit Teller, Henri Bendel, and Macy's. Our original business model began to fray. It was more complicated than our original thesis of just "buy low, sell high," but that was its essence: make something in Asia for $4 and sell it in New York for $12 to a retailer, who'd sell it for $25. We'd calculate our landed cost, the price to make the garment plus customs duty and airfreight charges. It looked like a high-margin business, but cash flow became our Achilles' heel. It began to eat away at our initial assumptions.

We had to pay for goods in advance, then we had to sell to stores on credit, often waiting ninety days for payment. When we started out, we were able to get away selling on a COD basis. "Struggling little guys," we pleaded, but the poverty pitch soon wore thin. Big retailers like Macy's would then take an 8 percent discount off the top. "It's standard," they'd say. We'd pay a 10 percent commission to our sales reps in Miami, LA, and San Francisco. Margins headed south and cash flow slowed. We could have $100,000 tied up in advances to our exporters. Laws precluded them from shipping anything to us until foreign currency was received. Our exporters were undercapitalized, too, unable to secure much credit, and they usually needed advances to purchase fabrics. None of these were unusual problems for undercapitalized small business owners. We had a line of credit with the Bank of New York to help fill the cash gap, but interest rates were high in those days, and even with business booming, it was never enough to cover our needs. I'd get stressed and had to scramble loans from family and friends. It was a far cry from the simple, lucrative business I had imagined on Mykonos in 1972.

These were also New York City's dystopian years. A recession was in full gear, and New York was the free-fire zone. The Bronx and Harlem were burning down. Parked cars had little signs in the windows that read "No Radio!," as if New Yorkers had lost faith in the police and were now pleading directly with the thieves. My Afghan pals refused to visit. "No, no, Mr. Tom, too scary . . . too dangerous in New York. Too crazy in America."

But like in India, in New York life went on. Something is always ascendant. Something is always recession-proof. In edgy, dangerous New York City, young, broke musicians were connecting with poets. New genres like punk and disco were emerging. Sam Shepard was writing a new play every season; Patti Smith and Talking Heads made the club CBGB famous; Martin Scorsese was filming his movie *Taxi Driver* with Jodie Foster. On my visits, I'd take full advantage of the musical feast underway in downtown Manhattan. Then, reinvigorated, I would return to my home in impossible Asia, where there remained a million other small frustrations.

The 1970s were India's most turbulent decade. They were days of fascination and confusion for me. The steamy, frenetic, fan-cooled nation was adding a million new citizens every month; annually India was adding a population equivalent to the entirety of Australia. Groups from every level of society filled the streets protesting something or other. Paralyzing strikes, blackouts, and riots were everyday affairs. To an outsider, the country appeared stuck in a vortex of discontent: a constant struggle with poor infrastructure, exploding poverty, a broken caste system, and an apparent official indifference to all of it. I wondered how long the insanity could continue. In 1975, as things bordered on anarchy, Prime Minister Indira Gandhi declared the "Emergency," suspended civil liberties, and began a campaign of forced sterilizations. It only made things worse.

On a sweltering 110-degree June day in Delhi, I endured an hours-long blackout, a dust storm, a fight with a textile inspector demanding more baksheesh, and news of a canceled airfreight slot for an already late shipment. "Anything has to be easier than this," I grumbled to myself. I did not feel like the pasha of Greater Kailash anymore. I stumbled into Khub Chand's shop. He poured some Johnnie Walker, which he served with his usual dose of wisdom: "You see, that is what business is, Mr. Tom. Business is problems. I tell you true."

Simple but wise. I had never thought of it exactly like that. I began to view my work in a new way. In the daily pileup of calamities, I saw problem-solving as the essence of my job. Whatever I was planning, I should count on it going wrong. My role was to put order in the chaos of the supply chain. One had to learn how to be calm and patient. I had to learn how to wait. With that small shift in focus, I found my satisfaction in managing to work my way through the cascading difficulties.

Whenever in New York, I'd always be thrilled to get back to Asia, back in the luxury of A2 or in Kabul. It was easy there to forget the cash crunch and other problems at home. I'm a good compartmentalizer. Asia was so alive. I lived very much in the present there.

Back then, very few Westerners worked in India. Westerners fit in one of four buckets: hippies and junkies, curious travelers on a walkabout, foreign students, and spiritual seekers who came searching for a flash of *satori*. Outside of diplomats and a handful of NGO types, none of them had a job. Getting more conscious, more educated, or more stoned were the primary options for foreign visitors. I was in the minority. In today's jargon I was a "purpose-driven entrepreneur." We were upping the locals' skill set and pumping cash into their thirsty economies. We set up factories with proper conditions. Our workers made money; their lives were improved.

I was tormented by fear of failure. I didn't want to return home with my tail between my legs and allow my peers to have the satisfaction of saying, "Freston wasted all those years. He never should have left Mr. Whipple."

Joe and I did keep the company growing. Sales went up every year, often doubling by millions of dollars. Our ambitions constantly increased, and our skills improved. We were designing, manufacturing, importing, and selling. By the end, we were even making our own fabrics. We had a game plan and were profitable, but, like most entrepreneurs, we flew undercapitalized, without a net.

We could have aimed to go bigger, take in more money, hire more people, and ramp up faster, but we were not out to be the biggest business. We were ambitious; the whole thing was ambitious, but I also had no burning desire to become a garment industry player; I was more interested in the adventure. I wanted us to stay unencumbered.

I built a wide network of Indian friends—writers, travel agents, other exporters, and strivers with small families trying to break into the new Indian middle class. I traveled whenever I had a chance; India had fourteen states then and I hit almost every one. There were many Indias to explore. Like some old colonial, I'd retreat to a houseboat in Kashmir in the hot months and go trout fishing. I loved to visit old British hill stations like Simla or Darjeeling, transplanted European alpine villages with rose gardens and clock towers.

In the 1970s, many royals began running low on rupees and needed new revenue streams. They began to turn their palaces into hotels. I loved it. I'd track them down. The smaller ones were in the most peculiar places, often quite rundown but enchanting nonetheless. I'd rent a suite and prowl around the opulent public rooms and gardens. In the bar room, I'd settle into a plush armchair under tattered old tiger heads and order up a gin and tonic, a maharajah for a day.

Like Mark Twain, I was seduced by the romance of India, its gorgeousness, the extravagant royal titles . . . the Nizam of Hydrabad . . . the Nabob of Jubbulpore . . . the exotic names of towns like Cannanore or Ranakpur. Whenever I went around a corner, I knew that anything could be there . . . perhaps an elephant . . . or a uniformed marching band. India was like another planet back then, home of the contact high. I loved to ramble for hours and lose myself in the crowded, narrow lanes and chaotic energy of markets like Chandi Chowk in Old Delhi, where each stall seemed to be blaring out the high-pitched vocals of Hindi pop songs. I'd feel I was dreaming. Learning to function in that India was vastly satisfying. I read everything on the country I could find.

But with the overabundance of nefarious characters, bad things began to happen. One day at high noon, Paul Ropp, a colorful, fast-talking New Yorker who lived nearby, hopped out of a taxi inside our gate. Laid out flat in the back of the cab was a dead man, Mark Jacobs, a friend from Kabul.

"Mark has left the planet," Paul announced in his cosmic fashion. Mark ran a store on Portobello Road in London and was an account of ours. The taxi was idling and after one look at the corpse, it was clear that rigor mortis was setting in. Our staff was horrified. "God, what happened?" Jill asked.

"Too much heroin, evidently," Paul answered. "I didn't know he was a user. Last night, he was depressed over a breakup." He continued, "I have to figure out how to get rid of his body. Hospitals will not accept dead foreigners. And the taxi driver is not crazy about driving him around." That was an understatement. The sun was scorching. The driver expected Paul to dump Mark's body in our driveway. My wingman Chander somehow got the body refrigerated and contacted Mark's parents, who came to India to bring home the remains of their deceased son.

Then, in the spring of 1977, the CBI, the Indian FBI, raided our house and found 250 pounds of hashish hidden in our garage mixed in with brass ornaments. That was a bad look. It made for quite a scene in our quiet neighborhood. I had hired a seemingly beatific young American woman to oversee production while Jill and I were away. She befriended an American smuggler from Boston, who convinced her our garage was the perfect staging area for his "export shipment." The CBI, along with the FBI, was tracking this dude and later busted him and ten of his pals outside Washington, DC, at Dulles Airport. The shipment contained over a thousand pounds of hashish. A cache of weapons and $120,000 in cash was found at his hotel.

"One thing another!" Khub Chand would always say whenever some new shit hit the fan. He shit a brick this time around. Joe and I figured this was the end of the line. But, improbably, we talked our way out of it. "We don't know nothing," I protested. We were never charged. But the worst was yet to come.

One thing I never had to worry about was Jill adjusting to Asia. It's been fifty years now and she's still there, living in a modern three-bedroom apartment in Bangalore. Chander Sawhney, Khub Chand's lively nephew and our one-time protégé, grew up to become a private jet-flying real estate mogul. He generously gave Jill an apartment as payback for all he learned at her feet.

"Karma," he explained.

CHAPTER FOURTEEN

A LONG RIDE IN THE HINDU KUSH

India was everything simultaneously . . . fascinating and fun, grim and utterly exhausting. It was easy to succumb to overstimulation. There was sadness and madness, but also a rush in surviving it.

Still, my heart was with forbidden, wild Afghanistan. India was tame by comparison. Afghanistan gave you the kind of rush you get when you meet a beautiful woman who seems half crazy. You know she's probably no good for you. She could be dangerous, but that's part of the attraction. That was how I felt about Afghanistan.

Whenever I wanted a jolt, I headed to Kabul.

Early in 1976, I picked up a copy of Eric Newby's travel classic, *A Short Walk in the Hindu Kush*. The Hindu Kush is a five-hundred-mile spur of the Himalayas that slashes right across the top third of Afghanistan. It's full of eye-popping twenty-thousand-plus-foot snowcapped peaks and it's the barrier separating the north and the south of the country.

I ran a company called Hindu Kush. Why the hell hadn't I been there? Forget a short walk. I was more ambitious. I was going to go up and over them, then break on through to the other side to the vast, mostly treeless steppes of Central Asia and Mazar-i-Sharif, sixty kilometers south of the Oxus River and the Uzbekistan border. I decided I'd arrive in time for for their New Year's.

The Afghan New Year, Nowruz, coincides with the arrival of spring. The Taliban tried to extinguish it as "a pagan rite," but it's like the Grinch trying to stop Christmas. Every March 21, Nowruz kicks off a two-week celebration. People buy new clothes for their children, clean everything up, and prepare family feasts. It is by far the biggest celebration in Afghanistan and nowhere bigger than in Mazar.

I rented an old German bus with a sign on the back that said "King of the Road." Then I invited a group of my Afghan friends and some very enjoyable characters from Kabul's small circle of foreigners to join me. "I rented a bus to go to Mazar for Nowruz. Get on board. It's spring break in Afghanistan."

We strapped our luggage onto the roof and our nineteen spring breakers filed in, picked an aisle or a window, and we were off. It was a brisk Kabul morning under a deep blue sky. We were off to ring in (the Persian year) 1355. Spirits were high. Everyone seemed pleased. I felt relief and a sense of accomplishment. Infidels that some of us were, we had a busload of booze and a harem of uncovered women.

As we passed the Kabul city limits, I noticed there was a swarm of jammed buses racing along with us, filled with excited Afghan men. We waved and honked at each other. They waved and flashed thumbs-up, happy to see our women. Mad-looking tribesmen were hanging off the ladders in the back, their turban tails flapping in the wind and their loose arms waving free. We were all headed to Mazar, going up-country, going to the big festival. I set up my tape deck and speakers and put on Canned Heat. We were headed to some place we'd never been before. Smoke started pouring out the windows. We looked like we were off of some Jimi Hendrix album cover, a sea of scarves, skullcaps, shawls, carpetbags, layers of ethnic jewelry, and all the odds and ends of Afghan haberdashery. We could have been headed to Monterey Pop.

The cusp of spring was the best time to be in the country. The delicate winter light turned brighter, the lowland snows cleared out, clouds melted away, and overnight the entire country bloomed. Brown valleys and farmlands turned green with new growth and the almond, plane, and mulberry trees that lined the roads (later chopped down by the Soviets) exploded with yellow and pink blossoms. We drove under canopies of color with the jagged snowcapped peaks of the Hindu Kush glistening and getting closer.

We maneuvered back and forth for hours, slowly puffing through switchbacks up into the mountains. When we reached the fabled Salang Tunnel, the world's highest mountain pass, thirteen thousand feet up, we were deep in snow. Jill had altitude sickness, so we stopped at a *chaikhana*, a teahouse, for a breather. We filed off the bus into an ancient world much to the delight of rifle-toting tribesmen who were perched on their heels on wooden platforms outside on the edge of a cliff, their mouths agape. Above were snowy mountain peaks and mud-colored homes that looked like they could slide into the abyss at any moment.

Our bus took a place in line and moved along through the two-mile-long tunnel in a cloud of leaded exhaust smoke so thick you could just about make out a faint glow of headlights and taillights. I felt like I was being tear-gassed. Then the bus burst into bright sunshine and a whole new world. We had passed into the land of the horsemen, the steppes of Central Asia, the "other" Afghanistan. Below was sun-kissed, green fertile farmland and flat grassy plains all the way to the horizon.

Spirits rose and the booze started to flow. We drove through the mountains and on to Mazar. Fields were full of red tulips. We passed a town with low-domed, yurt-shaped houses, then a series of long-abandoned villages. We slowed for listless herds of sheep and goats. It was on these same open plains back in the thirteenth century, in the Mongol Horde's Year of Zero, that lions and wolves feasted on thousands of corpses left from the carnage of Genghis Khan.

It was dark when we finally spotted the minarets of Mazar.

All travelers to Mazar first see the two large turquoise domes that dominate the skyline. They belong to Afghanistan's most beautiful building and most sacred place, the Shrine of Hazrat Ali. Ali was the son-in-law of the Prophet and is supposedly entombed there. It's considered a perfect masterpiece of Islamic architecture, a breathtaking array of turquoise-colored clay tile panels. From some angles the entire structure appears to float. Large flocks of pure white doves permanently encircle the shrine and its mosque. It is said that, if a dove with a touch of gray mixes in, it will turn white within forty days.

Great Islamic architecture can mesmerize with its simple unadorned beauty. The Shrine of Hazrat Ali was up there with the Taj Mahal in my book. Perfection and balance and harmony.

Today Mazar is a sprawling city of six hundred thousand. We pulled into a town of ninety thousand. It was still the biggest city in the north, inhabited mostly with Uzbeks, Tajiks, and Hazaras. Not many Pashtuns, the conservative tribe that dominated the south. Perhaps because of that, Mazar was said to be the most secular and liberal city in the country. Still, most women were covered.

I had booked us rooms at a brand-new place called the Hotel Caravan Serai. It was small and on the outskirts of town. A local entrepreneur built it in eager anticipation of a tourist boom that was never to arrive. There was a series of round, tricked-out, colorful yurts, each with a shower. It would be our base of operation. We drank the place dry.

The highlight of the trip was to be the buzkashi matches. Nowrouz was the Buzkashi Super Bowl, the grandest moment of Afghanistan's national sport.

Buzkashi means "goat grabbing" in Dari. Imagine polo with vicious, violent gangs of thugs. Instead of a ball with a mallet, the riders brutalize and whip each other over the carcass of a decapitated goat. They need to carry it downfield and dump it into a shallow pit. The game requires great bravery, strength, and skill. Uniformed horsemen wear fur-circled caps and high-heeled boots and gallop in packs battling it out. There can be more than a hundred riders. There are not a lot of rules. You cannot bite another player but that's about it. The violent character of the game and the fierce rivalry it generates is an apt metaphor for Afghanistan and its politics.

This was buzkashi country, home to the country's best horsemen. The long, flat, and sandy fields between Mazar and Balkh were the most exciting places in the country to see the game. Thousands of Afghans packed the perimeter of the field, on the ground or on tops of buses and trucks.

We rolled in, making an odd splash as we filed out of our bus looking like the Merry Pranksters. The field seemed to be a mile long. Watching the match puts one into a Genghis Khan time warp. Riders would thunder by. Huge clouds of dust would follow, then trail the packs of horsemen around the field. Within the cloud, the players would be beating the shit out of the horses and each other.

In a land short of heroes, the buzkashi players, called *chapandaz*, were the top of the line. They were the baddest asses in the land, more so than even the jacked-up drivers of the jingle trucks. Omar Sharif played a *chapandaz* in *The Horsemen*, a Hollywood take on the game made in the early 1970s. You might have seen it. Omar's character, like most of these king-sized men, was sponsored by brutish warlords. Like NFL team owners, they were looking for prestige and legitimacy.

The sun was high and warm on the skin. It was a perfect day for a match. There was a sense of great expectation. This was the Big Game. There was the odd foreigner here and there, but it was almost exclusively an Afghan crowd and virtually all men.

More than one hundred horsemen from the two teams were gathered on the other side of the field in front of a small grandstand. We decided to walk over there to see if we could get closer to the heart of the action. The grandstand was packed with local bigwigs. In the typical Afghan way, they enthusiastically waved us up into the stands and jostled to make room. Foreigners were like celebrities back then. The best action happened right in front of us. Every time the goat corpse was swung into the pit, the winning team would ride over to the center of the grandstand to bow in front of the governor. All eyes were on him as he congratulated the *chapandaz* and handed out prize money to the leading rider.

When the match was over, another man in Western dress came over and said that the governor would like to meet us. The governor was named Mohammad Alem Nawabi, a cheerful, mustachioed man with an aristocratic manner. He spoke English and said he was thrilled to have us all at the match. He asked where we were from and we told him we lived in Kabul, did business there, and loved the country. "That's so wonderful," he said. "Why don't you come to the palace tonight? I'm going to make a very special presentation in honor of the new year. It's a surprise and something that will lead Afghanistan into the future. Please give us the honor of coming."

Around seven o'clock our motley crew pulled up to the governor's palace.

Our bus was escorted right in and we were immediately ushered to the most prominent place on a platform in a large, dark ballroom. There were no security checks of any kind.

We were seated immediately next to the governor. Several hundred high-ranking tribal leaders and VIPs were in the audience below. We were the only foreigners. The governor came in and came right over to welcome us. He bowed, his right hand over his heart.

Something big was about to happen, but we had no idea what it would be. After a while, with great ceremony, a dolly was wheeled in by four uniformed men. Afghan kilims were covering up something secret. The governor made a speech about the new year, told of how the country was on the move, and that a wonderful future lay ahead. That the government was doing all it could to bring up living standards to modernize the country. Then he mentioned that new technologies were going to be embraced, things to accelerate the momentum forward.

With a flourish, the kilims were taken off. Voilà! A television! This was something. In 1976 probably no one in the room had ever seen a television set. This might have been the only television in the country.

After a short explanation, the governor had a man turn on the switch and black-and-white images appeared. A Soviet military band was marching around. The announcer spoke excitedly in Uzbek. It was a TV station from Tashkent just across the border.

It could have been the moon landing judging by all the gaping mouths and wide eyes. The tribesmen were blown away. Yes, there were a few movie theaters in the country, but this was a whole other thing: live images in a box. I studied their faces. They were transfixed, not taking their eyes off the screen, nudging the person next to them, grinning ear to ear. Something was happening here; a page was being turned. *This must be part of our new future*, these tribal leaders of northern Afghanistan thought, *even if it is in black-and-white.*

That moment in Mazar in the mid-seventies stayed with me. We can forget that television can seem a miracle to those who have never seen it before. Years would pass before TV really came to Afghanistan. Fanatics of every stripe would soon consign the country to decades of darkness. The Soviets made television a propaganda tool in the eighties. The Taliban would outlaw it in the nineties. People buried their sets like they were hiding diamonds.

When I returned to work at Afghanistan's first commercial TV network in 2007, that New Year's in Mazar thirty years earlier wasn't lost on me. Tolo TV, and its spin-offs, would become that window to a new future. It became the most influential media outfit in the country. Tolo probably did more to change the country than the $2 trillion Americans wasted on the military.

All this was in a distant and unimaginable future as our bus rolled back to Kabul. I think of that trip now and remember how alive I felt every day, how much I loved covering new terrain, and how sure I was that this was the life for me.

What I loved about Afghanistan was on full display . . . the extraordinary scenery, the sense of being totally unmoored and off the radar, the camaraderie with like-minded travelers, and the welcoming spirit of the Afghans along the trail. I was still young, still soaking it all in, and still had a sense that anything might be ahead, and I'd be okay. I was not thinking about where else I could be. I was right in the moment and right where I belonged.

CHAPTER FIFTEEN

SMUGGLER'S BLUES

Back in Kabul, my preferred hangout was a delightful bar and restaurant called the Columbus. It was set in a regal mansion in Share-Nau, surrounded by a spacious garden and high walls that cut it off from the hubbub of the streets outside. The garden was thick with dahlias and rosebushes, and on summer evenings, the night-blooming jasmine mixed in with smoke from the charcoal grills. You could enjoy a dinner under a starry sky and strings of Christmas tree lights. The clientele was a cross section of Kabul's quirky chattering class: diplomats, spies, government ministers, rich English hippie girls, expats, a wandering world traveler or two, and even a sprinkling of royals from the small Kabul elite. Not quite the *Cheers* bar, but conjure up a fantasy of an exotic Kabul saloon and dope den—and this was it.

Inside the Columbus, Uzbek ikats and suzanis, patterned Turkoman saddlebags, and other tribal paraphernalia covered the walls, alongside an arsenal of old rifles and swords. In Afghanistan, one was never far from a cache of weapons. Tribal rugs in the deep reds and geometric patterns of Central Asia overlapped each other on the terrazzo floors. Each room was lit with clusters of candles. Hanging lanterns with colored glass gave off a warm, welcoming amber glow.

In the separate barroom, you could sit on a velvet stool and order a very large bottle of Pilsner Urquell beer from Czechoslovakia or a shot of Johnnie Walker Red, useful things in a country where alcohol was hard to find. The Columbus was an oasis walled off from the raw, darker bustle of

Kabul. Every night, two Afghan musicians in traditional garb would gently take their place on a floral-patterned cushion at the head of the windowed U-shaped music room. Most Afghan musicians were "*charsis*," habitual users of Afghanistan's potent hashish strain. They'd swear to Allah that hashish created the perfect vibe for getting into the deep groove necessary to perform the trance-inducing ghazals for hours on end.

To start, these two smiling dervishes would meticulously roll two large hash joints, bow to the audience, then light them in tandem. I'd be slack-jawed, watching their almost superhuman powers of inhalation. Each would suck down what seemed to be a boxcar of smoke. They would hold their breath like they were underwater, finally exhaling to fill the room with a strong, sweet, and pungent narcotic cloud that would hover above us. It was a master class in hashish smoking. *They'd have to carry me out of here if that were me*, I'd think.

After a brief cough and a giggle, they'd bow again and politely pass on the joints to the audience for a communal smoke fest. Everybody must get stoned. Once the guests were properly ripped, couch-locked, had finished coughing, and were back to sipping tea or beer, they'd start their music. One gently began picking on his rubab, and the other slowly and rhythmically started drumming on the tabla that he gripped tightly between his legs. The hypnotic drone of classical Afghan music would transport the crowd deep into the mystical East.

One night, these peaceful, easy feelings were shattered when a violent brawl broke out after a hopped-up Afghan accused a foreigner of romancing his girlfriend. The Afghan man flashed a wicked-looking knife. Not to be outdone, the foreigner whipped out a thin dagger. They started crashing around the music room, screaming, trying to stab each other, knocking over tables, and colliding with unarmed bystanders. Their pals piled on. It was hand-to-hand combat in the dope den. The only escape was jumping out the windows, a drop of seven feet. I jumped; others followed and landed on top of me. I got up, dusted myself off, and ran back to my place, gasping in the high altitude. No one paid their bill that night. It was a metaphor, perhaps, for deeper tensions under the surface, a small, ugly prelude of what was soon to come.

Everything changed in the city and the country in April 1978. Early in the morning of April 18, four Afghan Air Force fighter planes swooped down low over Kabul and began to strafe the thirty-four-acre presidential palace. Residents across the capital looked up. They were hearing the sounds of a country starting a forty-plus-year descent into hell.

Coups d'états work best if they're a surprise. Not even the Soviets saw this one coming. Afghanistan's two small outlawed communist parties, gangs that really couldn't shoot straight, had pulled off a Pearl Harbor. They beheaded the sleepy government, which had pushed out the monarchy of Zahir Shah five years earlier. It happened in a day, with just a few thousand soldiers. The radio station was taken over. Tanks and gunfire filled the streets. The entire "despotic, treacherous, corrupt family" of President Mohammad Daoud was lined up in the palace and brutally murdered. Children, too.

Communist leader Nur Mohammad Taraki announced his "glorious Saur Revolution." The Soviets knew feudal Afghanistan wasn't ready for a Marxist transformation. But Taraki and his rebels didn't listen. Proudly independent Afghanistan, a country that had been forever neutral, a country that had famously repelled both the Russian and British empires, saw its flag turn red.

Joe and I had never given communism a thought. In 1978, we assumed it was going out of style. Who the hell wanted to go communist anymore? Afghanistan would be the last country on earth to give Marxism a shot, and there wasn't going to be any room for young capitalists in this new workers' paradise.

A good chunk of our business was ruined and with it my sense of invincibility. Joe and I were despondent. On my last run through the Khyber Pass, the Eagles were singing "Already Gone." So was I. Zipping through Pakistan, I made it to my house in Delhi three days later.

A few months afterward, the Americans managed to kill the rest of our business. The US domestic textile industry had grown increasingly alarmed at the flood of low-cost clothing coming from Asia. They put pressure on President Jimmy Carter to restrict clothing imports, especially from India. There would be a quota. Carter presented it as "protectionism," standing up for domestic industry and not allowing foreign factories that paid low wages to undercut American manufacturing. Joe and I were surprised for a second time, but this surprise turned out to be fatal. The day after the White House made the announcement, the Indian government proclaimed that the annual quota of clothing exports to the US had been filled. And guess what? All the slots went to big Indian companies with strong government connections. I protested, hired lawyers, and tried to organize a trade association. I even went to Kathmandu to see if we could set up an operation in Nepal. I found houses there to rent and turn into factories. But it was far too complicated. I was pissing in the wind.

After years of surviving strikes, blackouts, heat waves, rodent infestations, malaria, dysentery, dust storms, cobras, riots, drug raids, bribery demanders, cheaters, and thieves, Hindu Kush was going to be wiped out by President Carter.

The unkindest cut was that Hindu Kush had just finished its most successful selling season. We literally had tons of clothing in production. Our most important client, Bloomingdale's, was going to run a chain-wide promotion that summer, "India: The Ultimate Fantasy," with our clothes in their windows. Hundreds of thousands of dollars were tied up in the manufacturing to fill those orders. And now I could not get the clothes into the US.

A plan came into focus on my lawn in New Delhi late one night. All the drug smugglers I met in Asia loved to regale me with stories of sneaking pot and hash into the US or Europe. Jill seemed to make a habit out of dating them. My epiphany was: if those long-haired goofballs could do it, so could I. *Don't give up*, I thought. *Do something*. I decided I would smuggle our clothing into the States, collect payment, stand up for myself, and put a small dent in my debts.

Smuggling, I rationalized, would be righting a wrong done to me when the government changed the rules out of the blue. The big bad business guys were using government influence to stamp out us powerless little guys. Of course, anyone looking at this situation logically would have asked, if I was going to risk smuggling contraband into the United States, why waste the effort on clothes? Why not bring in drugs and make real money? But I just wanted justice.

Canada was the key. It still allowed clothes from India. I had a good commercial relationship with an import company in Montreal, run by a tall, bearded, flannel-clad character named Richard. I knew Richard and his wife from Kabul, where they came every winter to buy carpets. I had been shipping them Hindu Kush goods for years. Richard's father had been a rumrunner during Prohibition, sneaking booze into the US by boat. The family still had the fifty-foot boat and a yen for action. Richard said, "Ship me the clothes. We can smuggle them into America easily."

I did a dry run with Richard and his dad, the old bootlegger returning for one last adventure. We drifted out of Canadian waters, down the St. Lawrence River into the Thousand Islands, sailing among pine-covered islands sprinkled with summer cottages. We tacked south to a bigger island on the New York side of the border that connected to the mainland by a bridge. Peter's dad pointed to a dock at the end of an empty field where we could tie up. The place was alive with crickets. There was no sign of customs officers. It looked like the answer to my troubles.

Richard and I agreed on a price, and I shipped three tons of shirts, skirts, and sundresses from Delhi to Canada. We waited for a full moon and Joe and I made three runs over four nights, crossing from Ontario to New York State. We hauled the boxes off the boat and onto a rented truck, then drove our bootleg cargo down to New York City, arriving at dawn and punching the air in victory. I liked smuggling. We made our delivery dates.

That summer, I'd get a thrill walking along Lexington Avenue, seeing our clothes in Bloomingdale's windows, and thinking, *Yep—took that dress down the St. Lawrence.* But this was the end of the line for Hindu Kush. Joe and I managed to sell the company for a fraction of what it had been worth to an Iranian friend, who was desperate to qualify for a US green card to escape the Ayatollah's revolution. The Asia I had known and loved was collapsing behind me as I left.

Hindu Kush wasn't the biggest business, but our sales ran in the millions and we had created a respected brand. But success didn't come easily. Building a company in India as a foreigner, along with a parallel one in Afghanistan, easily ranks as the most difficult thing I have ever done.

It was a lot of work and a lot of fun, but in 1979, it vaporized. Like Ozymandias in Shelley's poem, I had built an empire and lost it all. Now I was thirty-three, deep in debt, and back in New York City.

CHAPTER SIXTEEN
CHANGES

It turned out that good fortune was still with me.

Passing by a bookstore near the Baronet Theater on Third Avenue and 59th Street, I spotted in the window the first edition of *What Color Is Your Parachute?*—the only self-help book I would ever purchase in my life. It was chock-full of good tips on changing careers and reinforced the notion that whatever skills you had were transferable. The book included an exercise to determine where your passions were and how to match them with your abilities. My answer was music. Rock and roll was my main passion. How could I get in on it?

My brother, Bill, worked at Columbia Records. He and his colleagues charged fancy dinners to their company credit cards, drove around in limousines, and invited me to concerts. I got to see two of Bruce Springsteen's epic *Born to Run* shows at New York's Bottom Line and Bob Dylan's legendary Rolling Thunder Revue. The life of a record company executive did not look much like work to me.

In December 1979, I read an interview in *Billboard* magazine with a man named John Lack. He worked at a new start-up, the Warner-Amex Satellite Entertainment Company (WASEC). They had just launched two cable networks, Nickelodeon and The Movie Channel. Cable TV was in its infancy. Lack was considering launching a third network devoted to rock and roll using music videos. I lit up; I'd seen music videos in Europe. This sounded like one of the greatest ideas of all time. Bill had a friend from CBS Radio who had gone to work at WASEC, and got me an interview.

In late January 1980, I entered 1211 Avenue of the Americas for an appointment with Bob McGroarty, the head of sales and marketing for WASEC. There was a poster of Bo Derek in *10* in the waiting area to let you know the company was in show business. I had gotten my hair cut and bought a $300 blue Giorgio Armani soft gabardine suit at a discount store on Orchard Street. I was nervous. I feared no one would want to hire me. I was reviewing my pitch when McGroarty came out to meet me. He had a boyish face and a playful manner. But with his suit and tie, he also had the buttoned-down look of a CBS radio executive.

I was worried that Bob might view this as a courtesy interview, so I went all out. I was looking for something ascendant and creative. I was a music fanatic. I explained that I was an entrepreneur, something they needed. I had started a legitimate business that had made millions of dollars, but I was driven out of Asia by a series of unfortunate events. I told him that I had an MBA from New York University, where I graduated first in my class. I had worked on Madison Avenue. I opened a leather portfolio filled with positive editorials about Hindu Kush from *Vogue*, *Mademoiselle*, and *Women's Wear Daily*.

It worked. Bob told me, "We need to hire a whole bunch of people in the next few weeks. I want you to meet my boss, John Lack, right now." John was a handsome man with close-cropped dark hair and a cleft chin. He wore a well-cut suit and a perfectly knotted tie, a Ralph Lauren man. On his feet were what looked to be slippers. He shook my hand and said, "What were you doing in Afghanistan? Smuggling drugs?" The way he said it, it sounded like a positive.

John did not have a desk, just a low table like you would see in a cocktail lounge. I told him the music channel idea was brilliant. I'd seen the power of music videos in Europe. He motioned for me to sit down and told me how cable TV was going to do to television what FM radio had done to AM. ABC, CBS, and NBC had every kind of program for every kind of viewer. They tried to reach everyone. They were broadcasters. That was old thinking. The future was in "narrowcasting." Each cable network would program one thing, all the time, 24-7, to a smaller, more select audience. New geosynchronous satellites made all this possible. "We are going to start a revolution, the TV revolution," he declared. "The music channel will only be the tip of the iceberg!"

John then threw out the unlikeliest line: "We're looking to hire smart people who have no experience in television. We have no money. We can't afford to produce TV like the networks do. We need people who don't know the old rules, people who can think outside the box and invent a new way."

I replied, "Goddamn, I'm your man. Not only do I have no experience in television—for the last eight years I've been living in places where they didn't even *have* television. And I'm an entrepreneur and a music nut." John sent me back to McGroarty, who offered me a job as head of marketing on the spot. "It's thirty-five thousand dollars a year. You start Monday."

This was going a lot better than I'd expected. I said, "Gee, Bob, that is so fantastic. You will never regret this. I'm the man for this job, but I can't start for a month. I have prior commitments."

McGroarty looked at me like he was already wondering if he had made a mistake. He said, "If you want the job, be here Monday."

"I just can't," I said. "I promised to finish up a thing or two."

McGroarty answered, "Look, Freston, if you come in Monday, the job is yours. If you can't commit, then all I can say is, come back in a month, and we'll see if the job is still open. We like you. We have a lot of slots to fill."

I thanked him and said I would soon be back. Then I took off with my girlfriend Margaret Badali for a few weeks of travel in Morocco, one last ride on the Marrakesh Express. I assumed that signing up for this new career would be a return to the straight world and to the corporate life I had fled in 1972—I had no idea that my adventures were just beginning.

Hindu Kush had managed to disintegrate at the perfect time. If it had been even a month later, I would have missed my greatest ride, hopping onto the MTV train. It could almost make a man believe in predestination. People talk a lot about luck, but timing is usually underrated.

On a rainy St. Patrick's Day, I reentered 1211 Avenue of the Americas. McGroarty had given the marketing job to a friend of Lack's, who had a more traditional, solid advertising background than I did. But there was still a place for me, McGroarty said. My desk was in a storage room turned office, where they kept cases of soda. For six months, my job was to sell

Happy hour, 1946.

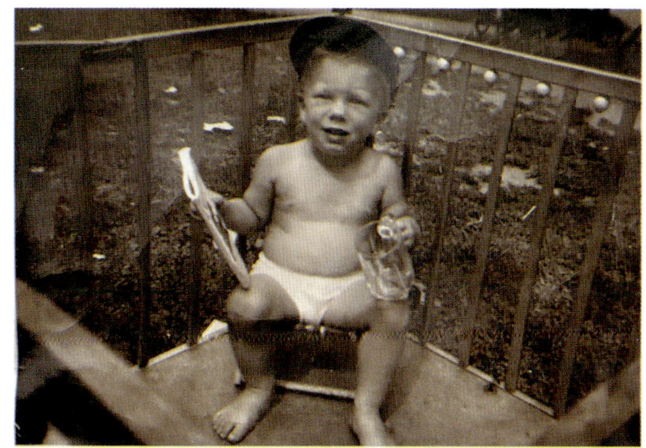

With mom and dad, 1946.

Sixth grade—braces with a flat top.

With my dad and mom and brother, Bill, circa 1970.

In the Hindu Kush, 1973.

Hitchhiking in England, 1972.

At the erotic temples in Khajuraho, India, 1972.

Hiking on Gomera in the Canary Islands, April 1972.

Rooftop riding into the Kathmandu Valley, 1972.

Suzanne Weil and Aquil Mohammad. Kabul Gorge, circa 1976.

Buzkashi match. Mazar-i-Sharif. March 1976.

My Afghan tailors on a trip home to Paktia. Aquil Mohammad is squatting on far left. Lol Mohammed is standing in center with rifle, 1974.

Khyber Pass, 1974.

Hindu Kush staff. Irvington, NY, 1977.

Joe Potter, my Hindu Kush partner, 1978.

Hindu Kush featured in *Women's Wear Daily* and *Vogue*, 1975.

Afghan tailor at work, 1974.

Me and friend Barbara Cooke at Mount Abu, Rajasthan in 1975. *Ken Cooke*

My staff at A2 in New Delhi, 1976.

Designers Jill Lumpkin and Lynn Ritchie in Kannur (formerly Cannanore), India, 1978.

New merchandising concept. Chandi Chowk, Delhi, 1974.

My local fruit stand. Share-Nau, Kabul, 1975.

The Himalayas, Nepal, 1978.

Fellow traveler Mike Dolan in 1978.

With (from left) John Sykes, Charlie Daniels, and Larry Divney at the March 1981 National Association of Recording Merchandisers (NARM) Convention in Florida, sporting our first MTV T-shirts.

Sumner Redstone outside the Video Music Awards at Pauley Pavilion, L.A., 1992.

With Mick Jagger, circa 1987.

Meeting Mr. Whipple, AKA Dick Wilson, at the 1996 Launch Party for TV Land, Universal Studios L.A. *Jeff Kravitz*

With Elliot Roberts and Neil Young at the 1993 MTV Video Music Awards at Universal Amphitheater LA. *Jeff Kravitz*

With Jon Bon Jovi, New York City, May 2005. *Photograph © Patrick McMullan*

FROM LEFT: me, Sumner Redstone, Courtney Love with daughter, Frances Bean Cobain, Rosemary Carroll, Danny Goldberg, and Kurt Cobain of Nirvana at the 1993 MTV Awards. *Jeff Kravitz*

The photo of the police boat that got us arrested on the Saigon River. Vietnam, 1993.

At the Royalton Hotel with my animated pals. October 1997.
Photo by Terry Doyle

At the opening of our India offices. Puja ceremony, circa 2000.

At Angkor Wat on a break from an MTV Asia management retreat in Siem Reap, Cambodia. 2002.

With Beyonce at the MTV Awards, 2003. *Photograph © Patrick McMullan*

With Lenny Kravitz at the 2001 My VH1 Awards. *Jeff Kravitz*

At the *War of the Worlds* premier in 2005, with Brad Grey and Tom Cruise. *Alex Berliner*

The orphanage Kathy and I built. Taunggyi, Myanmar, 2006.

With author William Dalrymple and Saad at Will's farm outside Delhi in 2018.

Bono with African ONE activists. Abuja, Nigeria. 2019.

Presenting the Asia Society's Global Vision Award to Aung San Suu Kyi at the U.S. Institute of Peace in Washington, D.C., September 2012. *Asia Society/Joshua Roberts*

Lunch at the Presidential Palace with Fidel Castro showing us his Chilean wines. Havana, Cuba, 2001. *Jonathan Brandstein*

Me and Jimmy Buffett at the Festival in the Desert. *Jonas Karlsson*

Jimmy Buffett and Carey Lowell at a rehearsal for *Escape to Margaritaville* on Broadway, 2018. *Rob Meder*

With Bono in Cape Coast, Ghana, circa 2010.
Jonx Pillemer/(RED)

With Oprah at the Jaipur Literary Festival in India, 2012.

With Michael Stipe of REM. Frankfurt, Germany. 2001.
Jonas Karlsson

Hiking in the Panjshir Valley with Amrullah Saleh, former head of Afghanistan's National Directorate of Security, 2013.

Me at an Afghan Premiere League football game. Kabul, 2014.

On the Rio Grande River in Jamaica. FROM LEFT: Gil Freston, Homer Gere, me, Carey Lowell, Andrew Freston, and his wife, Gemma, in 2023.

Andrew and Gil. Antiparos, Greece, 2016.

On top of Lake Como with Carey, 2023.

Nickelodeon and The Movie Channel to "pole climbers"—local cable operators in places like Fall River, Massachusetts, and Cooperstown, New York.

WASEC started having growing pains. Heads kept getting chopped just above me. In my lesser position, I was just below the swing of the axe. My boss left, and I was promoted to the job that I had been offered when I first walked in. In October, I heard that the Warner-Amex board was reviewing the business case for launching the new music channel. John Lack had brought in a young radio guy to develop it.

Bob Pittman was twenty-six years old and considered a star, the one-eyed hippie genius. He had never been to college and had already programmed some of the biggest radio stations in the country, last working with the legendary talk DJ Don Imus in New York. Bob liked my checkered past and was also convinced I'd been a hashish smuggler, which seemed to make him like me more. "Were you smuggling hashish?" he asked.

"Not really," I replied.

"Not really? That means you were! You're hired!" The smuggling thing was turning out to have been a good career move.

Bob was disdainful of traditional career tracks, and he liked odd. He once told me that he could not understand why people went to college. "They could've been out making money all that time."

I promised Bob I would give everything I had to this new channel. He made me his marketing chief, and I made the most of my shot. MTV was the opportunity of a lifetime.

The son of a Mississippi preacher, Bob was baby-faced and wore a suit to make himself look older and more credible. His slight drawl and quick patter could mesmerize almost anyone. Older folks thought he was some "youth whisperer," a guy with his finger on the pulse of a culture they did not have a clue about. He was one of the best bullshitters I had ever seen. I knew I could learn a lot from Bob Pittman. Bob was a great but demanding boss. This younger dude became a mentor to me. I was the oldest on his team, the only one over thirty.

Bob had hired eight of us for the original development team for the still unnamed "music channel." We set up shop in Manhattan's Sheraton Hotel in October 1980 and were told to turn his vague concept based around music videos into a new kind of cable network by August. In 1980, cable TV was considered low-rent and lowbrow. Cable programming was personified by Ugly George, a guy with a video rig on his head going around New York City asking women, "Show me your tits." It was not *Masterpiece Theatre*.

MTV was in many ways the ultimate start-up, a small group of crusaders in love with an idea. We were all music fanatics, and our mission, as we saw it, was to sweep the nation with this irresistible new musical invention. We shared desks strewn with old pizza boxes. The few phones all had call-waiting, the cheapskate's second line. We worked seven days a week, arguing and throwing out ideas. When we squeezed into new offices at 1133 Avenue of the Americas, we'd hold court well past lunch hour at Cafe Un Deux Trois, the unofficial canteen around the corner on 44th Street. Some nights we'd close the place, getting shuttled out with a bundle of paper tablecloths covered with crayon scrawls of creative ideas and business plans. No one made more than $35,000 a year. We would have worked for less. There were no stock options, which was fine—no one knew what they were.

America was still in the shitter in 1980. Inflation, gas lines, and the hostages in Iran dominated the news. In November, Ronald Reagan was elected. In December, John Lennon was murdered. If the sixties counterculture began with the assassination of JFK and the arrival of the Beatles, it felt like it ended with the arrival of Reagan and the assassination of Lennon. The music industry was in a "post-disco" slump and the labels were blaming home taping for all their woes. Media had been boring as hell. The three broadcast networks were dinosaurs coasting on past glories. It was the heyday of *The Love Boat*, *Fantasy Island*, and *The Dukes of Hazzard*. FM radio, with its steady diet of Boston, Kansas, and Styx, was starting to feel pretty square, too. It was a good time to offer something new.

We named the new channel MTV, although some on the team thought "MTV" was not catchy enough. MTV was originally built for baby boomers, eighteen- to thirty-four-year-olds, not teenagers. We were going to combine their two favorite things—television and music—in a new way. We had rich parents, Warner Communications and American Express, an unlikely alliance that wouldn't last. They barely knew we existed and treated us like an unwanted stepchild, shuttled out of sight on a meager allowance. Bob made sure we never saw our big bosses. We thought of ourselves as underground operators, hipsters crafting something new. We were going to draw more from the art and music scene of early eighties downtown Manhattan than from *Don Kirshner's Rock Concert* and *The Midnight Special*. MTV was going to be neither mainstream TV nor a seventies FM rock channel with pictures.

After nine months of prep, we launched at midnight on August 1, 1981, with 165 videos in our vault and a square logo that had cost us all of $1,000. About one hundred of us celebrated together at the Loft, a dingy New Jersey bar, about the only place in the New York City area where MTV was available. I brought Margaret, whom I had married eight months after we returned from Morocco—she had faith in my future.

The bar was ground control for our first flight. There were a few speeches, then a minute before midnight, a hush descended, and fingers were crossed. Were we going to make it to the moon or blow up on the launchpad? We all stared at the one television, counting down. . . . *10, 9, 8 . . . !* There was ignition, the rocket launched. The MTV flag was planted on the moon to a huge cheer. We were probably the only people on earth watching. John Lack did a voice-over: "*Ladies and gentlemen: rock and roll.*" And then came the Buggles prophesizing that video was going to kill the radio star. We were on our way. No one left before closing time.

The broadcast network people, in their three-piece suits and 95-plus-percent market share, laughed at us. We were just poor wannabes, know-nothings who didn't understand the economics of television, couldn't create quality programming, and were wasting time dreaming up crappy ideas that would never attract an audience, even if we ever actually managed to make them.

"Who the hell is going to watch music on television?" they screamed. *Everyone*, I thought. We were convinced the tide was on our side. We were so futuristic we were going to shoot our signals to satellites up in space. Fuck broadcast towers. A cornucopia of specialized new TV choices was going to shower down across the land. Soon, city after city began announcing they were granting franchises to companies to string coaxial cable down every street. The cable guys were coming.

This wasn't flying-car stuff, but it seemed to me that a new age was underway, and we were perched at the tip of the spear. CNN, USA Network, ESPN, and our sister network, Nickelodeon—the "narrowcasters"—were breaking new ground together. We didn't think of the other cable start-ups as rivals. We were fellow innovators, co-conspirators, brothers in arms. We knew the consumer was ready for us.

Anyone involved in a start-up dreams that their little venture will one day be enthusiastically received, turn a profit, and become a worldwide phenomenon bringing in boxcars of money and changing other businesses.

This is exactly what would happen with MTV. We went all the way from the New Jersey bar to worldwide conquest. And was it fun. The power of this simple idea would finally convert the skeptics—the cable and satellite operators, the advertisers, the music companies, and the government regulators. One by one they all joined the band.

CHAPTER SEVENTEEN

THE FIRST TIME

The girl at the Hertz counter at the Tulsa airport was staring at the little MTV button on my lapel.

"MTV! Wow . . . that's so cool. Where did you get that?" John Sykes—MTV's first director of promotion, the man behind that button, and my traveling companion that day—didn't miss a beat.

"Oh, I've got a bunch of them," he said, producing a fistful of MTV badges. "Take a few. Each one is different."

"How do you know about MTV?" I asked the young woman.

"You're kidding? Everyone knows about MTV."

At that moment, early October 1981, MTV was unavailable in New York, Chicago, Los Angeles, and every other big city. In fact, no one who worked for MTV got MTV at home. In 1981, cable was still mostly a rural thing; we had to travel to the heartland to look for proof of life. MTV might have been dreamed up in Manhattan with a downtown sensibility, but it was out in Middle America, in places like Tulsa—one of the few urban areas with a cable system—that the channel got its start. MTV descended upon an unsuspecting Tulsa at midnight on August 1, feeding into a hundred thousand living rooms. People stopped and stared at the weirdest channel they had ever seen.

Tulsa Cable was one of the world's largest cable systems, part of United Cable, and was managed by a smooth-talking, handsome man in a suit and cowboy boots named Mark Savage. Mark had signed up for MTV sight unseen before we launched. He thought it was a brilliant idea. He agreed to pay us ten cents per subscriber each month, an ungodly sum at the time.

We spent three days in full Oklahoma immersion. First, we cruised over to KMOD, the leading rock station. The program director told us, "MTV is making it much easier for us to play new music," like Squeeze, the Tubes, and the Buggles. Bill took us to a bar. MTV was on, and people were watching it like a football game. I stood there, quietly jumping out of my skin. When John started giving out swag, we got a hero's welcome. The next day, we made the rounds to the record stores: Sound Warehouse, Peaches, and Record Town. One guy at Peaches told us, "People who have never heard of Talking Heads see the video and come in to buy the single. . . . I say there's no single, so they say, 'Gimme the album.'"

John and I called Bob Pittman from a record store and put the manager on. On October 15, an ad with record store testimonials ran in the trade papers *Billboard* and *Cash Box*.

Mark Savage, however, gave us a dose of cable reality. "I really don't care if you're selling records. My only concern is, can MTV help me sell more cable subscriptions?" In this conservative city, some citizens regarded MTV as offensive, even sinful. MTV must be canceled, a group of ministers told Savage.

It's easy to forget how revolutionary MTV was back then. Most TV viewers had never seen music videos. Suddenly five guys in a group called Devo, a band no one had ever heard of, would pop up in red plastic hats, black shorts, and turtlenecks. One guy cracked a bullwhip at women and ripped off their skirts while chanting, "Whip it. Whip it good!" This was not the Captain & Tennille.

The first wave of MTV videos leaned toward what record companies called "new wave." We were heavy on Talking Heads, the Clash, Elvis Costello, Blondie, and Nick Lowe, along with some reggae—edgy stuff that was mostly the domain of college radio. Our second wave would be a new breed of British groups with striking visuals and hooky pop melodies: Culture Club, Adam and the Ants, Wham!, and Duran Duran, five handsome guys getting sprayed on the bow of a fast-moving sailboat surrounded by sexy women. We also had the Pretenders, a British band fronted by a singer from Ohio named Chrissie Hynde, who strutted around a diner in a waitress uniform singing, "I'm special," and the Stray Cats, dudes with elaborate ducktails playing rockabilly in an alley while angry neighbors throw shoes at the one plucking a huge stand-up bass. Random scenes, quick cuts, and total non sequiturs flashed in and out in seconds. It was hard to look away.

There were no shows. There was no plot. Only playful logo animations and "VJs," perky young people in a studio, interrupting the chain of music and images to tell you about David Bowie's tour dates or chat with a new Irish group called U2. Sometimes old people would appear on the screen in black-and-white, dancing the waltz. After ten seconds a big X would cover the screen and a voice would announce, "Don't watch that, watch this," and the picture would cut to Pat Benatar in black leather pants belting out a song in a dingy warehouse.

This format was not only different from Dean Martin and Glen Campbell; it was different from *American Bandstand* and *Soul Train*. *The Ed Sullivan Show* used to have something for every member of the family. That was the old broadcast television thinking. MTV clearly wasn't for everyone. We didn't want to be.

Perhaps the greatest gift Bob Pittman ever gave us was not giving us enough money to make slick things. It forced us to be scrappy and inventive. We couldn't afford to hire the corporate promotional firms that worked for ABC and NBC. We created imagery out of whatever we could get our hands on that was cheap or, preferably, in the public domain. Our creative director, Fred Seibert, discovered that we could use all the NASA footage we wanted for free. "Why not rip them off?" he said. "They have the best production values. They make rockets." The rocket launch cutting to an astronaut planting a flag on the moon ran at the top of every hour for five years. The MTV logo was on the flag. It would pulsate in and out in different designs. "It's the perfect rock and roll thing to do," Fred said triumphantly. "We're ripping off man's greatest moment."

We built an experimental, in-house creative team and staffed it with young misfits. In one early promo, we held a stencil of the MTV logo over a photo of 1600 Pennsylvania Avenue and spray-painted it. We graffitied the White House. We weren't just bringing the devil's music to Middle

America—we were defacing the nation as fast as the cable lines were being laid.

But we also needed to get viewers to our channel. We needed to get famous. That's where John Sykes and I came in. John was a good-looking, high energy, excitable guy of twenty-six with a case of restless leg syndrome. He came from the record business, where he had squired around the likes of Cheap Trick and Joan Baez, and developed a rare talent for relating to musicians, making friends with them, and getting them to help legitimize us.

A superfan himself, John understood rock fans' desires. After a few rounds of offering satin tour jackets and T-shirts, which any third-string local radio station could do, John created over-the-top contests where winners took private jets to faraway concerts and went backstage to meet the artists. We filmed these affairs and aired them on MTV. We offered access and fantasy. "A Lost Weekend with Van Halen" was an early contest. In the promo, David Lee Roth intoned, "Do you have the guts to enter this contest? It's destination unknown. You'll have no idea where you are, no idea where you're going, and you will have no memory of it when you return." We got over a million postcard entries. "You and a friend will fly in the MTV Learjet, take a limo to the show, get draped in MTV swag, and hang with the band." Even when we were struggling, we acted like we were big, bad, and nationwide. This contest almost backfired, as the band got the winner intoxicated and pushed a big cake in his face onstage. His friend leaned over to say, "He's doing okay for a guy with a steel plate in his head, isn't he?" He had no memory of it when he returned.

Entire offices would fill up with duffel bags of millions of contest entries. Someone would crawl in blindfolded to pull the winner out of the pile. These stunts put us on the map, but they didn't always go as planned. One time we gave away a "Pink House," a John Mellencamp promotion. You would win a home, and Mellencamp would come over and "paint the mother pink." John picked out a house in Indiana for $25,000. Our friends at *Rolling Stone*, happy to embarrass us, broke a story that it was sitting on a waste dump. We had to go out and buy the winner a second house.

But for our nervous bosses at Warner-Amex, we were behind on our business plan and badly needed to show some financial progress. Money was flowing out the door. Bob remained quiet about it with the rest of the staff. But I knew. It was clear that wherever MTV was, fans were plentiful and devoted. But our distributors were monopolists. There was only one cable operator for each piece of geography. There were no alternatives like satellite operators or internet providers in the early 1980s. In any place where the cable operators ignored us, we did not exist. They weren't about to give us a channel and then pay us unless we could prove we could bring them lots of new customers, which they called "lift." Without "lift," MTV was just another nuisance cutting into their profit margins.

Many of these cable guys were older, rural, and macho. Many weren't rock fans, or if they were, they listened to Elvis. They didn't like the haircuts of A Flock of Seagulls—or the gender-fluid Boy George. Some thought MTV was the devil's workshop. Capitalizing on that sentiment, Ted Turner launched his "Cable Music Channel" against us. He made it free. He told the cable guys that he'd only play good, "non-satanic," God-fearing, Christian-friendly music. He'd always cite the Twisted Sister video where the kid threw his father out the window. No parent was going to be thrown out a window on CMC.

Ted got this one wrong. What young person wants music that is designed to be safe and unoffensive? Statistically: zero. The Cable Music Channel lasted just 105 days. But in 1982 MTV's subscriber count stubbornly remained under 2 million homes and none were in major media markets. We needed a big idea. We needed a call to arms. And we needed it immediately.

CHAPTER EIGHTEEN

THE HAIL MARY PASS

Elvis Presley had just finished performing "Don't Be Cruel" on *The Ed Sullivan Show*. It was September 9, 1956, and I was ten, starting sixth grade. My parents, my younger brother, Bill, and I were huddled around the TV. Sixty-four million other Americans, almost four out of ten, were tuned in, too. I felt like a tornado had just passed through our suburban living room. "That was disgusting," said Mom. "How could a mother let her son dress like that? Look at his hair."

"That's a rotten kid," added my father. I think my parents thought they had just witnessed the start of the fall of Western civilization. They might have been right. Elvis was my first signal that I was going to grow up in a different world from the one my parents had struggled, through the Depression and the war, to preserve. At school, there was a new camaraderie among my friends. As we turned into teenagers, we would become increasingly fascinated with new haircuts, pegged pants, loud motorcycles, custom cars, and the shared joy and freedom that rock and roll brought us. This was our music.

That same September when Elvis shook his hips, Maypo, a breakfast food manufacturer in Burlington, Vermont, was struggling to sell its new maple-flavored oatmeal. It may seem like a stretch to connect Elvis to Maypo, but both were pure products of 1950s America that would identify and exploit a new demographic: the swelling numbers of children born after World War II.

Fletcher Richards, Calkins & Holden, Maypo's New York ad agency, came up with a campaign that played on the burgeoning generational cohesion and empowerment they sensed in these kids. Their radical idea: instead of gearing their pitch to mothers, they wanted to sell Maypo directly to children. Amid the Saturday morning cartoons and evening Westerns, they ran commercials in which little brats turned up their noses at Mom's breakfast and cried, "I Want My Maypo!" It was groundbreaking. Maypo sales shot up. "I Want My Maypo" became a famous baby boomer chant nine years before the Who released "My Generation."

It took a while for the long tail of Elvis to connect with the legacy of Maypo, but when they did converge, it saved MTV and my career. George Lois, a brash, foulmouthed Greek-American art director, was the ad man who took over the Maypo account when Maypo needed a reboot. Lois riffed on Wheaties' use of sports heroes on their boxes to sell their cereal. He enlisted Mickey Mantle and Wilt Chamberlain to cry on camera and whine, "I Want My Maypo!" It was ironic, it was satiric, it was bold, it was ridiculous. It was advertising that became more famous than the product.

By the summer of 1982, MTV was in desperate straits. We were still big in Oklahoma, but few other cable companies were adding MTV to their lineups. In American business, if you ain't growing, you're dying. We were in danger of being shut down if we couldn't convince more cable guys to carry us before the money ran out.

Enter George Lois and Dale Pon, a wild-eyed, smiling but scary-looking dude, whose specialty was "media promotion," which involved banging people over the head repeatedly with a simple idea, such as: "Love songs, nothing but love songs. WPIX FM." Dale and George were hired to help us beat the reaper. "Let's rip off that old Maypo campaign," George said. "I want my MTV! Fuck these cable guys. You got to go for broke." Being solicitous of the cable operators had gotten us nowhere. The next step was to get legions of spoiled young adult baby boomers to demand their MTV just like they had once demanded their Maypo.

So was born the campaign "I Want My MTV." Now we had to identify which stars were the rock and roll equivalents of Micky Mantle and Wilt the Stilt. George Lois answered that immediately. "You need to get Mick Jagger. He's the biggest star in the world."

Sure, George, no problem.

We had learned some lessons about big stars and MTV. Early on, we had struggled to get permission even to use photos of recording artists on the channel. Sykes and I realized we were asking the wrong people. To the record labels, we might as well have been a high school fan club asking for free pictures. They were oriented toward radio and print, not TV. It was worse when we tried to go through the lawyers. They said no as a policy. It seemed to defy logic, but we found that the easiest people to deal with were the hardest people to get to: the artists themselves. Rock stars lived behind insulated walls, but if you could get over those walls, more often than not, you were welcomed to the party inside.

We all felt that if we got the most iconic stars, the rest would follow, so we went off like bounty hunters to bag our targets. John's mission was Pete Townshend. Les Garland, our hilarious, new larger-than-life head of programming, went for Mick Jagger, whom he had met before. I drew David Bowie. This was our Hail Mary shot.

John waited for hours outside Townshend's manager's London office. When Townshend showed up, John went into his boyish charismatic mode. "Hi, Pete, I'm John Sykes! I'm with MTV, it's a new channel that plays music videos. Would you do a promo for us like you do when you visit radio stations?"

Townshend probably assumed his manager had set this up. He asked John when he wanted to do it. "How about right now?" Dale Pon had rented a garage across the street and had his camera set up. John led Townshend over. It took only a few minutes.

Garland took Dale Pon and a video crew to Paris to stalk the Rolling Stone. They all were holed up in a Paris hotel, waiting for Jagger to show his face. When he finally appeared, Les was on him with the full hustle of a seasoned radio veteran. Jagger remembered him. "All you need to say is 'I want my MTV,'" Les said.

"You want me to do a commercial?" said Jagger.

"It's really more of an endorsement, an endorsement for a new phenomenon called music videos."

"Yeah, that's a commercial. The Rolling Stones don't do commercials."

"Mick, we don't have any money. But, if this is about money, I'll give you a dollar." Les laid a dollar on the table. It could have gone either way, but Jagger laughed.

Then he said, "I like you, Garland. I'll do it."

Jagger told them to come back the next day. They did. He gave them five minutes, during which he said, "I WANT MY MTV!" a few times, giving it the weight of "I can't get no satisfaction!"

That single moment set us on our way to victory.

I still had to get David Bowie.

One of my true heroes, Bowie had been the first artist to allow MTV to use his photo in promotional materials. When I had approached him for permission, all he had asked about our channel was "Is this going to be good for music?" I explained, "We're going to put music on TV in everyone's home twenty-four hours a day." He said yes on the spot.

David had a very pleasant, somewhat mysterious associate named Coco Schwab. Managers came and went, record labels came and went, but Coco was constant. I called her. "Would David be willing to do an 'I Want My MTV' commercial?"

She responded a day later. "He'd really love to. But David's skiing in Gstaad, in Switzerland, right now. He's on vacation. He'll do it on skis, on the slopes there if you want. Are you up for a little trip? It'll be fun."

Was I up for that "little trip"? We were operating like *Mission: Impossible.* Along with Dale Pon and his crew, I took a plane to Zurich, then a train, and wound through the snowy Alps to posh Gstaad with a full load of heavy 35mm gear. Coco had us carry everything out into the snow and set up at the bottom of a remote hill. David skied down in great spirits. He was in his slick "Let's Dance" phase. On the slopes, he looked like a surfer with blond hair, dressed in a slim parka and shades. He directed himself for the spot. He wanted to ski down, swoosh at the bottom, rip off his sunglasses, and, with a broad grin, say, "I Want My MTV." He thought it would be fun to put our logo on his skis, too, in postproduction. We got the spot in a few takes. Mission: Accomplished.

When we finished, David asked if any of us wanted to ski with him. I am rarely starstruck by artists. Bowie, though . . . Bowie and the Beatles had a special aura for me, head and shoulders over everyone else. David made it easy in the Alps. He talked about books more than music. He asked about my background. I got some laughs out of him. I knew a girl who worked for him who dated my brother. That was another icebreaker.

Later when the sun was dropping, David said, "Hey, Tom, how about a sauna later to relax? Top off the day. Come meet me at the Palace Hotel." The Palace was the epicenter of Gstaad high society, the towering five-star, grande dame hotel in the valley. I rushed back to our hotel, a spartan lodge barely a cut above a youth hostel. "You're not going to believe this, but Bowie just invited me to take a sauna with him at the Palace Hotel. See you losers later," I told the crew.

David was waiting in the spa. We walked together into the sauna. There was only one other person there. He was sitting on a high bench up in the back, deep in the fog. I squinted. It was Paul McCartney! Jesus Christ. Somehow, I'd made it into the Sauna of the Stars. David and Paul, and Tommy Freston from Connecticut, sat around naked, wrapped in towels, taking turns throwing water on the hot rocks. We shot the shit for half an hour. They were easy to talk to and eager to hear about MTV. I was full of gratitude.

"Jagger's in," we told Pat Benatar. That was all she needed to know. Same with the Police. Our storyboard had Sting swinging a telephone receiver around like a madman, almost jumping off the screen and shouting, "America! Call your cable company and demand your MTV!"

I helped round up Billy Idol, Cyndi Lauper, Hall & Oates, and others. I traveled with Dale Pon and his camera crew all over the world. After a while, artists were calling us asking to be in the spots.

"I Want My MTV" became one of the most effective ad campaigns of all time. It saved us. It transformed us. After a three-week barrage, without fail, each cable operator in a market we targeted raised a white flag and signed up. We added more than a million new homes every month for more than two years. I had a map in the office to help us plot our next attack.

In the end, we closed in on the two major media markets, New York and Los Angeles. This was where the influencers, the opinion makers, the critics, the advertising agencies, the magazine editors and, most importantly, our employees lived. In rock and roll, it takes a long time and a lot of work to become an overnight sensation.

All of America got its MTV. Then the entire world got it. In 1985, a song came along that opened up new continents for us, "Money for Nothing" by Dire Straits. This was still the age of international superstars. Sting sat in and sang the chorus, the hook—"I want my, I want my, I want my MTV"—to the tune of the Police hit "Don't Stand So Close to Me." People in countries that never heard of us were now singing, "I want my MTV." It was a marketer's dream.

Dire Straits' lead Mark Knopfler had written the song as a takedown of MTV, a satire on what he saw as MTV's vapidity. We couldn't have cared less. Wherever I'd go in the world, Sting's chorus had beat us there. Even the guerrillas in Burma's jungle wanted their MTV.

It might have been George Lois's brainstorm to rip off his old Maypo campaign, but it was Dale Pon whose persistence and perfectionism made sure the campaign stayed on a roll until we mopped up every music fan we could—Dale parachuting in with his crew to ambush Townshend in a garage in London or capture Bowie on a ski slope in the Alps.

There is a long line of people who to this day claim credit for MTV's success. But there are two who never put their hands up to claim the acknowledgment they deserved. One was Fred Seibert. Fred set the playbook and sensibility for all the odd stuff MTV would become famous for. Fred gave MTV its cool persona and made it a cohesive place, not just a collection of unrelated elements. Later, with his partner, Alan Goodman, he did the same for Nickelodeon, Nick at Nite, and our other networks.

From Fred, I learned how small teams of young, offbeat creative people, not huge bureaucracies, were the way to go. He was an exceptional people picker, always rotating in fresh recruits and mentoring them to keep us on the cutting edge. I learned a lot watching Fred.

The other person is Dale Pon, whose perfectionism and contrarian thinking helped save MTV from the dustbin. I chased rock stars all around the world with Dale. I'd sit with him and his faithful sidekicks, Susan Kantor and Leslie Fenn, for hours straight in edit rooms making MTV commercials—painfully slowly, going frame by frame under Dale's intense direction. It took a lot of hours and fine detail work to make those ads look like they were tossed off. Dale was a difficult man, hell-bent. "Crazy-ass" was the conventional wisdom about him. But we owed him a lot. Dale had a list of simple maxims:

- Dominate the space. Be louder than everyone.
- You remember the first thing you see and the last thing you hear.
- Have one idea . . . and say it as simply as possible.
- Advertising is a "frequency medium."
- ANYTHING is possible.

We made almost everything possible in the years ahead.

CHAPTER NINETEEN

THE CRAZY YEARS

After we busted through the cable operator gates with "I Want My MTV," we became the new gatekeepers. Everyone wanted to be on MTV. Labels and artists lobbied to get their videos in heavy rotation. We could catapult nobodies to stardom in weeks. That was a lot of power to wield. Power doesn't always bring out the best in people.

MTV was also in the zeitgeist business, so we took a lot of chances with new things, not always successfully. If something didn't work, it died a quick death and we moved on. We decided we weren't going to grow old with our audience the way *Rolling Stone* magazine had—they were still writing about Bob Dylan and Eric Clapton.

We would refresh and reinvent MTV every four to five years as one group aged out and a new one replaced it. "Teenagers" were a radioactive group, although they loved us. But no one over twenty wanted to be associated with teens. We never had teens on the air and never used the word "teen."

Advertisers pay a higher premium to reach young people. The thinking is: hook them on Crest or Pepsi or Ford early on and you've got a customer for life. Plus, that crowd didn't watch much TV. When MTV said, "We have a direct line to them," Madison Avenue lined up at our door.

One by one, record labels agreed to give us clips for free, and they set up whole departments dedicated to servicing MTV. But they never stopped grumbling. They complained about the money they had to spend to increase the quantity and quality of their music videos. So we agreed to pay them millions of dollars through new, multiyear "output deals." Buried in those deals was a clause granting us exclusivity for six months over any other 24-hour channel on 20 percent of their music videos. The 20 percent of the videos we picked were all the big hits. No potential competitor could take a run at us without access to the hits.

I was against using hard-nosed tactics with the record companies and artists. Gatekeepers with a heart seemed the best way to prolong our prominence. As "the biggest radio station in the nation," I argued, we should be fair, humble, and walk softly; the labels were predisposed to resent us. My opinion didn't always carry the day. I watched some of our talent-relations people blossom into megalomaniacs. I guess it's human nature that if you are hanging out on boats with Billy Idol and partying with Van Halen and strolling into every dressing room while giving thumbs-up or down to anxious managers, it will eventually turn you into an asshole. I saw it happen again and again.

A recruit to the Music & Talent department with good ears and a deep knowledge of pop and rock might last three years. To fire them, we might have to find a concierge to kick down a door in an LA hotel and revive them after a three-day cocaine binge. We needed a strong human resources department. Top-notch music programmers with a good manner stayed for years. My goal was to build respectful, long-term relationships with artists and record label brass, to help us maintain our powerful position in the industry.

We were witnesses and eager participants in the last display of the legendary excesses of the music business. The party really kicked into gear when Bob Pittman made former radio DJ and label executive Les Garland the head of programming. Les was the one who had gotten Mick Jagger to scream, "I want my MTV." He referred to himself in the third person as "the Gar Man," which tells you a lot. Les Garland wasn't his real name. Like many former radio people on our staff, he created a radio name. "Les Garland" was really Lester Schweikert. Show business has a great tradition of welcoming people who want to reinvent themselves.

Les looked about my age, but to this day I don't think his date of birth has ever been revealed. He was an effervescent, good-looking guy with stylish curly brown hair, confident that he was the king of cool. In many ways he was. MTV's fingers were in every pie of the music industry machinery and for a while most things came through or went out from Les. He arrived with deep music business relationships, full of war stories from the rock and roll trenches of the seventies, which he recounted to entertain his younger minions. It was like David Lee Roth had arrived in an Armani suit and taken over the floor.

Amid towering speakers, gold records, stacks of videotapes, Sony Trinitrons, overflowing ashtrays, and a bar stocked with tequila and a lineup of squat green Dom Pérignon bottles sent over by the labels, the Les Garland Show streamed. Every time a big ad sale landed, he rang a huge bell. Grizzled label promotion men in satin jackets and facial hair would slink in and out, usually laughing. Rod Stewart would drop by to play his newest tracks. When female artists came calling, his staff would vacate, and according to office lore, the Gar Man would fornicate with a lucky few. At least that's the legend. With Les it was hard to tell what was true, what was myth, and what was scandal.

When he wasn't there, others would sneak in to have sex in his office. At one Christmas party, a staffer full of holiday bravado cozied up to Garland and said, "Les, I just want you to know that I fucked one of your assistants last night on your desk."

Les clinked his glass. "Congratulations, Bud." He walked away, without a follow-up question.

Big blowout parties became part of company mythology. "Tequila girls" in short shorts and cowboy hats, decked out in bandolier sashes packed with shot glasses, always circulated. Tequila bottles were nestled in holsters strapped across their hips. Bands like the Fabulous Thunderbirds would play. These parties could go on to three or four in the morning, sometimes devolving into after-parties. You could never get away with this kind of office party nowadays. Nonetheless, the next day, a line would form outside the human resources offices.

The Gar Man undeniably upped our game, our profile, our whole tempo.

To me, over in marketing, MTV was a lot like Kabul. An exotic new place with a crazy cast of wild characters and few rules . . . and fun as hell. A superfan myself, I had the privilege of attending any concert I wanted. Every day we dealt with the biggest stars in the world, along with all the black sheep and characters who handled them. Even though music drove the culture, the business of music was still considered the lowest rung of the entertainment ladder. To people in film and television, it was a lowbrow world of payola, shysters, and semi-gangsters in sharkskin suits. But these were the folks I liked the most. They had hustle, were clever, and loved music. They were also the most fun. Some label heads, like Gil Friesen, who ran A&M, Jeff Ayeroff, who ran Virgin, and Jimmy Iovine, who ran Interscope, became good friends.

Many in the MTV crowd had not been to or finished college. I went undercover with my academic credentials. It sounded a lot better to be "the man from Afghanistan" than the MBA from NYU.

People worked in flip-flops and bathing suits; some slept in their offices. In 1988, at 2 a.m., an overnighter flipped a lit cigarette into his garbage can and burned down a whole floor at 1515 Broadway. Nineteen firefighters were hospitalized. The local radio stations would play Springsteen's "I'm on Fire" and dedicate it to us.

"Exotic dancers" would be sent over by the music labels. Bands passed through all the time. Lemmy from Motörhead might wander by with a bottle of tequila. We had one receptionist who sold cocaine. Many of the staff found that convenient. Cocaine was rampant in the eighties, especially in the music industry. Even your dry cleaner was doing it then. People thought coke was the new No-Doz, a harmless pick-me-up powder.

One of the programming guys, a jovial, former radio hotshot whom Howard Stern had crowned "Pig Virus," kept his stash in a little plastic receptacle in his desk drawer, the place where you'd put paper clips. In a meeting, he'd nonchalantly open the drawer and take a hit off a collar stay, then politely look around. "Anyone need their beak packed?"

MTV wasn't a job; MTV was a life. We were a second family. People would duck out all the time to the bar around the corner. At night, there was always a smorgasbord of things to choose from . . . concerts, dinners, listening parties, movie screenings. We were in the middle of everything, so we were invited to everything. It was not unusual to make three stops a night—preview a new film, catch a concert, go to a party. Not everybody made it out the other side; there were casualties with all the late nights, alcohol, and drugs. No one except me had a family. Margaret and I had a young son, Andrew, at home, which kept me pretty much on the straight and narrow. Once he went to sleep, I could head back out on the town.

To try to prop up the business side and bring order to the chaos, Pittman installed a series of general managers. They didn't take. One, David Hilton, undermined his predecessor and then went down in flames. Hilton had zero music chops, which earned him zero respect. I've never seen anyone do a worse job at anything. He sent around a note to announce that if anyone was even one minute late to a meeting, they'd be locked out. He locked his door and put a chair under the doorknob. People would pound on it to no avail. Sometimes we'd all be purposely late so he'd have to have his meeting by himself. He became increasingly crazed. Hilton would often appear at my office door and shout, "Mr. Peepers!" That meant I was expected to follow him into the men's room to urinate next to him and hear his latest musings as we pissed away.

In 1984, MTV held the first Video Music Awards at Radio City Music Hall. It was a big step forward for MTV, a coming-out party we threw for ourselves. We were positioning ourselves as the irreverent alternative to the self-serious Grammy Awards. Bette Midler and Dan Aykroyd hosted. The Cars' "You Might Think" won best video, and Herbie Hancock's "Rockit" won pretty much everything else. Madonna rolled around on the stage in a wedding dress while singing "Like a Virgin" and a star was born. New York's mayor, Ed Koch, opened the proceedings.

When MTV began, we played almost any video we could get our hands on. As we proved our ability to sell records, the bigger stars with bigger budgets pushed aside the punkier stuff. The record companies began to crank up music video production. Instead of four or five new clips a week, we began to get fifty or sixty. Big star holdouts like Bruce Springsteen joined in. Older acts like ZZ Top reengineered their image. Lionel Richie spent a whopping $1 million on his "Dancing on the Ceiling" video.

As MTV became more influential, we also got more scrutiny, and not just from the Christian right. The criticism that stung was that we were not playing Black artists. In a very awkward interview with VJ Mark Goodman, David Bowie challenged him about the channel's color line. Rick James went on a public crusade about us rejecting his "Super Freak." He was right.

Rock radio went backward after the 1960s, when the Beatles and Stones shared airtime and formats with the Supremes and Aretha. The early MTV music programmers came from the world of seventies FM rock radio, which relied on a format called "album-oriented rock," or AOR. It was a very researched system, but predicated on an underlying racism. "Our audience wants to hear a guitar," was the refrain from the programming guys. AOR resegregated rock and roll.

In the 1980s, the record companies all had "Black Music" departments. The trade magazines, *Billboard*, *Cash Box*, and *Radio & Records*, all had separate Black Music charts. It wasn't just MTV. But we were the only music channel on television. Early MTV did play some Black artists who fit the AOR format—Joan Armatrading, Grace Jones, Eddy Grant's "Electric Avenue." We gave heavy play to Prince's "Little Red Corvette" and "1999." But that doesn't excuse the sad fact that the music department would put Hall & Oates doing R&B in heavy rotation, while ignoring Luther Vandross and the Brothers Johnson.

The wall was finally knocked down by Michael Jackson's *Thriller*, the biggest album of the 1980s. CBS Records chief Walter Yetnikoff always claimed that he forced MTV to play Michael Jackson by saying that if we did not, he would pull all Columbia and Epic videos from the channel. It's a good story, but I have never found anyone who worked at MTV who had any idea what Walter was talking about. "Billie Jean" was a smash from day one. We wanted that video on our channel. "Beat It" was even better.

By the time MJ released the video for "Thriller" toward the end of 1983, he and MTV were in a mutually beneficial relationship. We played his thirteen-minute mini-movie on the hour, every hour. I ran ads in *People* magazine with start times. Our ratings went through the roof and so did Jackson's album sales.

In the late eighties, we opened the aperture further. We were the biggest music outlet in the world; there was no need to follow anyone. MTV would be the first to mainline hip-hop into Middle America's living rooms with *Yo! MTV Raps*, hosted by downtown Renaissance man Fab 5 Freddy. Aerosmith and Run-DMC sanctified the rock-rap connection with the clever video "Walk This Way," and we were off into a whole new world.

But before that came our next powerhouse: the July 1985 sixteen-hour Live Aid extravaganza held simultaneously in London and Philadelphia. Bob Geldof, lead singer of the Boomtown Rats and the man behind the multi-star African famine anthem, “Do They Know It’s Christmas?,” was Live Aid’s organizer. He’d cut a deal with ABC to run a three-hour highlight program in prime time, but we committed to carrying the entire sixteen-hour concert commercial-free. At the time, it was the biggest satellite linkup and television broadcast ever. It raised almost $200 million for African famine relief and would set a template for the many all-star fundraising concerts to follow.

Paul McCartney, Elton John, and David Bowie were on the bill in London. Fans saw a career-making performance by U2 and a showstopper by Queen. Phil Collins performed at Wembley, then jumped on the Concorde to play another set at JFK Stadium in Philadelphia, where Mick Jagger tore off Tina Turner’s skirt.

I rented a car and drove from New York with Bob Friedman, my eager marketing foot soldier, known internally as “the V,” for reasons no one remembers. He wore Lacoste shirts and had an odd sort of Beatle haircut. When we got there, we realized our credentials were in the hands of a producer who had disappeared. This was the pre–cell phone era. There was no one to call. We finally found our way to the artists’ enclosure and jumped the fence. I landed in the dirt right in front of Bob Dylan’s trailer, dusted myself off, and then calmly strolled down lanes of trailers, striking the pose of someone who belonged.

It was like wandering through the Rock & Roll Hall of Fame trailer park. Signs read: Tom Petty, Santana, Madonna, the Beach Boys, the Four Tops, Neil Young. We finally made it to the stage, and I spent the entire show at our news desk, twenty feet from the action. Live Aid was the final step in the legitimization of MTV. We were now like “Kleenex” and “Coke.” That year, we made the covers of *Time* and *Newsweek*.

As for David Hilton, Pittman finally showed him the door and crowned me general manager. It was my fortieth birthday. I had finished my apprenticeship and was ready to run the beast. I got a very warm welcome. Always follow an unpopular person into a job if you can.

CHAPTER TWENTY

THE MOFOS

MTV's eternal challenge was to try to maintain an aura of hipness, but hipness expires like milk. James Dean and Jimi Hendrix retained their cool by dying young. For the living, it is a steady struggle. The hip factor let us get away with higher fees from cable operators and way higher rates for advertising than our modest ratings necessarily deserved. In adspeak, that's called the "power ratio." Advertisers paid a premium for their association with us.

We couldn't be too cool. We had to be hip by Middle American standards. Not Captain Beefheart hip, but David Bowie hip. Blondie hip. Our image spots were Talking Heads, but our music hours featured a lot of 38 Special.

By the mid-eighties, the sheer what-the-fuck novelty of music videos, even with their lavish budgets and star directors, was beginning to wear off. Radio programming had caught up with us. Other television began to look like MTV. *Miami Vice* was famously born of a two-word directive: "MTV Cops." Barry Diller and Rupert Murdoch were about to launch the youth-oriented Fox network.

As I took the throne as general manager, MTV's hipness quotient was dwindling. We were established and profitable, but there were whispers that we were just a fad. A reason for that was one built-in disadvantage of our main staple, music videos. They were short and self-contained. There was no through line to hold a viewer over commercial breaks. If you watched *Cheers*, you would sit through the ads to see if Sam and Diane were going to hook up. If you watched MTV, you might leave as soon as a bad video came on—and you might not come back that day. Our greatest nemesis was the remote control. The rise of that soap bar–sized device was turning out to be the most underrated television disrupter of all. Twitchy thumbs were now our executioners. One false move and goodbye.

Bob Pittman saw our strong ratings softening and was worried. Just before he quit, in late 1985, he organized us into a series of teams to try to reverse the erosion before the outside world caught on. Pittman made this a competitive exercise. What came out of these brainstorming sessions would create a blueprint for our future. Bob put me in charge of a team of nine. We called ourselves "the MoFos," short for "motherfuckers." Mine was a very astute, street-smart team. We all wanted to make a solid case that'd blow Pittman away, a jarring blueprint for the future. People all think they can be TV programmers. Like playing tennis or flying airplanes, it looks easy from the outside.

The MoFos felt that if we could expand a bit beyond the 24-7 music video format, we could make MTV a bigger place and establish a firmer business footing. A second generation of cable channels was just over the horizon. Media experts were predicting that someday soon a cable system would carry thirty-five channels. A few even said it could someday go as high as fifty-four!

"MTV is anti-authority . . . but we've become an institution. Real champions, like John McEnroe, know how to change their game plan." We pressed our point: "Our target audience, the young adult music fans have grown, evolved, and changed in the last four years. We're still stuck in a 1981 time warp."

Yes, music was our first name. Music brought us glamour, excitement, and controversy. But that meant we were totally at the mercy of the ups and downs of music trends. We had bound ourselves to the vitality of videos. We felt we could become more engaging by including some of the areas that music intersected with—fashion, art, movies, politics, sex. *Rolling Stone* magazine did this in the seventies. When music was not the most exciting thing going on, they would give their covers to actors, comedians, and political leaders. *Rolling Stone*'s most revered writer, Hunter S. Thompson, never wrote about music at all.

Our solutions weren't rocket science: Broaden our format to include other parts of the popular culture. And be more unpredictable, funnier, and more interactive with the audience, not just run videos all day. Since everyone seemed to want to be on MTV, we suggested making room for actors and comedians, even fashion models. We had thorough backup from our research folks, a serious brain trust who used all kinds of methods to get inside young people's heads.

Not everyone agreed with the MoFo position. The main opposition to MTV moving beyond just music videos came from—surprise—some in the music department. Along with the talent-relations people, they picked the videos like political kingmakers in their smoke-filled room. Many fought hard for the pure music position. My heart was with them, but my brain knew that battle was lost. We weren't abandoning music at all, we were just talking about adding some new flavor for only 10 percent of our 168-hour week.

The best thing to happen to me with the MoFos was getting to work more closely with Judy McGrath and Juli Davidson, two kick-ass, street-smart media savants. Creative people would line up to work with them, and they would help steer us away from the sexist, male-driven culture of the music business. Juli won countless awards for us in her various creative director roles, but she was at heart a musician and songwriter. Judy became a legend; she was the greatest talent magnet we ever had. She told me to "embrace the aberrant ones." She had come to New York to write for *Mademoiselle* magazine, which told her she was crazy to quit that institution to join a rock and roll (*echh*) cable (*yuck*) TV start-up. Judy eventually rose to president of MTV/VH1, then CEO of all MTV Networks, inheriting all my old jobs. We are great friends to this day.

A key reason for our success was women. We put women in many jobs traditionally filled by men. At the time, the television industry was still a men's club. Over half my senior team was female. Different, often better, thinkers, talented women would come to dominate almost every part of the cable business. MTV, VH1, and Nickelodeon were at the front of that wave.

The MoFos won the contest. Pittman gave us the green light to begin expanding MTV's purview beyond music. It was MTV 2.0. We unchained the VJs. Got them out of the damn studio and off on location. We hired other on-air talent, too. We began building MTV News. Doug Herzog, a music and news junkie who came to us at twenty-three from CNN, ran the news operation. He poached Kurt Loder from *Rolling Stone*. Judy McGrath brought in writers David Felton, Timothy White, and Charles M. Young. David's business card said "MTV's Oldest Employee," which took me off the hook. *The Week in Rock* became a must-see. Viewers saw it as "my window on the world."

Pittman left in 1986 before producers Joe Davola (immortalized in the 1990s as a character on *Seinfeld*) and Michael Dugan created a pilot for a game show set in a basement for $5,000. It was a zany send-up about TV trivia. The hosts were comedians who stood there smoking cigarettes and wisecracking, and it got us into the burgeoning NYC comedy scene. *Remote Control* cost $15,000 per episode and lasted five seasons. Hosts Ken Ober and Colin Quinn became celebrities. Adam Sandler and Denis Leary got their TV starts on that show.

This new direction was tremendously liberating. Ratings soared. We traveled the globe—from Daytona to the Moscow Music Peace Festival to the Montreux Rock Festival to Mardi Gras and the US Open of Surfing in Huntington Beach, California. Daytona Beach paid us to come broadcast the spring break bacchanalia festivities there. The city fathers threw us out, so we migrated to Panama City, then other places. We were never invited back anywhere.

There were always people who complained about any nonmusic programming on MTV, but when we asked them what current videos they liked, what new bands they wanted to see, we would get a blank stare. We came to realize that what the complainers wanted back was not music videos—it was their youth.

CHAPTER TWENTY-ONE

THE BATTLE FOR VIACOM

In 1985, Warner-Amex announced it might sell MTV Networks to Viacom, which got its start in the early 1970s as the syndication arm of CBS. Viacom (pronounced "Vee-a-com") sold reruns of *I Love Lucy* and *Lassie* to local stations. Government regulators forced CBS to spin it off into a separate company. Starting with the CBS programming library, Viacom went on to purchase a small group of TV and radio stations, a handful of cable systems, and then Showtime.

But the home of Lassie the collie and Lucy and Ricky, with their twin beds and headlining at the Tropicana, was not a natural fit for MTV. Sensing disaster, Bob Pittman had led our executive team in an attempt to buy out MTV ourselves using that ubiquitous 1980s financial vehicle, the leveraged buyout, or LBO. We had the investment bank of Forstmann Little ready to go and thought we had a done deal at $470 million, until Viacom upped its offer to $525 million. Our revenue was a puny $50 million. Steve Ross, CEO of Warner, chose Viacom.

"You never get a second chance to make a first impression," intoned the famous Head & Shoulders shampoo ad. That perfectly summarized our first encounter with our new Viacom bosses. After they defeated us at the battle of the leveraged buyout, they helicoptered to Montauk, on the eastern tip of Long Island, to declare victory and see what they had won. Our top people were at Gurney's Inn for a company retreat. The new bosses arrived at the property like it was a commando raid—quick in, hit us hard, quick out. We had set up a microphone in the basement ballroom.

The Viacomese marched in, and Terry Elkes, Viacom's no-nonsense CEO, stepped up to the mic and without even a word about our success or the exciting future they might see for us, went into a rant: "I know a lot of you have stock options."

Warner-Amex had taken one-third of MTVN public in 1984, and we each held a tiny amount. The options were scheduled to "accelerate and vest upon a change in control." This small reward was the only silver lining of the Viacom deal. "We've talked to legal experts," Elkes said, with all forty of us now on the edge of our chairs, "and we're pretty sure we don't have to pay you off." Then he riffed about cost controls in tedious detail. But we had stopped listening. All we heard was that he wanted to chop costs and planned to renege on our stock option payouts. After the speeches were over, the suits filed out and got back on their chopper, while we rushed to the bar. It was noon.

Fueled by tequila shots, we began to destroy Gurney's cocktail lounge. Someone hurled a shot glass. It smashed against the wall. We transformed into Led Zeppelin, a hotel-wrecking crew of enraged cable weasels. Tables covered in drinks were upended, more shot glasses were thrown, and six-foot potted palm trees were heaved over. Someone started taking fish out of a large aquarium, then the aquarium was overturned. "Fuck Viacom!" was the chant. When the carnage was complete, and the last fish had ceased flopping, I surveyed the wreckage. These vandals were my tribe.

We busted up a few more places in the years to come. It was an infantile ritual. We'd refer to it as "Wayning," as in John Wayne—"We Wayned the place," was the proper terminology. The *New York Post* ran the headline "Ten Years Old and Not a Day Older" about a tenth-anniversary party for MTV I threw in 1991 for all the original players. This time the victim was my neighborhood favorite, the Tribeca Grill. Bob Pittman kicked off the proceedings by throwing two shot glasses against a brick wall. Soon, the room was a shambles, and we were out on the street. But that first Wayning at Gurney's holds a special place in my heart.

With Viacom's arrival, a black cloud settled over our previously happy organization. Like the Beatles, we had enjoyed years of fun and glory. Now, like the Beatles, we were breaking up with anger and recrimination; many of the top executives, including John Sykes and Les Garland, left almost immediately. Bob Pittman briefly assumed control, but he quit in disgust. On the way out the door, he crowned me president. I was thrilled with the promotion, but part of me felt as if I were taking over as the captain of the *Titanic*.

My new Viacom boss, Ken Gorman, wasn't on board with Bob's decision to promote me. He wasn't sure I was ready, and he didn't trust me with advertisers. Money was a big source of the antipathy between the MTV Networks hipsters and the Viacom suits. Ken Gorman was pleasant enough to me, but he was an obsessive penny-pincher, more fixated on costs than opportunity. We were already working cheap, but Gorman thought we had been infected with Warner Communications's penchant for luxury, and he would always find reasons for outrage. Gorman insisted that I needed a "co-president," and he picked Bob Roganti, a hard-charging New Yorker, who was head of ad sales. Roganti wore dark sunglasses day and night and always kept his blinds down. Some joked that he was a vampire.

We tried to make it work, but split leadership is rarely easy. It also invites the staff to play the two bosses off against each other, the way kids will try to leverage mom against dad. A top item on Roganti's agenda was to shut down VH1, our adult music channel. Roganti felt it distracted from MTV. It would be much easier, he argued, to sell just one music channel. My argument against closing VH1 was practical. If we shut down VH1, we were opening a space for someone else to move in. Even when VH1 was playing Barry Manilow videos, it served as a flanker brand—keeping our rivals out of any music space. My argument prevailed. In 1994, John Sykes returned to the company to run VH1. He assembled a first-class creative team and built buzz and a separate identity for the network. With hit series like *Behind the Music*, *Pop Up Video*, and *Storytellers*, viewership soared and VH1's profits grew to hundreds of millions a year.

But to me, this bickering was also a sign of things to come. I could no longer pretend that the job was fun, and fun is an essential ingredient for me to stay committed to anything. Maybe, I thought, I should take the hint and leave as well.

That was where my head was when my phone rang inside my Tribeca loft late on a bone-cold Saturday morning in February 1987. Bob Pittman—the man who took me off the unemployment rolls in 1980—was on the line.

"Tom," Pittman said, "I just left the Carlyle Hotel. Had a meeting with this guy from Boston, Sumner Redstone. He'd love to meet you." Sumner was a mysterious Boston billionaire. He'd built a New England movie theater circuit, National Amusements, from a string of drive-ins. "Billionaire" was an unusual word in 1987, when people still dreamed of making a million dollars and retiring to a beachfront mansion. A billion dollars was almost incalculable. Leave it to Bob to hook me up with Redstone, shaping the company's future after he moved on.

At age sixty-three, Redstone wanted to build a Hollywood empire, and he sensed that Viacom could be the entry point for his ambitions. He had been quietly accumulating Viacom stock. By the time the Viacomese registered what Redstone was up to, he was dropping hints that he'd like to take over the company and oust the corporate robots who were making my life a misery. Next, he put a bid on the table to buy Viacom for $2.4 billion.

The Viacom executives talked about Sumner Redstone like he was the shark from *Jaws*. They refused to meet with him. As Redstone circled, Ken Gorman corralled all the senior managers into a conference room. His face was red with determination as he sputtered, "If anyone so much as utters a word to this guy, Redstone, I will personally fire you. Immediately. It's none of your business. If he tries to contact you, just say no!"

Thus, Pittman and I both knew how loaded his next words were: "I gave Sumner Redstone your number," Pittman said. "He's going to call you in an hour." This was a hanging offense.

"Redstone thinks they stole the company and he wants to send them packing, but needs to better understand the company's prospects. Go see him. What have you got to lose? The current guys suck. Maybe he'll be better." Bob was right. I had nothing to lose.

An hour later, Redstone phoned. He spoke with a thick Boston accent. Could I come to supper at his hotel? "Sure, I'd love to come to dinner, Mr. Redstone. You must know that you are persona non grata. Ken Gorman told me he'd fire me if he caught me speaking even one word with you. I'll be coming to the Carlyle undercover."

"Bring Gerry Laybourne if you can," he said. Gerry Laybourne, a brilliant, highly determined former schoolteacher, was the Nickelodeon version of me, who also arrived with no TV experience, and was now running our kids channel with a vision to make it bigger and cooler than the Disney Channel. I called Gerry. She was in. "Let's strategize on how to handle this," I said. "We're crossing enemy lines. I wouldn't say we're Benedict Arnolds. We're partisans, resistance fighters trying to liberate our territory from the invaders. It's treason for good reason. We need a savior."

"Badly," said Gerry.

"Our challenge is to see if the two of us can quietly sell a company we don't own to a devil we don't know. The odds are he'll be better than the Viacomese. I mean, he wants to start building a media empire at sixty-three? He must have heart."

Gerry agreed. "I don't think he is going to want to waste any time achieving moguldom."

"No, not on the cheap, either, I suspect. Let's just lay out our hopes and dreams. State how we're being held back. Make clear that there is an open field right now, and that opportunity is wasting away. We have little to lose."

"Except our jobs," said Gerry. "I'll be in the Carlyle lobby at seven tomorrow. Disguised."

Gerry and I slunk into the Carlyle Hotel like a couple of spies. We kept looking over our shoulders as we got off the elevator and rang Redstone's buzzer. Sumner greeted us warmly. His wife, Phyllis, was by his side. *Nice family people*, I thought.

I extended my hand. Sumner offered his purple, mangled right claw. It was his permanent reminder of the 1979 Copley Plaza Hotel fire in Boston that burned a good part of his body and almost killed him. He promoted a legend that he hung off a third-floor ledge by his fingertips while flames engulfed him. He was just too tough to let go. I can't say how true that story was, I wasn't at the Copley that night, but Sumner made his deformity a symbol of his unbreakable will.

Sumner was the first billionaire I ever met. I was expecting a lavish Carlyle suite, the kind of chambers where JFK might have courted Marilyn Monroe or Liz Taylor and Dick Burton polished their diamonds. It was deflating to see that the Redstones had just a modest single room. When I used the bathroom, I noticed a pair of panties drying on one of those retractable strings that pull out over the bathtub. *He's saving on hotel laundry bills*, I thought. Funny what you remember.

Redstone was calm, bright-eyed, and full of energy. A charismatic man, he had neatly parted graying hair and the face of a Boston Brahmin. His demeanor was grandfatherly. Decades later he'd brag to reporters, while holed up high over Beverly Hills with a harem of comfort women, that all he craved was steak and sex three times a day. But that side of Sumner was not on display when we met for the first time. He was dressed in a plaid sport coat with a pattern reminiscent of old car seat covers from the fifties. His pants were baggy, and his shoes were way too big. His feet had been burned, too. He spoke softly in his thick Boston accent, acknowledging our "bravery" for coming to see him.

We ordered dinner from the room service menu. Sumner ordered a rare steak. He went on to pepper us with questions about Viacom and its prospects. He was clearly thrilled to be finally speaking to people who actually worked there. A lawyer by training, he was very careful not to disparage the current management. Gerry and I were not so diplomatic. We ran down the company, our problems with the current management's lack of vision, and what a great road lay ahead if only we could get our hands on some cash to invest in our future. It was pretty much the same pitch we'd given the Viacom guys, who had been unmoved.

The through line was that MTV Networks was just getting started. With reasonable support, we could build a self-contained worldwide media colossus centered on kids, teens, and young adults. The world was changing. Other countries were beginning to deregulate their media, which meant that private satellite and cable operators would inevitably spring up. They would need lots of content quickly. Someone was going to become the first international television networker. Why not us?

We were like singers with a receptive audience, and we pulled out all our hits. We went into our brand strategy and why it was perfect for the coming era of media fragmentation. With hundreds of choices, we said, strong brands would have a powerful advantage, providing a shortcut for confused consumers. The old networks were defined by their hit shows. When NBC had *Bonanza*, it was unbeatable. Then CBS rode in with *All in the Family*. ABC was the sad number three until they launched *Happy Days* and *Mork & Mindy*. But the old network model rose and fell on hit shows.

We were not dependent on any series. Few of our viewers were going to remember the names of our shows. Our networks were "places." They didn't watch the *Top 20 Countdown*. They watched MTV. Children watched Nickelodeon. Thirty-year-olds watched VH1 and Nick at Nite. We were selling attitude and environment. And here was the bonus: because the networks themselves were the stars, the door was open to developing other streams of revenue. Nickelodeon toys. MTV films. Sumner's eyes lit up.

We explained how we mostly made our programming ourselves to save money and to make sure we created a unified presentation and look. Gerry and I said we'd built an unconventional, fun, creative culture, which was a huge competitive advantage. Other television companies rotated the same burned-out executives. We hired young people. When they left, we hired others. Our chorus: we were just getting going and needed capital.

For hours we fired all our cannons on Fort Sumner. The current administration, we complained, didn't get it; they wanted to harvest our business now, exactly the wrong impulse. He took it all in, and when Gerry and I finally stopped talking, he thanked us profusely. We could not tell exactly what our one-man audience was thinking, but after being under the thumb of the Viacomese, it felt good just to get it all off our chests.

As I was leaving, I said, "You should come by sometime and visit us. Just show up unannounced. It's really something to see." At the time, we were crammed beehive-style onto four floors in an old building at 1775 Broadway at 57th Street, over the legendary Coliseum bookstore. I hoped that once he witnessed the kinetic energy of the MTV and Nickelodeon operations, he'd be impressed.

He showed up the next day.

At 11 a.m., the receptionist called to say, "A Mr. Redstone is here to see you." My first reaction was shock. My crime was about to be exposed. Fuck it. I swallowed and headed to the reception area. Sumner was wearing the same clothes as the night before, only now with dried shaving cream on his ears. I gave him a tour of the two MTV floors, then with Gerry, of the two Nickelodeon floors. They were very unconventional working spaces for that era. Other companies had dress codes. We had one rule: "No frontal nudity."

The MTV workspace was as chaotic and messy as a college dorm, posters and gold records all over the walls, stacks of three-quarter-inch videotapes piled up on tables, and different music blaring out of each office. Everybody had a television on. I'm sure Sumner Redstone had never seen anything like it. It looked less like a workplace and more like a party.

He was probably the oldest person to ever stroll through the joint. Kids looked at him and smiled, probably thinking he was looking for a lost granddaughter. But Sumner could tell something was going on and, while he didn't know exactly what it was, he was energized. And apparently sold. These busy, engaged twentysomethings in T-shirts and jeans were set on reinventing television. Nobody was telling them no.

Five weeks later, Viacom's special committee of outside directors accepted Sumner's hostile bid of $3.4 billion for the company. It was one of the iconic takeovers of the 1980s, covered like the Super Bowl in *Business Week* and the *Wall Street Journal*. Nobody had squealed on me or Gerry. The overlords never found out who opened the gates and let in the Trojan horse.

Sumner's first move was to rechristen the pronunciation of the company to give it a Boston ring. "Vee-a-com" became "Vi-a-com." Sumner Redstone, just as he reached conventional retirement age, began his ascent to the pinnacle of the entertainment world. The company was saved and in much better hands.

Sumner's takeover was another stroke of luck for Gerry and me. That forbidden meal and office tour bonded me with Sumner. Instead of quitting, I was the golden boy. In August, Sumner hired Frank Biondi as the new CEO of Viacom. Over a quick get-to-know-you breakfast at the Warwick Hotel on August 9, Frank offered me the stand-alone job as CEO of MTV Networks. "Co-presidents never work," he said. *Decisive guy*, I thought.

I left breakfast and went straight to Bob Roganti's office. His shades were down. I told him he was out. He was surprised, but graceful. You can tell a lot about a person's character by how they handle being canned. Bob Roganti turned out to be a mensch.

We became all that we had promised Summer and much, much more. MTV Networks went from the smallest part of Viacom, with $75 million in annual sales, to becoming its fastest grower and largest division, with $8 billion in sales. Other divisions had plenty of headaches and issues over the years, but we never did. We were the low-maintenance, high-wire performers. We would launch new networks like Comedy Central and TV Land that came to be worth billions. We churned out hit after hit. *The Real World. Yo! MTV Raps. Beavis and Butt-Head. Cribs. Rugrats. SpongeBob. Dora the Explorer. Behind the Music. RuPaul's Drag Race. Unplugged. South Park. Storytellers. The Daily Show. The Colbert Report.* The Kids' Choice Awards. The MTV Movie Awards. The VH1 Fashion Awards.

We had our hands firmly on the levers of popular culture. For seventeen years straight, sixty-eight quarters in a row, our revenue and profitability grew by "double digits." We were a creative factory—the worst-dressed group of people in any Manhattan office building was a high-margin money machine.

Internationally, we launched MTV Europe in 1987, then Nickelodeon UK, and eventually more than 120 channels from Brazil to Japan to Russia to India. MTV's square, rule-breaking logo became one of the most famous on the planet. Thousands of great people cycled through our offices in those years. They'd leave and go on to prominent jobs all over the business. Invariably, I still run into people who say, "Hey, Tom, I used to work for you. . . . Those were my most fun years."

They were my most fun years, too.

CHAPTER TWENTY-TWO

THE NEW REGIME

Sumner Redstone rode into Viacom as a liberator: a boss who wrote the checks and let his team run things. No one talked about the crippling mountain of debt that he had saddled the company with as the price of acquisition. I should have known that the newlywed period was too good to last. The early Sumner-Biondi era of Viacom was the first time I had been in the engine room of a traditional corporation. Frank Biondi was a whole new kind of boss for me and not a rock and roller. Bob Pittman had been a fellow traveler, a countercultural spirit hiding in a suit. Frank was a grown-up, a calm, unpretentious, well-read family man, maybe the only entertainment company CEO to drive a Camry to work. Unlike Bob, he was not the type to hire a guy because he thought he was a hashish smuggler. Frank was a respected financial pro, schooled in the media and entertainment world. Hired by Michael Fuchs at HBO in 1978, Frank rose to become CEO in 1983. HBO was the first mover in premium cable programming. Frank would have happily stayed there forever. But Fuchs turned against him and sent Frank into exile.

Sumner found him in New York licking his wounds as CEO of Coca-Cola Television. Sumner offered Frank what he wanted most—a shot at taking on Fuchs head-to-head in the coming cable wars. A word to business majors and financial reporters: Don't assume that titans of industry are motivated only by greed. Vengeance is also a great driver of the capitalist enterprise.

Biondi was a real boss. We developed a mutual respect. He had a quiet sense of humor and believed in delegation. He gave me immense freedom to run our organization. Once, he let on that he had promoted me not because he thought I was some brilliant leader, but because he didn't have many choices. He wanted someone from the inside because there had already been enough turmoil, and felt I'd be a better choice than Bob Roganti. Later, in his memoir, he wrote that hiring me was his best business decision ever.

Frank saw right through the rosy picture Gerry and I had painted for Sumner at the Carlyle. He knew that our sales were in a rut and that MTV programming had miles to go. He wasn't overly impressed with Nickelodeon, either. We needed to score some wins to gain his confidence.

In October 1987, Frank scheduled our team to present an introductory dog and pony show, a debut performance for Sumner and him, where we would lay out our road map for the future. Not just ideas and vision—the kind of bullshit we were great at—but we had to produce the numbers that went with them. "How do you see yourselves looking in three years? What kind of growth are you going to ramp up?" It was to be a consequential day.

We worked day and night on the presentation. Our time slot was noon, Monday, October 19, 1987, in the conference room at 1775 Broadway. The room was dominated by live feeds of our networks that ran continually on three large, square Sony Trinitrons. Tall windows looked over West 57th Street.

I wanted to kick off the presentation with a powerful, rapid-fire video, with a driving music soundtrack. No one could make better tapes than MTV. You'd want to salute when they were done. This was the pre-PowerPoint era, so we also had overhead projectors and printed handouts ready to go. Frank, Sumner, and their team arrived just before noon. The kingpins sat at the far end of the table. There was some brief small talk and then I kicked things off with the video and an overview, and then we started talking the specifics of MTV and VH1. It was going well. Frank had a ton of questions. Sumner was quiet, listening.

In the days before digital communications, all you had to do to cut off the outside world was to say, "Hold all calls," and shut the door. So I was surprised when my assistant slipped into the room carrying a note. I was more surprised when she brought it to Sumner. He unfolded it, read it, and leaned over to whisper to Frank. Then he asked for a phone and called what sounded like his stockbroker. "Keep me posted," he said gruffly in his Boston accent. It did not seem to be positive news, but he did not explain, and our presentation resumed.

Ten minutes later, my assistant reappeared with another message for Sumner. This time he seemed more flustered as he grabbed the phone, unleashing a slew of "goddamnits" and "fucks." I remember thinking that he sounded like the possessed girl in *The Exorcist*. Not that calm grandfather I had met at the Carlyle. "There's something going on in the stock market," he barked. "A big fucking sell-off." Saying "fuck" was not a common practice in a business setting then, especially with women present.

We tried to resume. Gerry got up to make the case for Nickelodeon and Nick at Nite. More messages arrived. We were losing the room. Soon everyone was getting messages. "The Dow Jones is off one hundred points, falling fast," someone said, reading their note. A few minutes later, "It's fallen another one hundred points!" Fear was on every face. What did it mean? We had all grown up listening to our parents talk about the Great Depression, how dreams were deferred, and lives changed forever. We grew up prosperous and cocky, making fun of the old folks who hoarded string and tinfoil "just in case." Now I glanced around the room, wondering if our boomer attitude was about to go bust. I looked out at 57th Street and imagined breadlines forming.

Finally, Summer couldn't stand it anymore. He asked that we stop the presentation and turn on CNN. It was total mayhem on the floor of the New York Stock Exchange. This Monday turned out to be "Black Monday." By 4 p.m., the stock market's closing bell would record the biggest single-day drop ever, twice that of 1929, the Black Friday that kicked off the Great Depression. Here we were trying to get expansion funding while our bosses were contemplating a financial meltdown.

Before the closing bell, all eyes had turned to Redstone, who was on the phone, screaming at his stockbroker. "Buy every fucking share you can!" He kept repeating it. Frank sat quietly next to him. The room was Sumner's. This man was not jumping out any windows. We looked at each other in quiet disbelief. We were watching a man buy a condo while the building was burning. Black Monday was nothing but a discount-buying opportunity for the thick-skinned, battle-hardened billionaire.

This was the first time I witnessed Sumner Redstone summon the raging force that boiled deep inside him. He kept it well hidden beneath the senior demeanor, but it was always there, and it was frightening to see. In the beginning, there were few hints of the narcissism and megalomania that would infect his later years. The days of Sumner throwing plates at waiters were still in the future. But over the next twenty years, these eruptions would occur more frequently. By the end, they were as regular as Old Faithful.

But what I also saw on Black Monday 1987 was Redstone's unshakable faith in himself, his willingness to bet big, and his belief that Viacom would triumph. He was not going to let the moment slip by. The Dow would end up dropping 24 percent that day; Viacom hit its all-time low of $17. Redstone spent tens of millions vacuuming up every share he could.

No Depression would follow. The market fully recovered in twenty months. Redstone would make a lot of big deals in the years to come, but this little buying spree in the middle of a stock market crash had to be one of the most lucrative and satisfying. And he impressed the hell out of every one of his new employees.

His faith in us was reassuring, but I was nervous as hell leaving the room. Maybe my future would be dashed again. Sumner Redstone was not rock and roll by any stretch—but he had balls, had been around, and he understood business in a way that none of the rest of us did.

CHAPTER TWENTY-THREE

POLITICS IN A HIP-HOP WORLD

Every Monday morning at nine thirty, Frank Biondi would host a staff meeting in the twenty-eighth-floor conference room at 1515 Broadway, our new headquarters in Times Square. The district was still littered with porn theaters and their marquees with funny titles like *ET: The Extra Testicle*. All the division heads attended: Viacom Cable, Showtime, Viacom Entertainment, and MTV Networks. Key corporate executives were there as well, and Philippe Dauman, general counsel.

MTV Networks was the smallest division, basic cable was still the minor league, and I was the outlier among the top executives. I did not have the Ivy League pedigree or work experience of my peers. I was more of a street hustler who consorted with lowlife musicians and their handlers.

At these get-togethers, Frank sat at the head of the table. Sumner would sit quietly on the side. He had no pencil or paper, just a phone that connected him to his broker. I was impressed with how he held back and let Frank run the meetings. For me, these sessions were master classes on how every sector in the media/entertainment world worked—and how high-level corporate politics was played.

I always went out of my way to insulate MTV Networks from corporate anything. Building and maintaining our unorthodox culture was my primary goal—but now that we were part of a big public company, it was a real tightrope walk. Anything corporate was a turnoff for my group. No one came to work for Viacom. I didn't gather the general employee population and talk about Viacom's financial performance. I stayed focused on our creative work, our triumphs, and the need to stay fresh and take big risks. Some could argue that this was not good corporate citizenship, but Frank understood this approach perfectly and let it fly.

I probably spent less time with Sumner than anyone else in top management at Viacom. I noticed over time that familiarity with the man tended to breed contempt. He did not seem to have many friends. I kept myself scarce. But he always seemed happy to see me. In those early years, Sumner was pleased with our progress. He was also a regular at big events like the MTV Video Music Awards, where he'd get his photo taken with Rod Stewart, ZZ Top, and LL Cool J, though he had no idea who they were.

He only leaned in on one area—legal matters. The former antitrust lawyer had a mastery of the law. Lawsuits would become a healthy new profit center for us and were carefully plotted with his eager-beaver sidekick, Philippe Dauman. I should be careful how I describe Philippe. As he and I were destined to end on bad terms, the picture I paint of him might be unfair. Take my assessments with a grain of salt and a handful of sour grapes. In addition to being general counsel, Philippe was also Sumner's estate planner. As Sumner always maintained that he intended to live forever, it was a job predicated on theoreticals—a bit like listing which jewels and horses should be sealed up in the tomb with Pharaoh's sarcophagus.

Philippe and I would both have years as Sumner's favorites, would both run Viacom, and both be shown the exit when Sumner turned on us. I suppose if we ever found ourselves next to each other on a long airplane flight, we might have a drink and forget old feuds. Having said that, it's hard to want to bury the hatchet with the man who put a knife in your back.

The next MTV music revolution began in 1988, with Peter Dougherty and Ted Demme, a white twenty-four-year-old assistant in the on-air promotion department, our image makers. On-air promotion was an alternative world, our most offbeat group, our ears on the street. Many of our best ideas came from that outfit. The staff would hang downtown with Keith Haring, Sonic Youth, and Andy Warhol; *Andy Warhol's 15 Minutes* became a weekly series.

Ted, the nephew of the film director Jonathan Demme, became the in-house crusader for hip-hop. "No one is playing this shit," he'd say. "It's blowing up on the streets and it's not on the radio, not even on BET [Black Entertainment TV]."

"It's not our demo," said Lee Masters, the general manager, a talented former radio man who would soon revert to his real name, Jarl Mohn. "It's too street for us." But Ted was persistent. Finally, arguing that we had 168 hours a week to fill, Jarl gave him the green light to program an hour. It became the highest-rated music hour in MTV history. Ted had as much impact on popular culture as anyone who ever passed through MTV.

Yo! MTV Raps, with Fab 5 Freddy, was born. Ratings exploded. Once again, Black music saved our white asses. This time it was Run-DMC, Public Enemy, and Snoop, Dre, Tone Loc, Mary J. Blige. At first, their music videos were lo-fi and experimental, then they went way over the top with a bright, in-your-face aesthetic . . . sexy girls, cars, and plenty of sneakers. The rise of rap also gave older people a whole new reason to get upset with MTV. That was always good.

Our embrace of hip-hop injected some much-needed diversity awareness into our ranks. Not only were we overly white, laughably so, but most of us were fairly unconscious of that obvious fact. You can't successfully program an increasingly diverse music mix to an increasingly diverse young audience with just a bunch of white guys, I'd say. My dream was to get into our corporate elevators and see the faces of my fellow passengers resemble what I had just seen in the NYC subway.

I was naive as to how hard it would be to remedy our diversity problem. Hiring diverse employees was easy. Having them feel comfortable and included was more challenging. We had some false starts, but ultimately succeeded. By 2001, the place felt much healthier. It was one thing I was most proud of. It never should have been an issue, but in the real world, it was. Even at MTV Networks.

We also dipped our toes into politics. In 1990, partnering with Jeff Ayeroff of Virgin Records, we launched Rock the Vote, which was initially about censorship. Madonna, Lenny Kravitz, Iggy Pop, and others made PSAs that got lots of press. In 1992, at MTV News, Doug Herzog hired a twenty-three-year-old Tabitha Soren to head up our "Choose or Lose" campaign to help boost young voter turnout for the presidential election. Tabitha interviewed the Democratic nominees, Bill Clinton and Al Gore. They both did town halls with us. Clinton was asked if he wore "boxers or briefs" and it made coast-to-coast news, usually accompanied by tut-tutting about how far the dignity of the presidency had fallen. Incumbent president George H. W. Bush finally gave in and did a last-minute interview with Tabitha on the back of a moving train. He was barely cordial. He looked like he was submitting to a rectal exam. He lost.

Not ones to miss a self-congratulatory opportunity, we threw the "MTV Inaugural Ball" in DC when Clinton and Gore were sworn in. We did know how to throw a party. We ran it live and sold out all the advertising. There were eight inaugural balls in town and ours was the hottest ticket. Warren Beatty, Robert De Niro, and Jack Nicholson showed up. 10,000 Maniacs played. Members of U2 and R.E.M. performed as the one-time supergroup Automatic Baby. Don Henley sang a Leonard Cohen song: "Democracy is coming to the USA." Clinton came onstage and announced, "I think everyone here knows that MTV had a lot to do with the Clinton-Gore victory." I shivered. 1992 had the highest turnout ever for young people, up 20 percent, an increase that has never been beaten. We basked in a new legitimacy. Advertisers like American Express, who had once avoided us, came to the party. We continued to slip in new faces and franchises. We set Cindy Crawford up to host and produce *House of Style*, a groundbreaking fashion series. Chris Connelly hosted *The Big Picture*, all about the movies, which solidified our connection to Hollywood. I hired Downtown Julie Brown to host *Club MTV* to get in on the dance music resurgence.

In 1989, Bob Small and Jim Burns created *Unplugged*. Top artists came on to play acoustic versions—no electric guitars or synthesizers or the like—of their songs. What became *MTV Unplugged* was a phenomenal success both as television and at selling records. Paul McCartney released the first *Unplugged* album. Eric Clapton's *Unplugged* performance sold 26 million CD copies, his career bestseller, and won the Grammy for Album of the Year. After that, every musician wanted to unplug on MTV, from Mariah Carey to Lauryn Hill, Alicia Keys to Bob Dylan to Pearl Jam. Nirvana's

Unplugged became a posthumous classic after Kurt Cobain's suicide. Hundreds of millions of *Unplugged* records were sold, with MTV getting a royalty on each one.

By that point, we were eager to take more chances with different music. We had *120 Minutes* for alternative rock fans and *Headbangers Ball* for metal fans. We went interactive with a phone-in countdown show, *Dial MTV*. The record companies began hiring whole phone banks . . . demon dialers . . . to artificially jack up the voting results.

In the early nineties a lot of our young viewers were watching Fox's new prime-time soaps *Beverly Hills 90210* and *Melrose Place*. We developed a similar concept, but when Doug Herzog brought it to me, I said we didn't have the budget. It needed writers, which we could not afford. Doug went back to the young producers Mary-Ellis Bunim and Jonathan Murray. They decided to cast and film a group of kids sharing a loft in New York City. We'd track them with hidden cameras, then edit episodes together in postproduction, which we excelled at. Plus, we knew from all the MTV spring break productions that our audience liked it when the camera was turned on them. We called this new show *The Real World*—and the modern era of reality TV was born.

We followed up *Real World* with *The Osbournes*, another smash and the first "celebrity reality show." The reality format ultimately took over network and cable television, lighting up our lives with shows like *Naked and Afraid*, *The Real Housewives*, *The Kardashians*, and *The Apprentice* with Donald Trump.

MTV has a lot to answer for.

CHAPTER TWENTY-FOUR

THE ADVENTURES OF NICKELODEON

Nickelodeon was launched in 1979 as bait to help the newly formed Warner-Amex Cable Communications win big-city franchises. A hodgepodge of old cartoons, it was pitched to appeal not to kids but to cable operators as a "good for kids" network. Nick's new head, Gerry Laybourne, had come to Warner-Amex in 1980 as a former teacher with a master's degree in elementary education. She loved kids, and she respected kids.

With her rectangular glasses and straight blond hair, Gerry was a force of nature, a woman with a commanding presence and great confidence, along with a strong feminist bent. Gerry's number one rule: Nick would always take the kids' side. She felt Nick should have the opposite of the "eat your vegetables" approach of traditional children's programming. Gerry was a mother and was always conscious that Nickelodeon had to be cool enough for her kids not to be embarrassed by their mom's TV channel. Gerry was also quick to pick up on technological change. One day in the early nineties, she introduced me to the concept of email. I didn't get it right away. For starters, I didn't have a computer. Memos still arrived in brown envelopes. Gerry stayed on me until I got the hang of it.

From the outside, no one would ever mistake Nickelodeon for MTV. Nick was a well-dressed, polite operation of former educators and children's experts, and MTV was a raucous gang of music junkies in jeans and T-shirts. But the connective tissue between the two groups was strong. Plus, Gerry and I both shared a belief in the power of women in the workplace.

It could not have been easy for Gerry when I was promoted to CEO over her. She never complained or seemed bothered that her comrade had become her boss. I know how I would have felt if it had gone the other way, and I tried to always give her the freedom to run Nick as she liked. Nick's staff wanted to produce their own shows. Outside production companies were not making anything that fit, and we couldn't afford to use them. So, like at MTV, low-cost, in-house production became something that set Nick apart from its competitors, who relied largely on reruns.

In 1986, Nickelodeon broke ground with a game show, *Double Dare*. It was a mix of truth or dare, an obstacle course, and gobs of green slime called Gak and became the highest-rated non-sport show in the history of cable television. Countless new programs followed. The Kids' Choice Awards debuted in 1987. It would get more votes than the presidential election. Ask any millennial today and they'll talk warmly about *Dora the Explorer* and *Blue's Clues*, *Clarissa Explains It All*, *iCarly*, *Kenan & Kel*, *The Adventures of Pete & Pete*, and *All That*. Nick was "must-see TV" for children born in the eighties and nineties.

By 1989, we wanted to make the next big leap. Gerry's stated goal was to make Nick "the Disney of the nineties." We were ready to take on the Disney Mouse and create original animation: Nicktoons. It was the right direction, but an expensive proposition, and Viacom was still saddled with debt. Cash flow was tight, and Nick had a very specific financial problem: the channel had to spend a small fortune every year licensing Looney Tunes cartoons from Warner Bros. and series like *Danger Mouse* and *Inspector Gadget* from international distributors. Like any renters, as merely "licensees," our rights were few. We could be evicted or be subject to huge price increases whenever a licensing term was up. Plus, we could not exploit the gold mines of product licensing and feature films. It was a fiscal catch-22.

Then an opportunity popped up out of nowhere in Woodstock, Vermont. Frank Biondi decided to bring the senior management of Viacom's five divisions together, so we could get to know each other, socialize—and then, unbeknownst to us, do battle.

In October 1989, Viacom's five divisions were:

- Showtime/The Movie Channel
- Viacom Broadcast—a handful of radio and TV stations
- Viacom Cable—a small collection of cable systems
- Viacom Enterprises—broadcast TV production, syndication, and international
- MTV Networks—our heroes

The other divisions rolled their eyes and snickered when we suggested we were the future of the company. The broadcast guys were so old they thought cable was a fad.

We met at the Woodstock Inn's polished, well-equipped conference center. Over opening cocktails, Frank clinked a glass and welcomed the group. Then he detonated the bomb: "I know everyone here has been doing their best to help pay down the debt and get us on a faster-growth track. And I know each division has new initiatives they'd like to undertake. But we're still strapped for cash. Nonetheless, we've been able to gather up a pot of ten million dollars to invest in something new and smart that can bring great value to the company." The catch: Frank was going to give it all to the one division that presented the best idea. In the next twenty-four hours. It was *Shark Tank* in the Green Mountains. Winner takes all. New acquaintances who had been trading phone numbers now looked at each other as opponents.

For us, this contest was a gift from heaven. We didn't need any preparation. Sara Levinson, our crack business development honcho, and Gerry had just developed a concept plan for Nicktoons. Their eyes met mine across the room. I nodded. We were ready to go. The next afternoon, we listened to proposals to buy more radio stations. We kept straight faces through a pitch to fund additional episodes of *Matlock* and *Jake and the Fatman*. Then Gerry and I stood up to make the case for Nicktoons.

Nicktoons would not look like Hanna-Barbera's *Yogi Bear* or *The Flintstones*. A new animation movement was already blooming in comic books, video shorts, alternative weeklies, and graphic novels. We were going to find our animators there, kooky folks outside the factory system who had fresh characters living inside their heads. We weren't just going to create characters to sell toys. We were going to create characters we were in love with. Frank's head was nodding as we spoke. Our four opponents felt the money rolling toward MTV Networks. They argued that we didn't have the skills to do this. What did we know? This was a pipe dream—new episodes of *Matlock* were a sound investment!

Frank saw MTV Networks present a thoughtful, well-argued plan with a genuinely fresh proposal, apparently created in twenty-four hours! We won the contest. We put the $10 million right to work with three new series: *Rugrats*, *Doug*, and *Ren & Stimpy*. We'd eventually put sociopathic Chihuahuas, a cojoined cat and dog, and bachelor beavers on the air. Nick's ratings went through the ceiling. Creators beat a path to our door. Nicktoons signaled a new level of edginess for Nickelodeon and created billions in sales and value. We built our own animation studio in Burbank. When Joe Strummer, former front man of the Clash, came by for a meeting, he wanted to see Nickelodeon—he was a major fan of *SpongeBob SquarePants*, the brainchild of dropout hippie animator Stephen Hillenburg, whom we practically had to drag off the beach in Hawaii after the first season of the underwater yellow sponge and his crab and starfish sidekicks became a runaway hit. Nicktoons built our consumer product and film businesses.

In addition to becoming a full-fledged children's brand, Nick became the number one Nielsen-rated cable network, a title it kept for sixteen straight years. Nick would command over 60 percent of all kid viewing and 60 percent of the entire kid-advertising pie. Soon the Mouse was waving the white flag. Michael Eisner, Mike Ovitz, and Bob Iger, the Disney kingpins, began courting Gerry to come over to the other side. I was sad when Gerry accepted their offer, but I couldn't blame her. Gerry left Nickelodeon in 1996 to become president of Disney/ABC Cable Networks. I promoted the very able Herb Scannell as her successor, under whom the network broke new records every year.

No matter where I go in the world, it is rare to leave a country without spotting a *Rugrats* towel, or a beat-up *Dora the Explorer* baby stroller, or a line of schoolkids carrying *SpongeBob Squarepants* lunch boxes. That Sponge has become as universal an icon as Bob Marley.

CHAPTER TWENTY-FIVE

COMEDY WARS

On Tuesday morning, May 16, 1989, I was holding my weekly staff meeting when my assistant entered and slipped me a piece of paper. It was a press release from HBO.

"HBO has just announced that they're going to launch a twenty-four-hour comedy network in November. They are calling it 'the Comedy Channel,'" I said. "This is not good." Back then HBO was the industry powerhouse in premium cable TV. They had tons of money, a horde of Ivy-educated foot soldiers across the nation, and deep tentacles into the comedy world. They'd produced big-ticket comedy specials with Robin Williams, George Carlin, Robert Klein, and other luminaries for years. Now they were casting their eye on basic cable.

We all looked at each other. We'd heard rumors about this move and here it was. Mark Rosenthal, our head of affiliate sales, cut right to the point: "If they succeed, they'll be launching music and kids' channels before we know it. We need to get right onto a war footing."

The Comedy Channel was the pet project of Michael Fuchs, HBO's pompous CEO. It was based on Fuchs's "golden gut and entrepreneurial instincts." And it was modeled after MTV. They were going to run short-form comedy clips back-to-back . . . scenes ripped from movies, TV shows, and stand-up routines. Their versions of a VJ would introduce them.

We were fanatical when it came to defending our turf. When a competitor wanted to put their programming on the Nickelodeon satellite transponder after we signed off at 8 p.m., we hustled to foreclose that option by inventing "Nick at Nite" to fill up the twenty-four hours. We quickly licensed tired old shows like *My Three Sons* and *Route 66* for $5,000 an episode. We gave them a tongue-in-cheek context, packaged them with a cool nostalgic sensibility, and made Nick at Nite a huge, high-margin hit. In the frenzied cable era of the 1980s and '90s, you could sometimes make money just by throwing your hat into the ring without a lot of forethought.

We cooked up our comedy retaliatory plan in fifteen minutes: announce our own channel. It would do two things: ensure that our-yet-to-be-planned comedy channel was mentioned in every press article with HBO, and we'd help freeze HBO's ability to sign up new cable systems. Cable operators would not want to alienate either of us. In minutes we settled on immediately leaking that we'd be announcing a channel, since we didn't have a single detail to offer about what that channel would be.

I dialed Frank Biondi's extension and put him on speaker. He monitored all things HBO and had already seen the announcement. "Frank, I'm here with my team. We've got to do everything in our power to keep Mr. Fuchs out of our business. We think what they're announcing . . . short-form comedy clips . . . is a loser of an idea. We tried it on VH1. It does not work. 'Comedy interruptus,'" I added. "But if they get some distribution, they'll figure it out and change the format to something smarter. We have to stop them now."

I continued. "I suggest we announce our own long-form TV comedy channel, with complete shows, like Nick at Nite. We'll have time to figure it out. But the key, Frank, is that we do something today to steal their thunder." That resonated. Biondi still had a score to settle with his old boss. "We can leak our intention today," I explained, "then formally announce by the end of the week. By that time, we'll have a name, a rough format, and stuff to talk about. I don't know what this is going to cost or where it ends. But having Fuchs in our business is going to ultimately cost us a lot more."

"Do it." Frank sounded like he was smiling. My team cheered and high-fived. The Comedy Wars were on.

That meeting was one of the most gratifying moments of my career. We announced a new channel right out of the blue. Everyone was ready to buckle down and fight. We would make HBO's size a liability. We got on the phone to reporters immediately. By Friday, we had announced "HA! The TV Comedy Network," launching on April 1, 1990, April Fools' Day.

From that day on, we committed hundreds of millions of dollars, as did HBO. It was a hard-fought, wild battle that lasted for years. But cable operators were in no rush to add either our channel or HBO's. Systems were only beginning to upgrade from thirty-five to fifty-four channels, capacity was scarce, and new cable networks like CNBC and Bravo were hunting for slots.

By its November launch, HBO's Comedy Channel had 120 employees and was spending about $1 million a week, with an initial subscriber base of 4 million. A military man might say their supply lines were stretched too thin. Added to that, the early reviews were terrible. *New York* magazine called it "about as funny as root canal work."

We carefully plotted every countermove. I wanted buzz—we went after deals with marquee names, including Ron Howard, Brian Grazer, and Rob Reiner. I hired Fred Silverman, the comedy guru who had programmed all three broadcast networks. Fred said that he was "an admirer of MTV." We licensed all the shows in the Mary Tyler Moore library. We announced charter advertising deals with Coca-Cola, LA Gear, and all the major movie studios. We projected momentum and credibility. We also scooped up every piece of smart comedy programming we could get our hands on. I wanted to corner the market so that there'd be nothing left for HBO once they realized their format was a turkey. This culminated in a bidding war for the most desirable prize of all, the *Saturday Night Live* library.

I was in the back seat of a taxi late on a January night in a traffic jam on Canal Street and on my BlackBerry with NBC. I closed the *SNL* deal for $40 million. I punched the air. This was a big miss for Fuchs, and it began a wonderful relationship with Lorne Michaels. Top *SNL* cast members would soon help us schmooze cable operators at our annual February Vail ski weekend.

Fuchs could not believe that our little pack of basic cable weasels and comedy know-nothings was outflanking him. But while we were winning the psych war, cable systems were still not signing up either channel. They were waiting to see who surrendered to whom.

Most wars end through negotiations. With both MTV and HBO running up huge tabs, Biondi and Fuchs buried the hatchet in December 1990 and agreed to merge. The rationale was our two companies could much more easily build a strong comedy service working together than we could by slashing each other's tires. Some on my team were not happy; they wanted to vanquish HBO. But it was a major victory. Most importantly, HBO lost its appetite for basic cable and, from then on, stuck to pay TV.

The comedy joint venture would be located at our headquarters at 1775 Broadway. Its staff would combine employees from both networks and be run by an independent president brought in from the outside. The president would report to a board of directors made up of equal representatives. Fuchs and I would sit on the board.

The day before the press conference, Frank called me with a bit of news. "I don't quite know how to tell you this, but Fuchs had one last request."

"What was that?"

"He doesn't want you to be physically in the room at the press conference."

"He doesn't want me in the room? What a first grader. What an asshole. I'm the guy in the press release announcing it with him. What did you tell him?"

"Well, that's the thing. He was adamant about it. Like it was a deal-breaker. I didn't think it was that big a deal, and I just want to get this done and move on." Frank was war-weary. I was infuriated. But I calmed down and let it slide. It said more about Fuchs than me, I reasoned. The next day a handwritten note appeared from Sumner, which was uncommon. He congratulated me on our victory and said he knew how I felt about the snub. He complimented me on "statesmanship."

The network was soon renamed "Comedy Central," and it drifted along until 1996, when Brian Graden, the programming head at MTV, commissioned a six-minute animated video from two guys named Matt Stone and Trey Parker to send out as a VHS Christmas card to his friends. Stone and Parker's animation featured a pack of crudely drawn, foulmouthed kids with scatological obsessions in a bleak Colorado town named South Park. No Christmas card in history ever ended up making so much money. We green-lit it for Comedy Central in two minutes. *South Park* was Comedy Central's first explosive breakout hit that put the channel on the map. People signed up for cable just to get *South Park*. The show became a multibillion-dollar gold mine, including merchandise and feature films.

Our second hit, one that turned Comedy Central into a major cultural player, was when Jon Stewart took the helm of *The Daily Show* in January 1999. Jon's vision was to focus on smart political satire. At first, Doug Herzog, now the channel's president, pushed back. Political humor was a tough sell. Doug wanted more pop culture sensibility. Ultimately, though, we bet on Jon. We gave him total freedom, and he turned the place upside down. Jon and his team mainstreamed politics for a younger generation. At a time when most TV news maintained official objectivity, Jon was not afraid to call bullshit on politicians and journalists.

We had a rock-solid relationship with Jon. He said once, "You guys remind me of one of the great New York Yankees teams . . . more like a family than a business. Were it not for you all, I'd be bashing Viacom like a piñata." (By 2003, HBO had sold all of Comedy Central to MTV.) Everybody came on *The Daily Show*. Jon was on the cover of *Time* and *Rolling Stone*. He hosted the Oscars and the White House Correspondents' Dinner. He won twenty-six Emmys and gave Comedy Central gravitas and credibility. And he did all this from his position behind the desk. Following in Jon's footsteps, we created *The Colbert Report* in 2005. Stephen Colbert played, as he called it, "a well-intentioned, poorly informed, high-status idiot," a hilarious caricature of conservative personality-driven talk programs like Fox News' *The O'Reilly Factor*. It ran for 1,447 episodes until 2014.

We launched *Chappelle's Show*, Dave Chappelle's first TV series, another huge hit. Comics like John Oliver, Steve Carell, Adam Carolla, Jimmy Kimmel, Bill Maher, Samantha Bee, and, later, Amy Schumer and others all got their television start on Comedy Central. Only Lorne Michaels and *SNL* would be a better launchpad for comedic talent. Pulled out of thin air in ten minutes in a 1989 staff meeting, Comedy Central would go on to have more cultural currency than any of our other networks.

CHAPTER TWENTY-SIX

BUSTED IN SAIGON

We were always in search of new markets for MTV. But in 1993, even for us, Vietnam was a real outlier, just a cut above North Korea as a place you'd want to do business. For starters, the leadership had officially abolished capitalism. That's usually a red flag. Vietnam was also still under economic sanctions from the US, and the two nations did not have diplomatic ties. There was not a legal Coca-Cola to be had. But since 1986, under the new "Doi Moi" policy, the government had been cautiously opening up to a market economy. I figured it was only a matter of time before they would want their MTV.

In 1993, I was in Hong Kong with a group of colleagues visiting Star TV. MTV Asia was part of their initial five-channel satellite package that would revolutionize Asian television. Their satellite footprint covered all of Asia. MTV was already a sensation in China, India, and even in oddball spots like Burma. Saigon, now renamed Ho Chi Minh City, was just two and a half hours away by plane, no longer than a Friday drive from Manhattan to the Hamptons. In Hong Kong, I read that Vietnam was now offering tourist visas on arrival. We could be some of the first tourists to Vietnam.

I was curious to see what the austere regime in Hanoi had done to tame the former South Vietnam capital, once known as the tropical "Paris of the East." I had heard that the city formerly known as Saigon was anxious to reclaim its old glory as Vietnam's commercial capital. This would be the last chance to see it before capitalism, defeated on the battlefield, sneaked in through the back door. My fellow travelers on this jaunt were

Gerry Laybourne; Sara Levinson, who ran business development and international; Greg Ricca from business affairs; and my wingman at MTV Asia, Vinnie Longobardo. "Let's fly to Saigon for a three-day weekend," I said. "We can scope out prospects for MTV. MTV in Vietnam would be a mind-boggler of a press story." I told them it was the chance of a lifetime. There was not a ton of initial enthusiasm, but nobody wanted to be the one to say no.

I had been hoping for this trip for years. I had tried to go in 1972. Not as a soldier, Lord knows, but as a tourist. Tourists were encouraged and welcomed in South Vietnam throughout the war. The South Vietnam National Tourist Authority and Air Vietnam printed posters with exotic Vietnamese backdrops imploring travelers to see the war up close. I only got as far as Laos.

This time, I found an old tourist guide in a Hong Kong bookstore, and we booked round-trip tickets on Cathay Pacific. My adrenaline was flowing. Landing at Tan Son Nhat airport put me right into a 1960s time warp. The terminal was a relic. Battle-scarred concrete huts, once hangars for US fighter jets, lined the runways. We grabbed a van and headed to the Hotel Continental. The Continental, along with the Caravelle across the square, were landmarks from the French colonial era and had been home to many a journalist, soldier, and spy during the war. In 1975, Hunter S. Thompson famously chronicled the war's end for *Rolling Stone* without ever leaving the Continental.

The Continental had seen better days. A long row of worn-down cyclos (rickshaws) sat out front, drivers slouched in the passenger seats. The sign at the front desk said "No Weapons Allowed in Rooms." I got a room overlooking the street with beat-up, mismatched furniture, a small black-and-white TV, and a stand-up wartime vintage GE refrigerator hooked up to a voltage converter. No minibar. The carpet was stained and rippled from the humidity and air-conditioning.

We set out to see the city. Most of the historical landmarks were in District 1, the French colonial section, which was still officially called "Saigon." The streets buzzed as swarms of bicycles and motor scooters raced by in a constant onslaught. There were few cars or trucks. To cross a street, you had to step out and keep going, praying to God that everyone would swerve around you. Women wore the traditional ao dai, men were in dark pajama-style clothes.

The city's main street, Dong Khoi, ran right by the Hotel Continental. It was French Saigon's version of the Champs-Élysées and shaded on both sides by rows of tamarind trees. During the American war era, it became known as Tu Do Street. GIs packed into a tawdry Times Square–like strip of saloons, full of bar girls and cover bands from the Philippines. Now the sidewalks were jammed with vendors and ragged street children selling old *Herald Tribune* newspapers and gum. Old, engraved Zippo lighters left behind by American GIs were piled on blankets ("When I die bury me face down so the whole world can kiss my ass"). Next to them were tin airplanes and helicopters made from Tiger beer cans. The war was still here.

We walked down Dong Du Street, coming to a full stop at a sign that said "Apocalypse Now," indicating a small bar with a large open window, "Born to Be Wild" by Steppenwolf blasting out of it at a deafening volume. "Do you think Marlon Brando could be in there?" asked Vinnie.

Los Angeles had Planet Hollywood. London had Claridge's. Saigon was going with Apocalypse Now. Say what you will about capitalism, it conforms to human nature better than any other economic system. If America's leaders had glimpsed the future here, maybe they could have spared both us and the Vietnamese a lot of misery. Inside, there were a few customers at the bar, mostly Vietnamese, drinking Vietnam 333 beer from cans and nodding their heads to hit after hit from the Vietnam War songbook: Aretha, Creedence, Otis Redding, and Jimi Hendrix. Helicopters were painted on black walls. On the ceiling, the helicopters were painted upside down, so their rotors became ceiling fans. "Do you smell what I smell?" asked Sara as we scoped out some seats.

"Geez," said Vinnie. "Beer, grass, and the Doors. The only good things I associate with the war." He went over to the bar and came back with a broad grin. "I asked the bartender where one could buy some grass and he handed me this pack of pre-rolled joints. Ten dollars US. There must be twenty reefers in here." It was a Lucky Strike–sized package, shrink-wrapped and all, labeled "*Cigares de Joy*" in French, or "Joy Cigarettes." Their marketing was years ahead of its time. "Purple Haze" came on. Miss Nickelodeon torched up. She coughed. "Welcome to Saigon," she offered, as if it were a toast.

"Give me a hit on that," said Greg. Large, serious, and straight, this was not a man used to smoking reefer in a bar. As a lawyer he was always careful, warning me not to do this or that. He took a hit. We all watched him. He explained with attorney-client formality that the smokes must be legal with packaging like that. He passed it to Sara, the Ivy League stoner of the group. She inhaled. We were a merry band at this point. The weed was highly potent and quickly took effect. "Jeezus . . . How did we ever fight a war on this stuff?" asked Gerry.

"As I recall, not too well," I said. We stepped outside into the humid night air. My head was buzzing. Prostitutes and street children followed us, tugging at our sleeves. I had not expected such poverty. I thought the communists were supposed to share the wealth, but maybe there was no wealth to share.

Next door was yet another bar, B 475. That meant "before 1975." The next joint across the street was Good Morning Vietnam. I decided if we stumbled upon a bar called the Deer Hunter I would keep walking. We kept barhopping, grabbing drinks in each place. The Rex Hotel, which had been transformed into an officers' barracks during the war, had a famous rooftop bar with crazy-looking topiary shrubbery. We opted for a nightcap at a fancy spot called the Q Bar inside the historic Opera House. An American ran it.

The next day, I woke up with a nasty hangover. I imagined myself as Captain Willard, the Martin Sheen character in *Apocalypse Now*. I wasn't breaking any mirrors and covering myself in blood, but I decided I needed a mission. Could I put together a detail and head up the river? Make it a reconnaissance detail for MTV? We would not terminate anyone; we'd just float out of town on Sumner Redstone's cash. I walked down to the quay, past the Majestic Hotel, and found a boat and an eager captain, who barely spoke English. A Vietnamese man nearby helped translate and we made a deal. It was a rusted old tub of a cabin cruiser, but it had plenty of room for us and a head. Mission accomplished, I went back to rustle up my crew.

We bought a bunch of beers, and I hooked up my portable speaker and Walkman, cranking up "Satisfaction" by the Stones. We drifted past rows of shanties on stilts lining the riverbank. Plastic garbage was everywhere. Several freighters, mostly from Eastern European countries, were anchored in the waterway. I spotted a big Samsung billboard in the downtown area with an empty billboard next to it. "We should put up an MTV logo on that billboard there," I said. "A big colorful psychedelic one. When Western businessmen begin to arrive, they'll be impressed." The empty space had a Hong Kong telephone number on it. I told Greg to make a note.

Technically, MTV was already in Vietnam. The Star TV signal was available to anyone in Asia with a satellite dish. The locals knew about it. When we went into a club or bar and mentioned MTV, we got the royal treatment. People loved the idea of MTV even if they had never seen it. God bless Dire Straits' "Money for Nothing," with its "I want my MTV" refrain. It was the gift that kept giving.

As we cruised up the river, I was taking lots of pictures with my small camera: villages and small motorized fishing boats. I noticed an old rusty boat anchored near the jungle-covered shore with shirtless men under a canopy playing cards. I snapped away, not realizing it was a police boat. The men dropped their cards and snapped to attention. Then they began heading our way, siren on, waving for us to stop. We couldn't imagine what the problem was. "Should we try and make a run for it?" joked Vinnie, beer in hand.

The police boat pulled alongside, and one soldier jumped aboard and herded us all near the stern. He motioned for us to put our beers down. He spoke no English, but gesticulated madly in Vietnamese. At least he kept his gun in his holster. The police boat bobbed up and down, hitting our boat. Our angry captain was ordered to follow the police boat. We were confident we had not done anything wrong, but we were thinking like Westerners.

Ten minutes later, our boat pulled up to a dock on a small island in the middle of the river. All our captain could manage to say in English was "This is jail." We exited the boat, the cadre of policemen surrounding us. The head cop led us to a courtyard. More police came out of the building. We were herded into a holding area, and they took our passports. Americans. We might have been the first Americans these men had seen since the end of the war. The police circled around us. One left with our passports. The main man spoke no English, but remained very animated, sputtering in

Vietnamese. He kept waving his hands in an X to make clear that we were in a forbidden zone. That was bad enough. He came over to me. Maybe he figured I was the ringleader. He held up his hands in front of me, mimicking using a camera. I got the message and handed over my camera.

Our captain came over to repeat what seemed to be his favorite English word, "Jail. Jail." I was glad I had a lawyer with me, but Greg seemed nervous. I fantasized about him preparing to negotiate a side deal, leaving the rest of us in the pen. It dawned on me that they were about to search us, and I remembered Vinnie's pack of Joy cigarettes. Maybe they were not as legal as we thought.

These guys were mad as hell, jumping up and down, yelling at us. I got the impression we were accused of being part of a spy ring, taking photos of forbidden locations. A dope rap on top of that would turn a nostalgic trip into Midnight Express. The Vietnamese jail cells were a mere twenty feet away. It was my fault. But I hoped to use a talent I developed with the bullies in my hometown: I can almost always find a way to put people at ease, which has helped me to get along with everyone from Indian gangsters to monopolistic cable operators. A gentle bearing, a bit of humor, and projecting a sense of good intention and sincerity were how I usually talked myself out of a jam. I stepped forward and pulled out one of Vinnie's business cards with a big MTV logo on it. I pointed to the card and started repeating, "MTV, MTV!" They stopped jabbering. "We . . . we are MTV," I repeated and repeated. "We are MTV. Not spy."

I had their attention. These policemen had seen MTV at least once on someone's satellite dish. To them, MTV was a very good new thing. It's hard to beat nice music and pretty girls when you are cooped up in the jungle, dodging snakes and sleeping dormitory style. They knew no English, but knew our logo. I told them again, "Not spies! MTV!" The whole team joined in, nodding and chanting, "Not spies! We MTV!" Now the cops were smiling, nodding their heads up and down, and saying "MTV" to each other.

I pointed to my bag and took out the Vietnamese phrase book I had picked up in Hong Kong. Many of its translations were for military things like "How do I dig a foxhole?" I did not want to excite the situation by saying that, but the book had the basics for simple vocabulary.

I was nervous as I flipped through the pages. Finally, I pieced together a succinct but unique confession I hoped would win them over. Two sentences. "My name is Tom." They leaned in to listen. The second sentence was the clincher . . . "And I am sorry." I repeated, "My name is Tom. And I am sorry." I added one more "MTV" for good measure. Smiles broke out all around. They were laughing. We started to laugh with them. We went from being a spy ring to emissaries from the great and joyous MTV.

The captain and the police chief huddled with a couple of others. They came over and gestured that we were free to go. Vinnie, always looking for documentation, waved his camera and asked if it was possible to take some group photos. Everyone took out their cameras. We stood in the door of the prison, smiling with our former captors, snapping away. We made the peace sign and gave the thumbs-up. They thought it was hilarious. After they ushered us back to our boat, we shook hands. As the boat pulled away, everyone waved like old friends. I noticed that the head cop had Vinnie's MTV card in his hand. I reminded the group that a small downtown company called Manhattan Design had helped us create our logo in 1981, and we had paid them all of $1,000. I told Greg to send those guys a bonus.

CHAPTER TWENTY-SEVEN

SUMNER DOES BANGKOK

The 1990s would prove to be Viacom's high-tide decade, right before the digital revolution would begin its decimation of the entertainment ecosystem. By 1995, the sky was the limit. Sumner Redstone seemed more energized than I'd ever seen him. The man who had waited until retirement age to start to assemble a media empire was exuding a new sense of confidence and ease. Even his style changed. In the early years, Sumner would wear the mismatched clothing of his movie theater operator days. He had a wide selection of ill-fitting, rumpled sport coats in loud plaids. Gradually, the sport coats were replaced by Italian suits with ties. He began to dye his hair. At the same time, he became increasingly convinced of his infallibility and hungry for public adulation. In his mind, he had turned himself into the embodiment of the corporation. He would proclaim alternatively, "I am Viacom" or "Viacom is me."

He was also a titan and a raider, waging a forever war. Whether they were lawsuits, acquisitions, or personal feuds, he won most of the battles he started. He kept an eagle eye out for any predators. He also had his grievances; at the top of his list was the cable industry itself, our primary customers. Sumner saw cable as a penny-pinching, price-gouging group of monopolies out to eat our lunch.

Until Sumner came along, the cable industry was like a country club. The members were polite and anything but litigious. Disputes were settled peacefully, usually in favor of the cable system owners. Sumner was perfectly happy to join the club as the turd on their golf course. He had trained as an antitrust expert, something in short supply at the club. This orientation kept him always alert to the slightest sign of price or marketing discrimination against us, especially against Showtime, the closest rival to HBO. In 1989, he went after both HBO and Time Inc.'s cable systems for $2.4 billion for "conspiring" against Showtime. That might have been a stretch. But his genius was to strike exactly when Time Inc. was seeking government approval to merge with Warner Communications. Steve Ross, Warner's CEO, wanted nothing to distract from getting the big deal done. At Ross's command, Time Inc. ate crow and settled the suit for hundreds of millions of dollars, along with distribution commitments for Viacom's cable networks.

Sumner liked to say, "I hate litigation." But this was a man who regularly sued members of his family. He and his legal sidekick, Philippe Dauman, made lawsuits a new profit center for the company. Peace never came. Sumner and Philippe struck next with a 1993 lawsuit against TCI, the largest cable company. Once again, it was for discriminatory practices against Showtime versus HBO. The key point of leverage here was to go after TCI CEO John Malone personally with an incendiary second lawsuit. Malone was the Darth Vader of cable. No one messed with him. Sumner was happy to. He called Malone out as an "evil monopolist" who used "bully boy tactics." This was something everyone knew was standard TCI behavior. Sumner bet that Malone would not want to risk his personal assets.

Fearing blowback to MTV Networks, I had counseled Sumner not to sue. TCI was our biggest distributor, and we were in the middle of an important negotiation. After I ran down my rationale, he got up, walked over to where I sat, bent down, got inches away from my face, and blasted me like a drill sergeant. "Listen, Freston," he screamed, "no one shits in my mouth!" That was a new one. Almost blew me off the chair. The rest of the room was motionless and silent. Sumner knew how to pick his targets. The TCI lawsuit was also settled on favorable terms, and Viacom sold $2.3 billion worth of cable systems to TCI.

After spending years sitting quietly at the meetings Frank Biondi ran and absorbing Frank's knowledge of the cable business, in 1996, Sumner fired Frank and crowned himself CEO. That was a shock to all of us. Frank's light touch and sound advice had won him many fans inside the company, me among them.

I had a very warm relationship with Sumner in those years. After all, it had been my secret meeting with him at the Carlyle that helped convince him to go full bore to get Viacom. I'd also delivered on the vision for success and global expansion that I had laid out in his hotel room nearly a decade earlier. MTV Networks had become both the star and central growth engine of the company. We were up every quarter and always breaking new ground.

But I didn't seek to build closer ties with Sumner. My strategy was to make myself scarce and keep things between us short. Better to keep a bit of mystery about our business and myself and stay out of any corporate politics. I'd seen other executives get too close and then they'd be gone. Sumner also did not seem to have many real friends. I figured he burned through them, too. I was not looking to be in any inner circle at Viacom.

Indeed, I went out of my way to insulate MTV Networks from corporate Viacom. No one approached us to be part of a large conglomerate. Sumner and I rarely lunched, but there were the occasional dinners, often with his wife, Phyllis, or sometimes just he and I, or sometimes Gerry or one of my other business leaders would join. These were largely social meals, gossiping about the industry or world events. I found him to be quite funny and enjoyable company. He had his favorite haunts; places like Scalinatella (there was a "Chicken Redstone") or Elio's in the East Eighties. He was not a cheap diner, and usually ordered fine red wines and, always, a Gavi di Gavi for Phyllis. Eventually, though, he'd be banned at Elio's, Le Cirque, and other dining spots for abusing the staff or throwing plates at the waiters. Sometimes I thought I was seated with a werewolf.

My star with Sumner continued to climb when MTV produced an *Unplugged* episode with Tony Bennett, a hero from his era. Tony's son Danny, a hip reader of the zeitgeist who was now his dad's manager, wanted to shake up Tony's image. He looked at an *Unplugged* as a game changer for Tony. It turned out to be a ratings and press bonanza for both Tony and MTV and introduced Tony to a whole new audience. Tony Bennett, the most gracious of men, came into our life and became part of the MTV family.

For Sumner, this was pure heaven. He was starstruck at last and tried to become Tony's friend. They were contemporaries. There would be dinners, Tony would sing at his birthdays and at his second wedding. After I left the company, I heard that Tony had asked Sumner for a major donation for an arts high school, the Frank Sinatra School of the Arts, that Tony was opening in New York City. It was to be Tony's charitable legacy. Sumner gave a paltry donation. I was mortified. That defined Sumner's ungracious spirit in a nutshell.

In part because I probably spent less time with Sumner than anyone else in top management and ran the least traditional division at Viacom as his least traditional top executive, Sumner imagined me to be a bit friskier than the others. Added to this was the fact that the other Viacom executives were proper married people. In 1995, I was in the last stages of a painful divorce. Sumner imagined that a single man on top of the freewheeling world of MTV surely must walk on the wild side. That was far from the truth. When he would ask about my dating life, I tried to change the subject.

But Sumner began to share things about women and sex with me, drop hints, raise an eyebrow here or there. I would just laugh, and he would give me a knowing nod of the head. I thought it was hilarious, that this grizzled old fellow with the gnarled hand saw himself as a hot ladies' man. He was not a predator like (as we later learned) our advertiser Harvey Weinstein. He imagined himself more a Casanova, along the lines of Hugh Hefner, his near contemporary.

One of my favorite topics with Sumner was regaling him with tales of MTV's adventures in Asia. I told him about the huge potential lying in wait for us: five hundred channels were coming, and music traveled faster and easier than almost everything else. MTV was well on its way to becoming what I had dreamed we'd be—the first global TV network. I kept egging on Sumner to go to Asia. Asia was the most optimistic continent, and Sumner was a wild-eyed optimist. I wanted to turn him into a leading champion for our Asian conquest.

In November 1994, Sumner called me up to his office. "Tom, I'm finally ready to take that trip together to Asia. It's important, I know. Let's plan it for early February. It's one place I have not visited and need to." According to his bio, Sumner had helped break the Japanese code in World War II—but he did it from the USA. "I cannot make it a long trip, but I can make it easier on us. We do have our own jet now, a Gulfstream," he offered. Gulfstreams were the status symbol of the age and a luxury he could easily rationalize. The key perk of a mogul. Sumner Redstone would never hold a boarding pass again.

"Let me put some options together for you," I said. "It will be a great opportunity for us to get some high-level access." MTV had opened our new Asian headquarters in Singapore, and we were trying to get distribution deals throughout the continent. We were set to launch our first twenty-four-hour service, MTV Mandarin, in May 1995, serving China, Taiwan, and Singapore. We had plans for a separate service in India in Hindi and in Indonesia in Bahasa.

But Sumner's first and only choice for the trip was to visit exotic Bangkok. This was not one of our top target markets at the time. Thailand had few distribution opportunities. There was a vibrant music scene there, however, and we were working with some local producers. The biggest media player in Thailand was the CP Group, a huge family-controlled conglomerate. They had just started a new division, UTV Cable. I figured the CP Group would be a fine place to deploy Sumner. And a taste of Bangkok, a vibrant, booming city, was bound to please.

Dhanin Chearavanont, Chairman of the CP Group, was elated to meet Sumner Redstone, a fellow family-controlled businessman and billionaire. We planned to leave New York on February 8, 1995.

A few days before our departure, Sumner took me aside. "Listen, Tom, I can trust you, yes? There is a little secret I do not want anyone to know. I am going to bring along an old friend of mine on the trip. I've known her since the seventies. I would like you not to share this with anyone else at the company." I was now entering the closely guarded domain of Sumner's private life. Sumner's wife, Phyllis, evidently, would not be joining us.

"Sure thing," I said, caught off guard. "My lips are sealed."

"And tell me," he added, ". . . tell me what you know about the sex clubs in Bangkok."

"Well," I said, taking on a worldly tone, "Bangkok is the world's most famous commercial sex capital, you know. You can see almost anything there."

"I know that. Do you think I'm an idiot? But what's it actually like?"

I had been to Bangkok many times, but was never a regular at Patpong or any of the other red-light areas. Not a prude, but not a fan. I only went to a sex club once, dragged along with a group after some cocktails. I found it depressing. I wondered what pressures had put the women there. Plus, it was hard to think about sex after seeing ping-pong balls firing out of a vagina into the chests of older Japanese gentlemen.

"What about people fucking?" Sumner asked. "I want to watch people fuck. Can we see that?" Now I was getting the picture.

"Let me see if that could be arranged."

"Well, arrange something good. I'm counting on you," he said, ending the conversation. This was all to be our little secret. I was now to be an advance man for Sumner's Asian sex tour. There was little mention of our agenda with Mr. Dhanin and the CP Group.

Sumner was an obsessive man, but his obsessions had seemed limited to two subjects: (1) Viacom and (2) how to forestall his demise. There was always some new diet involving cruciferous vegetables or acai berries or obscure antioxidants. For years he was an Atkins man, eating almost exclusively meat. But now there was clearly a third topic, at least with me. Sex. I began to realize that Sumner Redstone was an aspiring swinger—and he figured I was one, too. Next time we met one-on-one, he suggested that I was welcome to sit with his girlfriend and him and watch people have sex in Thailand.

I first went to Bangkok in the 1970s. It was a much smaller and less complicated place back then. One of the legacies of the Vietnam War for Thailand was the birth of the sex industry. In the 1960s and early '70s, thousands of battle-fatigued American soldiers flocked to Bangkok from Vietnam on American Airlines flights for five days of R&R. "Rest and Recuperation" they called it, but to the GIs it was more like "Intercourse and Intoxication." Places like Brown Sugar, the Horny Toad, and the Thigh Bar opened to cater to lustful GIs. Bangkok became the world's most notorious sex destination. Now chartered planeloads of creepy passengers arrived daily from the former World War II Axis powers of Japan and Germany for "sex tours," to run wild in Thailand's red-light neighborhoods.

On my first trip to Bangkok, I flew in from Calcutta. It was hot and humid. When I got into a taxi, before I could even tell the driver where I wanted to go, he turned around and looked at me, a sweaty Caucasian, and his first words were "You want fucky-fucky show?" I laughed. The last time I heard that offer, I was in Tijuana. I told him to just take me to my hotel.

As I planned Sumner's trip and started to focus on the sex club thing, I called Vinnie Longobardo, MTV's international all-around utility player. Now based in Singapore, Vinnie was a happy, easygoing guy with a ponytail. Everyone liked Vinnie. He had an encyclopedic knowledge of world music, and he loved being out on the frontier, heading the "MTV Foreign Legion," as I called it, working in Japan, Brazil, and elsewhere. No Ugly American, his humble style and music cred were perfect and allowed him to build important relationships, even with the dodgiest of people.

I had several memorable adventures with Vinnie, including our near-arrest in Vietnam. On a trip to Taipei with Bon Jovi, we hit a wet market called "Snake Alley." Men hung live snakes on strings and slit them down the middle to squeeze out the blood into glasses. A mob would fight each other to buy a glass and then swill it down on the spot. If there was a man to research the sex emporiums of Bangkok for me, Vinnie was that man. He would meet me in Bangkok.

"Tom, this is my very good friend for many years, Delsa Winer," Sumner said, introducing me as we got on the plane at the Teterboro Airport. I had expected a younger woman. Delsa was sixty-eight. Sumner was seventy-two. Turned out these lovebirds had been an illicit item for decades. She was with him at the famous Copley Plaza hotel fire in Boston in 1979, the disaster so central to Sumner's legend. I used to wonder why a guy with a home in Boston would be spending nights in a hotel there. Now I knew. He was doing the hanky-panky.

Delsa was a pleasant surprise and nice company, a good conversationalist, curious, and with a sense of humor. She was a mother of grown children and an accomplished writer who'd won several literary prizes for short stories. Holding her hand, Sumner seemed thrilled to be in her company.

They seemed a far happier couple than Sumner and Phyllis, who I'd seen yell insults back and forth for hours on plane trips. Delsa brought out a sweet side of Sumner, a side I had not seen before. We were all in good spirits. Like winners of some extravagant contest, we were headed west in our private jet at 10 a.m. A One Night Stand in Bangkok awaited over the far horizon.

The early G2 Gulfstream jets did not have much range. We had to refuel three times before our first destination, Bali. We touched down in Alaska, then in Sapporo, Japan, where Sumner asked that a case of cold Sapporo draft beer be delivered to the plane. *Nice touch*, I thought. In Alaska, I had told him that was my favorite beer. We drank all the way to Taipei, our last refueling stop. When we landed in Bali, it was midafternoon, two days later on the calendar. The door opened and warm, humid air rushed in. We left our winter coats on the plane and a hotel car whisked us into the mountains. Bali is one of the greenest places on earth. For an hour or so, we drove through spectacular tropical scenery. With volcanoes looming on the horizon, we passed rice paddies terraced up to the lush highlands of Ubud.

I had booked suites for us at the ultra-luxe Amandari. Each suite had an outdoor garden and a private pool. We checked in and went to our rooms. Soon, over the fence, I could hear Sumner and Delsa laughing and swimming in the pool. While I was talking to my children in New York, I had to cover the receiver with my hand; Sumner was audibly moaning in the background. Dinner was off. Sumner and Delsa would not leave their love nest. I didn't see them until we checked out the next afternoon to fly to Bangkok.

Bangkok was about the only Asian place the European colonialist set never got their hands on. The gentle and romantic Kingdom of Siam stayed independent. Now the whole country seemed to be a boomtown, full of things that were forbidden at home. It also had probably the worst traffic in the world. Endless, horn-honking caravans of vehicles, tuk tuks, and motorcycles snaked through the narrow streets. Bangkok's canals, which had given the city such character, were being filled in to make roads. In 1995, it could take four hours to get from the airport into town.

But not for us. Mr. Dhanin had sent a limousine to greet us, along with a police escort. We left the airport with the siren blaring. Sumner was beaming. He was arriving triumphantly, like a king. His Viacom would soon be conquering a new land. The siren wailed nonstop as we inched ahead, trying to pry our way through the logjam. Periodically the police car would veer off and go up onto the sidewalk to keep us moving. Our limo would follow suit, bulldozing pedestrians out of the way. There was a small flagpole on the fender. I suggested we needed a Viacom flag.

I had booked us into the iconic Oriental Hotel, on the banks of the Chao Phraya River. Graham Greene, W. Somerset Maugham, and James Michener had stayed at the Oriental whenever they came to town. Not only was it the most luxurious hotel in Bangkok, the Oriental was rated number one in the entire world. It had more staff than guests. I explained to Sumner that this was known as "the Asian level of service." At that time, most of the world's top-rated hotels were in Asia.

Sumner was heralded like a head of state. An entourage came out to welcome us. The manager bowed with his hands together and proceeded to place orchid wreaths around our necks. We were quickly spirited away past the towering floral displays in the dazzling marble lobby to the older nineteenth-century Author's Wing. I had arranged for Sumner to have the Noël Coward Suite. His grand entrance could not have been grander.

We met in the lobby for dinner. I took the couple down to the river and into a boat to go to a Thai restaurant on the other side. The humid night air felt as smooth as silk. There was a scent of jasmine. We sat at a perfect table, at the river's edge under strings of lights. The Chao Phraya is the most scenic and efficient highway in Bangkok. Golden temples and palaces line its banks. Barges and long water taxis filled with passengers motored by us in both directions. Longboats bobbed up and down, their unmuffled engines roaring. If you used your hand to cover a couple of new skyscrapers on the skyline, you could imagine yourself back in more romantic times.

Sumner and Delsa were transported. We had a delicious meal and talked about the next day's meeting at the CP Group. Afterward, jet lag kicking in, they wanted to head back to their suite. Tomorrow was Chairman

Dhanin and a full workday. As we approached his suite, Sumner turned and gave me a sly look. "Remember, Tom, tomorrow's our big night. . . . The sex clubs."

After a quick change of clothes, I went down to the lobby to meet Vinnie for some porno reconnaissance. Of all the odd things I had thrown Vinnie's way over the years, this was the oddest. He and his wife had flown up from Singapore for the weekend. "But she's got something else to do tonight," he said. I was relieved and added, "Then you both should join us on Sunday. I've arranged for a private boat cruise for us. I'd love for Sumner to spend some time with you. Just don't say 'Patpong.'"

We jumped into a tuk tuk outside the hotel. It was immediately liberating to be in the open air and energy of the city. The driver gunned the scooter. The wind blew my hair back. The sweet mix of exhaust fumes, Thai street food, and sewage smacked me in the face. We were off to the red-light district. Patpong is the centerpiece of Bangkok's seedy underbelly. It was Friday and crowded. A clutter of neon signs for bars and clubs ran up and down every building . . . Super Pussy, Fetish, Hot Male, Sixty-Nine Bar. We were headed to a bar to meet a Thai music producer, who knew the scene here and was going to pass on some helpful hints and wisdom.

When we arrived, women sitting at tables outside gestured to us to come in. Barely dressed go-go girls danced onstage to rock music. Our man was at the bar, Vinnie introduced me, and he took us to a corner booth. I ordered a Singha beer. Two Westerners were getting hand jobs at the bar. They were standing there talking to each other while getting their penises gently stroked by two short, half-dressed Thai women. "You don't see that every day, Vinnie," I said, pointing in their direction.

"You do around here," said our new Thai pal.

Vinnie mumbled, "Somehow I don't see Sumner Redstone doing that."

"He's like Chauncey Gardiner in the movie *Being There*," I said. "He likes to watch."

"You really have to know how to safely get around here," declared the music producer. "Many foreigners who come here get ripped off. There are so many scams. You have to know the right places. I've asked around and have some options for you. Super Girls is right down the street. It's sort of famous. There is a bar downstairs and upstairs; they have both a 'ping pong' show and a sex show. Even Thai people go there. No one will rip you off." He went on to explain the finer points of the Patpong entertainment mix: The ping-pong shows were not actually people having sex, but more an acrobatic thing. Think of everyday activities you do with your hands or mouth and imagine them being done with a vagina instead. You can see a vagina blow out the candles on a birthday cake. There are girls with vaginas that can smoke cigarettes, he said, even open a bottle of soda. The Japanese love this stuff, he added.

The "sex shows" were just that. Couples or threesomes of men and women running through the Kama Sutra catalog. But the local laws were tricky; if you wanted the real deal, you had to know where to go. "What's the other place?" asked Vinnie. Our friend explained that it was kind of new and was in a basement of a shopping complex, nearby but off the beaten track. There was no sign. You had to be in the know. "More classy," he said. "They have lots of real sex onstage." He said that he could take us to both places so we could scope them out. This would also have the advantage that, when I brought Sumner and Delsa here, I could weave them through the crowded streets like a man who knows how to put the "bang" in "Bangkok."

We headed out to Super Girls. The streets were set up for a night market with stalls crowded together. Each seemed to sell versions of the same stuff; cheap fake watches and jewelry, T-shirts, counterfeit DVDs, and, at one stall, rows of dildos hung upside down like sausages. We trudged through backpackers, grizzled-looking Western men arm in arm with young Thai girls, some frat boys, and hustler after hustler hawking "ladyboy shows," lesbian shows, and more. Scantily dressed women sat outside.

Ahead was Super Girls, with a Superman logo in stained glass on the front door. A big sidewalk sign outside proclaimed "'Super Girls is the very best sex club in town'—*Rolling Stone* magazine."

"I did not know that *Rolling Stone* was rating sex clubs," said Vinnie. "Maybe you should have just asked your pal Jann Wenner where to go."

"You can't always trust them," I said. "They hated Led Zeppelin. Let's check for ourselves."

The doorman greeted us. The place looked pretty legit. Almost like a regular bar. Classier than the semi-bordellos we'd been passing. It was jammed, and not just with bar girls or johns, but a real crowd including couples and many Thais. There was a show upstairs, but the man at the door said they had some "surprises" from time to time in the bar area. I told him I'd be back tomorrow night with friends. "Remember me."

We left to see the other place. After a few twists and turns, we came to a nondescript building in a small strip mall and descended a concrete stairwell. A Chinese man in a tuxedo stood at the door. He was the maître d'. The club did not seem to have a name. I took that as a good sign. The maître d' greeted the music producer by embracing him, an uncharacteristic gesture in Thailand. Then he turned to me. I said how happy I was to meet him and explained that we were preparing for a VIP couple, who wanted to come the next evening. We wanted to make sure they would be nicely accommodated, nice seats and all that. The producer spoke to the maître d' in Thai to further explain who Sumner Redstone was, a Hollywood billionaire mogul out for kicks. Vinnie and I peeked in. A couple was having sex on the stage. The seats all seemed to be filled. "Very popular here, eh?"

"Good crowd every night. Popular here," said the maître d'.

"Well, I'll be back tomorrow night with my friends," I said, "What's a good time to come?"

"Late show begins eleven p.m. Come earlier. That's better," declared the man in the tux.

That was our dry run. Research was done, venues picked, and proper directions through the red-light district mapped out. I was glad to have that over with. I would be back with the eager couple after dinner tomorrow night.

The CP Group had their own office tower on Silom Road about five minutes from the hotel. Sumner and I headed over at 9 a.m. Chairman Dhanin was tickled pink to have Sumner Redstone in the building. Asians are known for both their veneration of elders and their fascination with Hollywood. Sumner checked all the boxes; he was a celebrity to the Asian executives. After introductions and pleasantries and tea, Chairman Dhanin and his top associates gave us an impressive rundown on their company. To kick off our presentation, I had brought along a slick mixtape that went through the entertainment assets of Viacom. They paid close attention after that.

Sumner was on top of his game, convincingly communicating our interest in Thailand as he ran down the Viacom story. When he was on, the man really could exude passion and sincerity. Viacom was the love of his life, and it showed.

We were done by 5 p.m. We were loaded down with gifts as we made our way to the car. Chairman Dhanin gave me a large gilded wooden pagoda. As we headed back to the Oriental for a nap, Sumner was very pleased. He liked this new frontier of ours and sensed its potential. One mission accomplished. I said we could compare notes at dinner. "Dress casually, the both of you. It is going to be hot out there tonight."

I already had an exit strategy for the evening.

At 9 p.m., I was waiting for Sumner and Delsa in the lobby. They came down the hall looking like elderly tourists from the heartland dressed for the tropics. Sumner had on a light-colored short-sleeved plaid shirt with gray pants and Delsa had on a light blouse. "Are you guys ready for action?" I asked.

"We sure are," said Delsa. "Cannot wait."

We took a car to Patpong and then I led them through the congested streets. So many overweight foreigners, bulging out of their T-shirts, were holding hands with their slender young dates. As we edged past the stalls of knockoff merchandise and sex toys, Sumner made an abrupt stop when he saw the racks of DVDs. *Forrest Gump*, from our movie studio division, was right up front.

"These are all counterfeit, Sumner," I offered. "But look how well they are made, right down to the shrink-wrap." He picked one up and closely examined it, dumbfounded. "This is illegal," he barked at the stall keeper. I thought for a minute he was going to confiscate it and maybe take a swing at the man, but he let it pass. He had bigger things on his mind. I bought one to take back to New York for show-and-tell at the staff meeting.

Super Girls was just ahead. "*Rolling Stone* says it's the best in town, Sumner." He nodded, making a beeline to the entrance. The man at the door recognized me, and I put my hands together and bowed slightly. "Nice to be here." Then, I said, "This is Sumner Redstone and Delsa Winer." He put his hands together and welcomed them. Count on the Thais to be polite. "Come in. And big show upstairs starts soon. Crowd is building."

I ordered three Singha beers at the bar. Everyone was standing shoulder to shoulder. I was impressed at the number of Thai couples. Sumner was scanning the room. He was at last in an Asian fleshpot. There were respectable-looking people here; Sumner was probably the oldest in the room. "Where is the sex?" he asked.

"It just may appear when you least expect it," I said.

A few minutes later there was the faint purr of a motorcycle from inside the barroom. Then someone gunned it. Ever so slowly, a small Harley-Davidson motorcycle descended from the ceiling into the room on chains. There was a nude couple on the bike. Their bodies were hairless; slender and shiny, like they had been oiled up. The man was entering the woman from behind, one hand around her left breast, the other on the throttle, gunning the engine. They stopped, smiled at the festive crowd, and continued to copulate, just feet away.

If there were to be a "greatest hits" reel of Sumner Redstone images inside my head, this one would be front and center. Here he was, like a deer in the headlights, mouth slightly agape, moving slowly into the crowd to get even closer for a better look. The show went on for a few minutes. The rest of the room had pretty much gone back to their conversations, as if they couldn't care less about the acrobats fucking on a running motorcycle just over their heads. But Sumner could not take his eyes off the fornicators. Finally, he leaned into me and said with great enthusiasm, "I've never seen anyone fucking before." Oh, God, was the man happy. His smile was wide. He was filled with joy.

"Haven't you been to an orgy or anything?" I asked, sounding like a libertine.

"No," he snapped, still not for a second diverting his eyes from the nude couple. Delsa seemed delighted, too. The copulating went on for a couple more minutes, then there was a roar of the engine, and the motorcycle was off, pulled back up from whence it came, through the trapdoor on the ceiling.

People started to go upstairs for the main event. "It's showtime!" proclaimed a very enthused Redstone.

"Listen, Sumner, they have a good show here," I said, as if I knew, "but trust me on this, there is a much better one at a more exclusive place not far away. It's off the beaten track, but my friends here in Bangkok say that is the one to see, a sex show for the cognoscenti."

"You sure know your way around these whorehouses, Tom. I'm impressed." I was not sure if that was what I wanted to be known for, but I got them outside, and we plowed our way through the massage parlors and dildo salespeople to the waiting car. At the strip mall, I led them to the basement, very glad that Vinnie and I had done the dry run the night before.

Our Chinese friend was at the door, in his tuxedo, looking perfect. I almost laughed. I put my hands together in greeting and then, in a move that might give my career its most indelible boost, the tuxedoed doorman approached and put his arms around me in a bear hug, like I was some kind of sex club soul brother. *Perfect*, I thought. I turned to introduce "the great Sumner Redstone, Chairman of Viacom," and "Delsa Winer, his wonderful girlfriend and an award-winning writer." The doorman extended his hand, and Sumner shook it. "We are honored to have you, sir," he announced. "Great show tonight. Let me take you to your seats." He showed us to three seats in the center of the second row. Ugh. We were up close.

The room probably held sixty people. It was nearly full. There were a couple of Western men, one other woman, and the rest appeared to be mostly Japanese businessmen sitting upright in dark suit jackets. There was a small, rounded stage about three feet off the floor and covered by a curtain. Soon the curtain opened, and the MC appeared and introduced two naked young Thai women, who laid down on benches facing the audience.

I won't go through the details of their routine, but there was a program detailing their many skillful feats: "Pussy Shoot Balloon, Pussy Open the Bottle, Pussy Shoot Banana, Pussy Write Letter, Pussy Electric." The host assisted them like a ringleader. It went on and on. After "Woman and Snake," there was a break before new performers came out to have actual sex.

Two people right in front of us got up to leave. Sumner grabbed Delsa, and they scrambled to take their seats. He turned around as if to say, "How lucky are we and I hope you don't mind." Finally, after all those miles in the Gulfstream and all those years he probably spent anticipating a moment like this, he was ringside at the great sex show in a musty basement in Bangkok. A new threesome took the stage, one man and two women. They started in. It seemed kind of mechanical. That was enough for me. I tapped Sumner on the shoulder. "I have to head back to the hotel." He barely paid me any mind, turning back quickly so as not to miss any of the intercoursing. "The car will be outside when you are ready," I offered. "Remember, we have a boat trip through the canals. See you in the morning."

Having delivered on my assignment, I found the whole thing more than uncomfortable. What were these women's stories and how did they find themselves here?

Sumner went on to become the greatest high roller for commercial sex the world might have ever seen. In his later years, well after he cashiered me, he spent over $150 million on a squad of comfort women. Cash, apartments, jewelry, you name it—all of it just flew out the door. Two of the women that he liked made so much money off him that they opened their own charities. Say what you want about him, just as he did for his executives, the man paid well for what he wanted.

After that night in Bangkok, more than ever, I was Sumner's golden boy. He figured we were on the same wavelength, connected by shared values and those dirty times in Thailand. As the years went on and Sumner adopted more of a playboy pose, getting divorced and remarried and divorced again, and spending all that money on hired girlfriends, I often wondered if that trip to Bangkok marked the moment when Sumner Redstone saw what he wanted to surround himself with in the years that remained in his life.

CHAPTER TWENTY-EIGHT

MY LUNCH WITH FIDEL

Newsweek splashed "It's an MTV World" on its cover in 1995. It was true. In the nineties we moved across the globe like Coca-Cola. We slid into the opportunities that followed the fall of the USSR, the liberation of Eastern Europe, and a general loosening of government broadcast monopolies all around the world. Local entrepreneurs were opening new cable and satellite TV systems and MTV was a hot commodity. Music traveled well. Our $1,000 logo became a global icon, like McDonald's golden arches.

After the fall of the Berlin Wall, a new interconnected generation was emerging. We used to say that a kid in Amsterdam and a kid in New York had more in common with each other than they did with their parents. It was a great line, but of course it really wasn't that simple. When it came to music, local tastes usually prevailed. MTV International was not culturally imperialistic. We knew enough not to force American tastes on other countries.

Our viewers, hundreds of millions of them, received locally programmed MTVs. Each mixed international and local programming with common MTV branding elements. There were over one hundred feeds . . . in Mandarin, Russian, Bahasa, German, French, Spanish, Italian, Portuguese, and on and on. MTV India mixed Hindi pop and Punjabi hip-hop with Bollywood film music, dropped in a little Michael Jackson and Metallica, maybe even a touch of global flavor with Nigeria's Fela Kuti.

There was a small circle of international superstars who were popular everywhere—Madonna, Tupac Shakur, U2, Mariah Carey—and our talent departments juggled requests for them to play every awards show from Singapore to Barcelona, but local music and local culture was king.

However, while MTV spread from Argentina to Istanbul, we were locked out of a musical mecca ninety miles from Florida. Cuba didn't have MTV, but it was having an exceptional period of musical creativity with fresh strains of salsa, dance, and rock music—the soundtrack to the arts explosion that followed the collapse of their patron, the Soviet Union, in 1991.

When the USSR disappeared, Cuba was cast adrift. The economy contracted by 40 percent. Communism had failed, but Fidel Castro, the truest believer, wasn't giving up. The Cuban people might have gotten poorer, more alienated and pissed off . . . but their music had never been better. In 1997, the great American musician Ry Cooder made an album with the Buena Vista Social Club, a collection of veteran Cuban musicians, that demonstrated their mastery of various styles—son, danzón, and bolero. The Buena Vista Social Club album was a sensation, the bestselling "world music" album ever, that led to two award-winning documentaries and international concert dates. That was just the tip of the iceberg. The new music from the Cuban streets included rock bands like Los Van Van and, hands down, what had to be the most punk band ever, Eskoria, who injected themselves with HIV to protest the Castro government's AIDS policies.

I had always wanted to go to Havana. The more stories like that I heard, the more Cuban records I fell in love with, the more determined I was to go.

The USA was the only country in the world that could not do business with Cuba. We were forbidden to even go there. It was easier to enter North Korea or Iran. I yearned to prowl the Malecón in the back of a 1950s Cadillac convertible, tap into this music, drink it all in, and hustle up some deals to feed our ravenous international network.

My brother, Bill, had gone to Cuba in 1979 to work on the Havana Jam, a rock festival with Stephen Stills and Kris Kristofferson. He was still talking about it. But that was back in the more liberal times of the Carter presidency. I was attempting to get in, in early 2001, the first days of the new and less-generous Bush-Cheney administration. My lawyers told me, "Don't even think about it. It's a fifty-five-thousand-dollar fine."

I needed a fixer, a loophole-finder, a Man in Havana. As I asked around, one name kept popping up: a thirty-one-year-old American named Jonathan Brandstein. By day he was a Hollywood comedy talent manager. Cuba was his passion and side hustle. He'd been there six or seven times. Mariel Hemingway told me Jonathan got her in to visit Finca Vigía, the estate where her grandfather wrote *A Moveable Feast*.

I called Jonathan. "Look, no way we could ever launch MTV into Cuba, Jonathan, but I want to go, get smarter, and start some relationships in the creative community."

"This will be a piece of cake, Tom. I can get you all organized. I'll even come with you."

Boy, I thought, *that was easy*. Then I got a half-hour fire hose of encyclopedic patter about the country, the government, the music scene, his connections there. Jonathan was personable, hysterically funny, and a music nut. I had found my Man in Havana.

"The first thing is to apply for a cultural exchange license with the US Treasury Department. I can help you with that. You qualify easily. I recommend you fly to Cancún, then charter a flight to Havana from a Mexican company. It's about an hour. You can get a Cuban visa on arrival. I can handle all your arrangements in Havana. You have to stay at the Hotel Nacional. Real history. That's where all the gangsters stayed in the Batista era. Remember *Godfather II*?"

I asked how to rent an old Cadillac, like the used one my dad used to have, in which I got my driver's license.

"No problem. I'll get you a driver, too. And a cell phone. Yours won't work there."

"Great! What about music?"

"It's everywhere. I know a lot of these bands. I'll check to see who's playing when you arrive. And you have to meet with the Minister of Culture, Abel Prieto." Jonathan talked about him like he was a pal. "He's a really good guy, a commie with a mullet haircut who's a massive Beatles fan."

I'd hit a home run with Jonathan. One man to do it all. I asked Bill Roedy, the head of MTV Networks International, to join me.

I shot my mouth off about this impending adventure to my movie producer buddy Brian Grazer. "I'm headed to Cuba to look around and try to wrangle some deals." Without missing a beat Brian said, "Can I come?"

Brian told Jim Wiatt, who ran the William Morris Agency. Jim told Brad Grey, who ran the talent management firm Brillstein-Grey and was a producer of *The Sopranos*. Brad told Les Moonves, who ran CBS. Brian also told Graydon Carter, editor of *Vanity Fair*. The moguls all wanted in. I found myself host and tour guide to some picky travelers to a tropical island full of communists where I'd never been. This would now be a whole new kind of trip.

We touched down on February 7, 2001. Havana's historic eight-story, four-hundred-plus-room grande dame Hotel Nacional towered over the city. Winston Churchill and the Duke and Duchess of Windsor had stayed there. Walt Disney, too. Like the rest of Havana, it was faded and crumbling. The hotel seemed to be staying afloat on the fumes of its gangster yesteryear. Brian Grazer scrambled to score the Meyer Lansky Suite. Graydon took the Lucky Luciano Suite. I went for a more proletarian single accommodation, which had beat-up, mismatched furniture, cigarette burns everywhere, and an old dial phone I was told not to use. "It's tapped," Jonathan told me. Water trickled out of five or six pinholes of my showerhead.

Jonathan rented two vintage convertibles—a 1953 black Chevy Bel Air and a cherry-red 1957 Cadillac Eldorado. The drivers wore proper chauffeur hats. He distributed a bunch of Cuban cell phones, each about the size of a loaf of bread. "They're tapped, too!"

In this period of economic misery, small shoots of capitalism were finally allowed to emerge in Cuba. Early entrepreneurs opened restaurants in their homes called *paladares*. They had to be run by family members. They had charm and atmosphere. The coolest spot and hottest table in Havana was chic La Guarida, a cluttered series of high-ceilinged rooms up two flights of stairs in a ramshackle mansion right out of Belle Époque Paris. It buzzed like New York's Odeon. Jonathan had scored us a reservation and we were joined by Jorge Gonzalez, a short, rotund, jolly minder from the Ministry of Culture. He stayed glued to us the entire time.

Our spirits high, we piled into convertibles after dinner and motored through Old Havana. After a century of neglect, the city had been described as a "prince in pauper's clothes." To the exiles in Miami, it was an open-air ruin. For us, it seemed a dreamy time machine, filled with art deco, Moorish, and Spanish colonial architecture, the streets full of all the cars from our youth. The soft breeze off the sea on the Malecón was sultry and salty. We passed under the towering steel Che Guevara mural in the Plaza de la Revolución and stopped by the legendary Havana Riviera hotel for more mid-century gangster vibes. Built by Meyer Lansky, it was a mid-century architectural gem that appeared to have been dropped in from Vegas.

We spent two days rambling around city streets, clubs, and bars, hearing lots of music. I met Ricardo Alarcón, president of the Parliament, the third most powerful Cuban figure after Fidel and his brother, Raul. Alarcón was gracious, but curious about my intentions. He spent most of our time berating the US for the travel ban and embargo. After he finished the tirade, he relaxed and said he had lived in Manhattan for a dozen years as Cuba's Ambassador to the UN and enjoyed recounting some of his good times there.

On our third day we gathered around a large roundtable meeting at the Ministry of Culture with the minister, some vice ministers, some recording executives, and other government functionaries. Minister Prieto was fascinated with MTV and glad to learn that we wanted to take Cuban music to the world. They were very friendly, but it was clear that the government intended to continue controlling everything, which was not a good omen. They asked CBS chief Les Moonves questions about American news coverage.

As we were leaving, Minister Prieto called out, "Hey, would you guys like to meet with Fidel?" We skidded to a stop.

After dinner that night, Jorge Gonzalez took us to a hot spot called Habana Café. It was close to the Presidential Palace and was packed with happy, well-dressed Cubans letting off steam after a long communist workweek. There were beautiful women and deafening disco music. People were dry humping against the walls.

"Fidel wants to meet you all tonight around midnight," Jorge declared. "He's out of town now speaking to a group of schoolteachers. We have to wait for the call."

The call would come on a pay phone outside the club at 2 a.m. Like criminals, Fidel and his handlers were pay phone users. Not even burner phones for them. Anything that might indicate his movements was top secret. We waited like spies for a signal.

Jorge walked in. "The call has come."

We were hustled outside and gathered around the phone booth in the humid night.

"Fidel's speech ran longer than expected," Jorge said, hanging up the pay phone. "Over three hours." The dictator's windbaggery was legend. "Too late now. But the president would like you all to come to the palace at noon for lunch. What do you think?"

We were scheduled to leave for Cancún the next morning. We caucused.

Jim Wiatt said, "Not sure I can do this, I've got to get back to LA for an important meeting."

I was floored. "Are you kidding? You can meet with Fidel Castro or someone at Fox and you pick the studio executive?"

"Of course we'll be there," I told Jorge. "We'd be honored." I couldn't believe it. We were going to meet El Jefe himself.

At noon the next day our two convertibles pulled up to the front of the Palace of the Revolution. Jorge greeted us and led us up the stairs.

Castro came out to meet us in his trademark olive-green fatigues. No medals. An imposing man at six foot three. It was as if a statue, a figure from history, had appeared in front of me. The man who had been a stone in America's shoe for over forty years, who had totally dominated every aspect of Cuba's government and society, a full-on authoritarian, a dictator, but also a hero to much of the developing world, was waving at us. Our government tried to assassinate him eight times. We tried infecting his diving suit with tuberculosis. We tried to poison his cigars and drinks. What might El Jefe have on his mind as he looked at this collection of sunburned gringos?

He spoke almost entirely in Spanish that day. His translator, Juanita Garcia, was a very able woman who stayed about half a sentence behind him, but his opener was in English. He had an important question.

"Who of you makes *The Sopranos*?"

Brad Grey, the shortest of the group, pushed to the front and sheepishly raised his hand. "Me. That's my show."

Fidel had overthrown a gangster-infested regime to seize power. The

CIA had hired gangsters to kill him. Maybe Brad thought he was going to be shot.

“That’s my favorite show,” Castro proclaimed. Cuba’s only HBO subscriber then went on a bit about Tony Soprano. He patted Brad on the shoulder.

Nice icebreaker, Fidel, I thought. Brad was glowing. We were ushered inside, into “the Hall of Ferns,” a long white neoclassical marble chamber where Castro received international leaders. We were getting the full monte. We were swarmed with waiters in crisp white uniforms carrying trays of daiquiris and mojitos. Castro announced, “A vodka martini for Mr. Carter.” Our late-night trawling through Havana had been monitored down to drink preferences. Castro snatched a mojito.

The cocktails went on for an hour. Good vibes with the dictator. Fidel posed for photos. We each introduced ourselves. We stood in a semicircle, drinks in hand, chatting it up. Fidel gravitated toward Les, putting his arm around his shoulders. Les spoke decent Spanish and kept smiling and nodding at Castro, which pleased him. He had seen Brian Grazer’s film *Apollo 13*, but had something else on his mind about Brian. He rubbed his hands through his hair. “How do you got your hair to stand up straight that way?” Brian talked hair gel with the president of Cuba.

After all this small talk, we were ushered into a dining room. There was a long table. Place cards were set. Minister Prieto, President Alarcón, and Jose Gonzalez joined us. I had the place of honor, just to Fidel’s right. His translator sat to his left. In bold letters his place card read: “El Comandante El Jefe Fidel Castro.” (I stole it later.)

Fidel asked if we’d like a little wine. There was a small cheer. He got up and rolled over a mobile wine rack with a full range of Spanish Riojas, Argentine Malbecs, and more. The dictator leaned over and bantered with me about the various choices. He highlighted the Algerian reds, grown by his once-fellow revolutionaries. Fidel said he loved wine, but had recently had to give it up for health reasons.

He toasted all of us for our bravery to come to Cuba, our appreciation of their music, and hoped that we would bring back good tidings to our countrymen.

I was feeling comfortable enough to remind our host that in 1964 he had banned the Beatles' music. Two months before our arrival an artist unveiled a statue of John Lennon on a bench in a small square called "Parque Lennon."

"Why the ban and what caused the change of heart?"

"Early on, it was a defense against cultural imperialism, a defense of the revolution," he explained. Since then, he had learned the futility of censoring the Beatles: "Lennon was a dreamer and I share his dreams. I have seen my dreams turn into reality."

The lunch was not that of an impoverished communist regime. Course after course arrived, new wine bottles kept opening. There was lobster and fried beef and roast pork, rice and beans and salads. For dessert it was piles of ice creams. Fidel famously loved ice cream. I asked if revolutionaries usually ate this well. He told me it was a "modest lunch."

They shoveled food my way, but Fidel was given small portions and barely ate. He was too busy talking. At seventy-four, he was still trim and fit. He told me that he worked out on the treadmill for an hour every day. He stretched and pumped iron, too, and had largely traded in his combat boots for sneakers.

El Presidente wanted us to bring a message home. Looking to Les, he said he'd been upset about the single-engine planes that "counterrevolutionaries" had been flying from Miami over his island to drop anti-communist pamphlets onto Havana. "They violate our airspace. It's pathetic," he said. "In 1996 I dispatched MiG fighter jets to move their two Cessnas out to sea. We shot them down off Havana."

Fidel wanted Les to pass along the message to President Clinton that he practiced great restraint, warning them not to do this, but finally had to do what any national leader would. He wanted Clinton to know his desire for better relations. The strange thing was that Clinton was no longer president. Fidel seemed to be motivated less by international policy than by a desire to repair a personal relationship.

"We will get Clinton that message," Les promised. "I will let him know."

Castro spent five and a half hours with us, holding the floor for at least five hours of that time. I started out mesmerized, hearing the litany of his revolutionary triumphs right from the horse's mouth. However, as the hours passed, I became increasingly bored. The chatterbox had an elephantine memory, down to the price per kilowatt of electricity near Santiago de Cuba, but how much of such detail can any listener take?

This was his default mode, I thought. We were getting full on Fidel . . . powerful, unfiltered, supremely confident and unassailable . . . a narcissist blowhard with undeniable charisma and the nonexistent self-awareness that grows with decades of dictatoring.

I would periodically get up to go to the bathroom, exhale, do a reality check, and realize that while I came innocently out of curiosity and for the music, I somehow ended up having a boozy lunch with the last Western communist, a tyrant who ran prison camps, imprisoned homosexuals, and worse. The novelty of hanging with El Jefe had worn off.

At five fifteen, Fidel stood up. Lunch was over, but the party had just begun. A cart was wheeled out. There was a stack of wooden boxes full of cigars. Castro gave us each two boxes. "These are of my favorites," he said as he signed the boxes of long thin Cohiba cigars from his personal stash. Then his photographer, Roberto Salas, entered with a stack of large black-and-white photographic prints. Salas was an American communist who moved to Cuba in 1953 to help document the revolution. A handsome man, he spoke with a Bronx accent. He had become a confidant of Castro, one of his official photographers, and was a friend of Jonathan's to boot. He had sold some of us prints of iconic Castro images—Castro with Hemingway, Castro lighting a cigar for Che Guevara.

Fidel began signing them. This kicked off a frenzy, the kind you see after a concert when the artists come out, do the meet and greet, and sell and sign CDs. Fidel signed away. We jostled each other like fanboys to be next. There were pamphlets with his speeches, place cards. Fidel signed everything. Grazer hadn't bought a photo, so he stuck out his chest, smiled, and asked Fidel to autograph his new white guayabera shirt with his Sharpie. Fidel demurred.

"Come on," Brian pleaded. Castro signed the shirt.

"Fidel never ever does anything like this," Salas told me, laughing. It was a scene to make Cuban exiles wince, I thought. It would not be a thrilling sight for old revolutionaries there, either. Here we were, the media elite of the USA, lining up to kiss dictator ass in Havana. These were men paid to not lose their cool.

Fidel escorted the short, smiling Brad outside by the hand. He was a touchy guy. The old convertibles waited. "Now, please come back again," he said, holding me tight with his arm around me. We had shown the despot a good time, I guess. He waved goodbye. It was pouring, but as soon as we pulled out of the palace grounds, the clouds ripped open, and the tropical sun burst out. The tops went down. There was a rainbow. We were off to the airport with a shitload of free cigars. We were dazed and quiet Americans. Brad broke the ice. "So where are we going next?"

A week later the *New York Post* gave us the Page Six headline: "Media Mavens Hug Thug in Havana." The story, making it sound worse than it was, reported, "They had a blast sunning on beaches, visiting jazz clubs, drinking lots of white rum, even taking a 5-hour lunch with dictator Fidel Castro."

My well-intentioned fact-finding excursion was playing in the press like a beach party with America's number one pariah. In Miami the headline was "Media Moguls Must Answer for Cuban Fling."

A week later I received a registered, one-inch-thick package from the Treasury Department. "We understand you went to Cuba in violation of the Trading with the Enemy Act to meet with Fidel Castro." I was commanded to fill out an extensive form documenting exactly where I was, who I saw, what I did for every fifteen-minute interval, and did I spend more than $100. I was being fined $55,000, as predicted.

I called Jonathan. He got one, too. "I thought we had the proper licenses to go? This shouldn't be an issue, right? They gave us permission, yes?"

"Definitely. But I think we might've jumped the shark by lunching with Castro. Let me look into getting us a good lawyer." We got Ry Cooder's lawyer, the man who defended him when he was charged with a similar offense after he went to Havana to produce the Buena Vista Social Club.

Attorney Richard Popkin was a revolving-door man. He had worked years at the Treasury Department prosecuting people for exactly this. He explained that, while the Treasury Department had issued us proper licenses to look into cultural exchange issues, that didn't include mojitos with El Jefe. We were criminally liable. But he could get the fines reduced to $2,500, so, of course, we all hired him. The catch was his legal fees were $30,000 a head, $210,000 in total. Of course, Graydon Carter, as a journalist, was not charged. It's definitely a better living outside the Treasury Department.

Les Moonves paid the biggest price. David Letterman was renegotiating his contract for the *Late Show* at CBS and went to town on the network boss.

"On one hand, you have a ruthless dictator, surrounded by yes-men," Letterman announced on the air. "On the other . . . Castro."

Letterman staged a series of "dramatic re-creations" with actors, a bit called "Lunch with Les and Fidel" in which Les would say inane things like "I have the biggest office in show business," and "At your Grammy party, you let me whip political prisoners."

The public mockery drove Les crazy, but he had to take it. Letterman was his biggest star.

It was embarrassing for me, too, but I had to admit, we probably had it coming.

I still have a whole bunch of Cohibas.

CHAPTER TWENTY-NINE

MY BEATNIK UNPLUGGED

We covered a vast expanse of cultural ground at MTV Networks: music, film, comedy, animation, politics, fashion, you name it, in over one hundred countries. I met almost every major musician, movie star, comedian, and US president, along with a long line of showfolk, artists, athletes, supermodels, magazine editors, and other business leaders. My assistant, Diane, kept a series of two-foot-tall Rolodex wheels with addresses and phone numbers. A few years ago, my son Andrew found them in a closet and started going through them. "Geez, Dad, you've got Eric Clapton's fax number! Bet no one has that. Let's see if it's still hooked up."

You never knew who was going to come by. One day Muhammad Ali came to talk about his humanitarian projects and how MTV Networks might help. It was a very moving meeting. He was fighting Parkinson's, but he still commanded the room as he struggled to tell stories of the less fortunate. Ali was a different level of fame from other celebrities who came through. People huddled around my office door to see if there might be a chance to get his autograph. They never did that for anyone else.

The next day, Rodney Dangerfield appeared. Yin and Yang. We were in the early days of Comedy Central, and the team gathered in my office to meet the great man. "I just wanted to come by and introduce myself," he announced as he breezed in and settled into a chair. After a quick salute to the majesty of *Caddyshack*, I began to lay out our comedy plans. Rodney looked around and said, "So this is MTV? Looks like a pretty cool place, right? It's okay to smoke a joint, right?"

Before I could reply, he was lighting up a reefer while everyone watched in wonder. He took a toke or two, then passed it to the executives on the couch. "Here ya go, man. Good shit!" My colleagues weren't sure what to do. It was still okay to smoke cigarettes in the office back then, but this was marijuana. Well, no sense being rude to a comedy legend. Pretty soon everyone at the meeting was happily toking away. Except for the business affairs guy. He was probably looking out for loopholes and liabilities in our free-flowing, stoned discussion with the man who became famous because he "got no respect."

But there was one group I still had never met. The Beats. They'd had a profound influence on my early life. Their novels and poetry resonated with me in the conformist suburbs and set me on the path of experience and adventure. Without them, I probably wouldn't be who I am. I would certainly not be where I was. I had met Bob Dylan and Mick Jagger. I bought some Andy Warhol paintings and then his house. But the still-living Beats remained out of my orbit.

In the mid-1990s, I went to an exhibition of Allen Ginsberg's black-and-white photos at the Fahey/Klein Gallery in LA. There were evocative shots of the old days on the beatnik trail in Tangier, in India, in San Francisco, upstate New York with Timothy Leary, out on the road with Cassady and Kerouac. I already collected photography. I bought five of them. When Ginsberg heard that "the head of MTV" had purchased five of his captioned photographs, he spotted an opportunity. This was one crafty beatnik.

Allen Ginsberg had always wanted to be a rock star. He had a mad crush on Bob Dylan, and I suppose at one time Dylan had a man crush on him. He's hard to miss in Dylan's 1965 "Subterranean Homesick Blues" video, looming down the alleyway while Bob flips the cue cards. Ten years later, Allen toured with Dylan's Rolling Thunder Revue, banging a tambourine ecstatically in a trancelike state. He collaborated with all kinds of musicians, Patti Smith and the Clash, U2 and Jeff Buckley. He performed and recorded loads of his poems over music, chronicling all his obsessions, the CIA, capitalism, sodomy, Buddhism, cops, Vietnam, FBI creeps, politicians, Richard Nixon, and altered states of consciousness.

In 1996, he was set to do a reading of a recent poem, "The Ballad of the

Skeletons," at the Royal Albert Hall in London, going after the windbags Newt Gingrich and Rush Limbaugh. He wanted musical accompaniment, so he rustled up Philip Glass to play piano, and on guitar, Paul McCartney. McCartney's appearance brought down the house. The Beats' influence on the Beatles was right there in their name. "It's the closest I'm going to ever come to being in the Beatles," Ginsberg said.

When Allen later performed it, accompanied by Patti Smith's guitarist Lenny Kaye at Carnegie Hall in New York, Danny Goldberg, the savvy president of Mercury Records, was in the audience. Danny invited Ginsberg to rerecord the song for Mercury and released it as a CD single in two versions, one with sanitized language for radio. Allen Ginsberg's showbiz dreams were coming true. He was seventy years old and going for a hit record.

You can imagine what happened next. "Tony Bennett's on MTV, for God's sake, Danny! I'm seventy, too! This Freston guy is a fan of mine. Let's make a music video. I want to be on MTV!" Danny hired Gus Van Sant to make the video. Allen wore an Uncle Sam top hat and sang deadpan, almost talking-blues style, in his flat baritone voice. All the beatnik bogeymen were featured. Satan sat in an electric chair and set off an atomic bomb. As Danny wrote later, Allen "wanted to regale Freston with stories of the beatniks one night at my house. That, he figured, would make it almost impossible for MTV to reject his video." Danny was a friend, and he called me. "Come for dinner with Judy McGrath at my place in the Village." He added almost as a throwaway, "Allen Ginsberg is going to join us." How smoothly Danny baited the trap. Then he added a nudge I did not need: "More than almost anyone, Allen helped create the culture we all prosper in."

There was a lot of truth in Danny's statement, particularly for me. I had faithfully retraced Ginsberg's steps in India, right down to burning ghats in Varanasi, where he obsessed over the sight of flesh peeling off burning bodies. Ginsberg had said that it was in India that he first developed a real sense of empathy. It was the same for me. If it were not for him and his beatnik wingmen, I might still be peddling toilet paper.

It was a wonderful dinner. Allen was a lively cat, very funny and gracious. I was in Beat Heaven. I must have asked him a hundred questions. I got the name of the hotel in Tangier where he sat with William Burroughs doing the cutups for *Naked Lunch*. I swore I'd track it down and I did. Even though I was the mark in this Danny Goldberg–engineered schmooze, I think we genuinely got along. Allen didn't even have to ask. His "Skeletons" video would get a good run. The 1996 election was a month away. MTV put it in the "Buzz Bin" rotation, a big deal, and shouted about it from the rooftops.

I brought up *Unplugged*. "How about an Allen Ginsberg *Unplugged* as a follow-up?" That took about a second. Allen lit up and said he'd start working on a treatment immediately. Our music guys were totally into it. The septuagenarian poet was thrilled. We agreed to do the *Unplugged* taping in September. But "The Ballad of the Skeletons" would turn out to be Allen Ginsberg's last project. In April, what he thought was hepatitis turned out to be liver cancer. He quickly passed, peacefully in his bed in the East Village, surrounded by friends including Patti Smith, Roy Lichtenstein, and Gregory Corso. The painter Larry Rivers blew a saxophone to send Allen's spirit on its way.

Judy and I attended our new friend's memorial at St. Mark's Church in-the-Bowery on East 10th Street, prime Beat territory. Allen Ginsberg was unplugged for real. Kaddish.

CHAPTER THIRTY

TOM GOES TO TOMBOUKTOU

During my last couple of years at Viacom, I developed an Africa obsession. The birthplace and ancestor of all the music we loved was the missing piece in MTV's global conquest.

For years at the company, I mentored Alex Okosi, a smart, young guy from Nigeria. He was six foot six, a basketball player who came to the US on a boarding school scholarship. After college, he got a job at MTV Networks, where he discovered that he and the CEO had gone to the same small college. We bonded immediately. Alex was ambitious and very capable. His first assignment was selling MTV and Comedy Central to cowboy types at cable systems in Wyoming and Idaho. They loved him. From there, he went to our Los Angeles office.

Alex's dream was to go home and start MTV in Africa. I encouraged him to move to London to get some international chops and then use his inside track in Africa to put together a business plan. I believed he was entrepreneurial enough to make it happen. If we got up and running in Africa, not only would our worldwide network be complete, but I would have a good reason to travel to a continent that I yearned to more fully explore.

In 2003, I took Dave Matthews and Trey Anastasio from Phish to Dakar, Senegal, to make a documentary for VH1. The special focused on Orchestra Baobab, the iconic Senegalese dance band that defined the Afro-Cuban sound of the 1970s and '80s. Both Dave and Trey were great admirers of Orchestra Baobab, and Dave had African roots, having been born in South Africa. Joining us were my friend Brian Grazer and VH1's

Bill Flanagan, who would produce the documentary. We spent a week with Orchestra Baobab and made the musical rounds of Dakar. The entire trip was a wonderful experience. In my mind, it was time for MTV Africa.

I helped Alex with his plan, and, despite pushback from higher-ups, in London, he launched MTV Africa (MTV Base) in February 2005 with a huge concert in Johannesburg, South Africa, mixing African acts like Fela Kuti's Egypt 80 and American stars like Will Smith and Ludacris. MTV Base became a solid business and is still the greatest single music force on the continent.

As MTV Base's first anniversary approached, I spoke with Bill Flanagan about shooting a film on the legendary "Festival in the Desert," held every January deep in the Sahara at an oasis called Essakane, northeast of Timbuktu. Correctly billed as the "world's most remote music festival," it was attended largely by Tuareg tribespeople, traveling in camel caravans. A few adventurous foreigners were always sprinkled in. Robert Plant had come back raving about it. Flanagan told me that the next Desert Festival was slated to feature forty-five different acts over three days, representing music from all parts of Mali, as well as from neighboring countries like Burkina Faso and Senegal, a veritable Woodstock in the Sahara.

We decided to go to scout the situation. While we were making plans, U2's Bono called and asked me to join Bobby Shriver, the Kennedy family nephew and an activist, and him at a lunch at the Four Seasons in New York with Graydon Carter, the editor of *Vanity Fair*. Bono, ever the salesman, was going to pitch Graydon to let him guest-edit a special edition of *Vanity Fair* focused on Africa. He was going to bring in all kinds of star power, make Africa relatable to Middle America, and cover the progress his new (RED) organization, which he had founded with Bobby to help combat AIDS in Africa, was making there. Graydon said yes on the spot.

Bono then volunteered that *Vanity Fair* should commission me to write a piece about the Festival in the Desert. "Let's show people that Africa can be fun!" Graydon nodded. I loved writing, loved this idea, and now I'd gotten my first assignment in a corner booth in the Grill Room. This one-off assignment would lead to another thirty-some pieces for *Vanity Fair*. Later, I would be listed on the masthead as "Our Man in Kabul."

Music is Mali's most famous export. Any visitor to Africa will quickly notice that music comes at you from every angle. The air is like a mixtape. This part of Saharan Africa is home to the hypnotic desert blues sound, best exemplified by the late Ali Farka Touré, and the more danceable rhythms of Salif Keita and Amadou & Mariam. You've heard this music. Snatches of it are all over movie soundtracks and TV commercials.

I needed some fellow travelers who were West African music afficionados. Flanagan was in. I reached out to Jonathan Brandstein, my man in Havana. He'd been to Mali, too, and knew the ropes. I also convinced my old pal Jimmy Buffett, whom I'd known since the seventies. The Caribbean troubadour piloted his own plane, the "Jimmy Jet," and wanted to land it in Timbuktu. Kino Bachellier, Jimmy's longtime road doctor and fixer from St. Barth, was in. Topping it off was the legendary Chris Blackwell, the founder of Island Records, a man with a talent divining rod. Aside from having signed Steve Winwood, Cat Stevens, Bob Marley, and U2, Chris had founded Mango Records, a label that specialized in African artists. It would be one of the most epic trips any of us would ever take.

After a short stopover in the Cape Verde Islands, we headed to Bamako, Mali's low-rise, gritty capital, where we embarked on a wild music crawl, lasting until 5 a.m. Chris said it was the best single night of music in his life. Hours later, we landed in Timbuktu. It was a dusty, brown town that appeared to morph into the surrounding desert. Locals rushed the plane selling daggers. That was the first sign of trouble.

I noticed that they spelled the name of the city "Tombouktou." I started to introduce myself that way around town. Jimmy Buffett would never call me anything else for the rest of his life. I was Tom Bouktou. He was Jim Bouktou.

Jonathan had recruited a smooth travel guide named Syndou from the Ivory Coast. He accompanied us and served as translator. Syndou set off to hire a local who could guide us across the desert to Essakane, the site of the festival, one hundred kilometers away.

We spent the night in a run-down hotel, and in the morning Jonathan scored some weed, and we wrapped blue turbans around our heads, cranked up the music, and set out in three 4×4s in tight formation. I imagined us as Cheech and Chong in the Sahara. There were no roads, just endless braids of tracks in the sand in, around, and over sand dunes.

After about four hours, the burly security guide we'd hired in Bamako called for us to stop. We were headed northwest, not northeast, he said. He yanked the local guide out, they started shouting at each other, then he put the guy in a headlock and then a pistol to his temple.

"I'm going to kill him," he screamed. "Right here. No one will know. He's a bad guy."

He was a very bad guy. This guide was attempting to deliver us to the local al-Qaeda outpost. We were being kidnapped. Al-Qaeda had been making a nice business kidnapping foreigners and holding them in a camp in Mauritania for ransom. We were on the way there, just fifty kilometers from the border. Some German tourists had been held there for a year already.

I was a little shaken. I just went out for a little music and here I was . . . in the middle of the Sahara, buzzed with the sun burning down, about to witness a killing with a blue turban on my head.

Jimmy, always the good-natured, barefoot individual we imagine, stepped forward. He looked the guy over, took a beat, and said, "He may be a bad guy . . . a kidnapper and a terrorist rolled into one, but we don't have to shoot him. Let's just leave him here." Off we went.

If you ever think of traveling to Timbuktu, don't arrive in a private jet. You might as well have a sign around your neck saying "Kidnap me!"

Later, we spotted a wandering nomad. "Have you seen a festival around here anywhere?" Not only had he, but he played us a Bob Marley ringtone on his phone, which thrilled Blackwell. "Hop in," said Chris.

We got to Essakane three hours later. Upon arrival, we were offered sandy snacks and assigned low tents made of animal skins tied to wooden poles, trimmed with decorative tassels, but without door flaps. I went to sleep as a sandstorm raged and woke up surrounded by a foot of sand. The music went on all night. No one seemed to sleep. Around the festival's edges were military jeeps with mounted .50-caliber machine guns. Six adventurous American college students were nearby, running up and then rolling down the dunes. They told me they were tripping on LSD.

The festival was a West African musical feast; Jimmy was able to weasel his way onto the stage, a short white man bopping up and down with a guitar behind a towering rhythm section of tall Black men.

It capped off with Tinariwen, the superstars of the Sahara. They were a ragged-looking, visionary Tuareg rock band in turbans and scarves . . . six electric guitars, three female singers, and a percussionist. They grew up in southern Libya as refugees. In the camps they discovered electric guitars and beat-up cassettes of Santana and Dire Straits, whose influence they blended with Bedouin traditions. They wrote songs about revolution and freedom. This new music traveled all over the Sahara by cassette and would inspire an entire generation of young Tuaregs. Tinariwen's music was officially banned in Algeria and Mali, which only added to their rebel allure. They had traded their Stratocasters for rifles to join in the Tuareg rebellion against the Malian government. One of them was shot. It was as if the Rolling Stones went off to war.

The Festival in the Desert was a beautiful cultural oasis, welcoming wanderers from all over the world for years. In 2011, I advised Bono to go. But in 2012, the radical Ansar al-Dine group, an offshoot of al-Qaeda, overran Timbuktu and imposed Sharia law, burning ancient manuscripts, cutting off the hands of musicians, and ripping out the tongues of singers. They invaded the festival grounds and destroyed the stage and all the instruments. Eventually, French forces drove them out, but Mali still boils with political unrest. Our near-miss with the kidnapper was just a harbinger of what was coming to Timbuktu. I am grateful to have experienced the dream before it ended.

Later I'd embark to other musical hot spots across the continent: Addis Ababa, Cape Town, Zanzibar, and on and on. Each place had its distinct sound and musical soul. It's no surprise that blues, jazz, ragtime, gospel, rock, rap, and even some country all have deep roots in Africa. If you want to know how much America was shaped by its African population, just turn on the radio.

CHAPTER THIRTY-ONE

MILLENNIUM APPROACHES

The twentieth century was ending. Sumner was nearing eighty and was at the peak of his powers. He next set his sights on acquiring the blue-chip media empire of CBS, from which Viacom had originally sprung nearly thirty years before. When CBS chief Mel Karmazin agreed to sell CBS to Viacom for $36 billion over Labor Day weekend in 1999, Mel negotiated for himself the top leadership spot of the combined company for three years. He also demanded that Sumner fire Philippe Dauman.

Many people made the mistake of thinking they could outlast Sumner. When analysts asked him about his succession plan, Sumner's comeback was always: "I am never going to die." No matter how good a job Mel did, anyone who truly knew Sumner would have bet that Mel would be pushed out, and Sumner would claim the combined CBS/Viacom as his own.

Mel was a media star with a throng of admirers on Wall Street. He had a short gray crew cut that looked a bit like Brillo and matched his bushy eyebrows. He always had a twinkle in his eye. He joined Viacom like a man on fire. Mel referred to MTV Networks as the "arts and crafts" people. We called him the "Melvinator." I loved him. We all did. And I loved my job. By then I had run MTV Networks for twelve years. We were still Viacom's hottest division. Why would I ever want another job?

Mel was a private man, proud, and not big on deference. Bit by bit this wore on Sumner's nonstop thirst for adulation. He invariably refused Sumner's lunch and dinner invitations. The fifty-yard corridor from his corner office to Sumner's was a path rarely walked, with only a few exceptions.

When Mel heard that Shari Redstone, Sumner's daughter, was in the building meeting executives, he stomped over to tell Sumner that this was off-limits, saying, "This is not Take Your Daughter to Work Day!" Mel's failure to kiss ass became a thorn in Sumner's grizzled paw.

In 2004, Sumner began to refer to Mel as "KarmaFuck." When I heard Sumner shouting this "nickname" to Bernadette, the elderly woman who prepared food on the executive floor, I knew Mel's end was near.

Late in the afternoon of May 18, Sumner called me in my office. "What are you doing, Tom? Why don't you come up to the Carlyle for a drink?"

"Be right there." I grabbed a cab and drove up through Central Park in bright spring sunshine. Sumner's Carlyle apartment was charmless. It looked like a corporate rental. His most prized possession, a DirecTV dish, sat precariously on a window ledge. He smiled when he told me it had been illegally installed.

Sumner poured me a vodka soda and sat down, face-to-face. Calmly, he leaned forward to tell me he had decided to fire Mel. Mel had been making "bad moves" and he could not stand by and watch it happen anymore. I was dumbfounded. The company was prospering. But it drove Sumner nuts that everyone saw Mel as the real player at Viacom, not him. It was the same reason Frank Biondi had been canned. An article in the *New Yorker* had come out about Frank making smart moves, and a couple weeks later Frank got the boot. I felt for Mel and would miss him. Mel had been a winner his entire career.

But I sensed what was coming next. Sumner moved closer and started sweet-talking me, saying, "I want to appoint you as the next CEO of Viacom." I took a deep breath. I was flattered, of course, but I realized the day I had long feared had come. I had always been an ambitious guy, but I was not a corporate climber and never aspired to work directly for Redstone, a man who fixated on the daily stock price. It also meant answering to a man who could never be pleased.

This exact topic had come up the week before. I was talking with Jeff Bewkes, a good friend and the CEO of HBO Networks, as we wound our way down Broadway on a gorgeous spring afternoon after a Comedy Central board meeting. "You know," he said, "the two of us have the best jobs in town." I nodded. He added, "Now the only thing that could fuck that up was if they promoted me to CEO of Time Warner and you to CEO of Viacom."

I had turned down overtures for more lucrative jobs at Disney, Warner Music, Bertelsmann, and others over the years. Yes, CEO of Viacom had a tantalizing sound—it'd be the fever dream of most executives. I'd be leading a Fortune 500 company. Making big bucks. But how long until I'd be ejected? Still, I did not want to seem ungrateful. In my head, a voice was saying, "Don't be myopic." Who would not want this?

Sumner probably expected me to jump out of my chair and fall to my knees in gratitude. But after seventeen years, I knew an obsessive narcissistic personality when I saw one. This is not to say Sumner did not have his good qualities; he had nerves of steel, liked to bet big, was brilliant, built a fortune legitimately, and certainly had a wild-ass fire in his belly. But this was a nasty man with a complete lack of empathy. Think Donald Trump, but smarter. He probably assumed that everyone on earth dreamed of working for him and running his company. He expected an immediate and enthusiastic "Yes!"

I asked some questions on timing and how it would work. I ended by saying, "I'm so flattered that you believe in me, Sumner. This is such a surprise, such a big deal. Just let me talk it over with my wife, Kathy. Give me twenty-four hours." I left knowing that he was greatly annoyed. Was I playing hard to get? Or was I just a loser? I was just trying to buy time to game Sumner's offer in my head and concluded that I'd be excited to take the promotion. How in the world could I say no? If I declined, I knew Sumner would give the job to my colleague CBS chief Les Moonves, and I'd probably be gone. Les did not let rivals survive.

The next day I walked into Carnegie Hall for the annual CBS Upfront presentation—the roll-out-the-stars event for advertisers. It was a full house. As the show started, I slipped into a reserved aisle seat right next to Sumner. Sumner was staring at Les Moonves, who was onstage bashing NBC, cracking jokes, and going on about CBS's ratings leadership. "Sumner," I said, "I'd be thrilled to take the job. Thanks for your belief in me." Sumner was sulking. He pointed to Moonves dispassionately and said, "I've already offered it to Les. He immediately accepted."

I couldn't believe it. "Not fair. My twenty-four hours isn't up." Sumner grunted and said that he could not recant on Les. "You cannot recant on me, either," I told him. Les and I ran Viacom's two top-performing divisions. I had MTV Networks. Les had CBS Inc. Sumner could never admit he had made a mistake, but his impulsiveness had put him in a jam. He did not want to lose either of us, but by offering us both the same job on the same afternoon, he had pretty much guaranteed that whichever of us he reneged on would walk.

The next day he came back and said we could both have the job. He split it in two. We'd be co-presidents of Viacom, a setup that Les and I both knew rarely worked. Les knew Sumner had picked me first, but we never discussed it. Sumner's childish ego started an inexorable process that would result in one of the most monumental mistakes of his career.

Ten days after Carnegie Hall, on Memorial Day weekend, 2004, Mel Karmazin left. He might say he resigned in disgust. I sat in a conference room at our outside law firm's offices with Redstone, Les Moonves, along with Viacom's general counsel, the head of communications, and some outside advisers to tee up an announcement. Les and I were to be named "Co-presidents of Viacom," a mouthful of a title. I would be responsible for MTV Networks, BET, and Simon & Schuster. Les would have CBS, Infinity Radio, the outdoor billboard business, and Showtime Networks. Paramount, Sumner's studio acquisition, was to be split into two pieces with the television operation going to Les and the feature film part coming to me.

At the end of the meeting, everyone was assigned people to call that night to give a heads-up on the announcement. The most important call was to Jon Dolgen, Chairman of Viacom Entertainment, who ran Paramount Studios. Sumner and Frank Biondi had hired Jon in 1994. Sumner now would have to tell him that his job was being eliminated and fire him over the phone. The corporate announcement went out at midnight. Sumner never made the call. He let Jon read about his termination in the press.

Early the next morning, my phone rang. It was Dolgen. "I'm reading these articles, scanning the press release, and see no mention of me. Where am I in this?"

"Didn't Sumner call you last night?" I asked.

"No, no call from Redstone, no call from anyone." Jon was a tough guy, but his bravado was gone. I felt bad for him. I had to do the dirty work. Jon went on to a new and, I think, more pleasurable chapter in life, on boards of high-flying companies like Live Nation and nonprofits like the Simon Wiesenthal Center. Splitting Paramount into separate TV and film businesses was a terrible error. Both Jon Dolgen and Sherry Lansing, the gracious, uber-connected Chairperson of Paramount Pictures, said it at the time, and they were correct.

The co-president jobs were an adjustment for Les and me. It was a setup for a clash, but we made an awkward situation work pretty well. That is not to say there were no frustrations. Both of us would have found it easier to control the whole enterprise. We had to agree on capital allocation, who got what of the limited money we had for reinvestment, or for the acquisition of new assets, especially digital ones.

Viacom continued to grow with Les and me at the helm. But these were the last glory days before YouTube, Netflix, Google, Facebook, Apple, and the digital horde began to kick down the doors of the closed systems that media empires had created. MTV Networks would soon be consigned to the unenviable "legacy media" category unless we could quickly transition into this new world.

Les and I were more collegial with Sumner than either Frank Biondi or Mel Karmazin had been. We did go to dinner with him. He preferred old-school joints with red-checkered tablecloths like La Dolce Vita in Beverly Hills or Dan Tana's in West Hollywood. Sometimes we'd bring our wives. You could get an early bird special at these restaurants at six or six thirty. Conversations hovered around Sumner's two favorite subjects: himself and the stock price. If the stock had been up that day, it would be happy Sumner. He might ask a wife a question. If the stock was down, he might curse the waiter or throw a plate. The silver lining was we'd be done by seven thirty. I'd often say goodbye to him and go off for another meal with friends.

Sumner had gone full-bore Hollywood. There were fewer trips back to New York. He had divorced Phyllis, his wife of fifty-five years, and in 2003 married Paula Fortunato, a third-grade schoolteacher from New Jersey who was forty years his junior. They had their wedding at Temple Emanu-El on

Fifth Avenue and a lavish reception at the New York Public Library. He had me book Tony Bennett to perform.

The happy couple moved their base from the Carlyle Hotel into a large home in Beverly Park, a gated neighborhood off Mulholland Drive full of sprawling mansions. Sumner bought his house from his new next-door neighbor Sylvester Stallone. There, high in the hills overlooking Franklin Canyon, among Stallone, Eddie Murphy, Rod Stewart, and various Saudi royals, Sumner was living the life he had fantasized about as the owner of a chain of New England movie theaters. He would swim naked in his pool, check the stock ticker all day, and summon us when needed.

CHAPTER THIRTY-TWO

SUCCESSION AT PARAMOUNT

My being handed the metaphorical keys to Paramount Pictures in 2004 was highly ironic, given my earliest Hollywood experience. In the early eighties, when MTV launched, we occupied the two lowest rings of the entertainment solar system, the cable and music businesses. The feature film was king. Next came broadcast television and premium cable. Basic cable was lumped in with local access television and the music industry was seen as existing in its own lowbrow world. Hollywood was the last thing on our minds—and we were the last thing on theirs.

Film studios did not return our phone calls. But when it became clear that Hollywood's most desired movie audience demographic was hanging out on our channel, Tinseltown began to embrace us. Music-driven films like *Purple Rain*, *Footloose*, and *The Breakfast Club* did huge box office, riding on MTV promotion. Multi-artist soundtracks became an integral part of movie marketing. Music videos extracted from these new films populated the MTV and VH1 playlists.

Soon, almost every big Hollywood movie had sequences cut like a music video, big rock songs blasting as convertibles tore down desert highways, montages of action sequences edited to the beats of hit records, and love scenes backlit like a Madonna clip. Tom Cruise supposedly did not make musicals, but what were *Days of Thunder* and *Cocktail* but Elvis movies without Elvis?

Before we knew it, our New York offices were crawling with Hollywood agents and movie-marketing mavens. And we started spending more time in LA, where there was plenty to like, especially in the winter. We got to know everyone. Adventurous young producers like Brian Grazer and Billy Gerber became friends. We cruised the canyons in our rented Mustang convertibles and took meetings at the Hotel Bel Air and the Sunset Marquis. In American entertainment, all roads lead to Sunset Boulevard.

Pretty soon, the people at the film studios wanted to produce movies with us. At first, I resisted. It looked like a time suck to me. I wanted to keep our creativity focused inward. But the gravitational pull to the center of the universe was strong. We did realize that making MTV movies could be a smart extension of our brand, especially if we did not have to finance the films ourselves. Our creative people were itching to go Hollywood. Everyone, deep down, wants to make movies.

David Geffen was as sharp about the movie business as he was about the music business. Geffen Records had been the first to grant MTV rights to air music videos in 1981. Now Geffen would also launch us into the film business. In November 1994, David called me at home in New York on a Saturday morning to say, "I watched your first episode of *Beavis and Butt-Head* last night. It's hilarious." The man did not miss a thing. "Let's make a movie with them."

Just as we were finalizing the deal, Sumner Redstone went and bought Paramount Studios, after a fierce bidding war with Barry Diller. Sumner wanted a Hollywood studio and Paramount was his lifelong dream. He had quietly struck a deal with Marty Davis, CEO of Paramount Communications, to buy it for $8.5 billion. Hearing this, Barry immediately stepped in. Redstone outbid Diller three times, finally winning the prize for $10 billion. Once again, he leveraged us to the hilt. Paramount became the jewel in Viacom's crown, though it never came close to generating the cash flow of MTV Networks. But Paramount secured Sumner a seat at Hollywood's most exclusive table.

When Sumner made his play, Paramount had been as cold as a corpse, at the bottom of the Hollywood ladder. Frank Biondi hired studio veteran Jon Dolgen and paired him with Sherry Lansing, who ran Paramount Pictures, and the hits started rolling in. Paramount went from worst to first. *Clear and Present Danger* with Harrison Ford kicked things off, then *Beverly*

Hills Cop III with Eddie Murphy, then *Naked Gun 33⅓*. Next came the unexpected blockbuster *Forrest Gump*, directed by Robert Zemeckis and starring Tom Hanks. The film generated $675 million at the box office and swept the Oscars with six wins, including Best Picture. Redstone was giddy.

As for MTV's project with Geffen, *Beavis and Butt-Head Do America* grossed a respectable $65 million. But it took a while for me to realize that Viacom's acquisition of Paramount would forever constrict MTV's and Nickelodeon's future dealings in Hollywood. We were consigned to be a captive supplier to Paramount in the name of "corporate synergy."

We produced a slate of forty pictures at Paramount over the next twelve years. The total box office was $2.1 billion. Titles included: *Napoleon Dynamite*, *Zoolander*, *Jackass: The Movie*, *Team America*, *The SpongeBob Movie*, and *Nacho Libre*. In the beginning, we were thrilled just to learn how to make films. The little cable weasels could run with the big dogs. A part of that thrill wore off as we learned more about how the motion picture business really worked. Paramount kept the lion's share of the profits. Welcome to Hollywood, where the house never loses.

Jon Dolgen was right out of central casting . . . a brash, chain-smoking, number-crunching, no-bullshit studio head from Queens. Known around town as "the King of Pain," he converted his conference room into a large freezer, which was nicknamed the "Meat Locker." He'd preside over legendary marathon negotiating and budget review sessions there. Stacks of cigarette packs, mints, and candy bars were piled on the table. It all signaled "you're going to be here a very long time."

We were fellow division heads, and I served my time in the Meat Locker, rarely making any progress. Despite that, I came to really like Jon. A hard-ass on the outside, he had a good heart on the inside, plus a quick wit and sense of humor that was generally underappreciated. Talent like Chris Rock loved him. The two of us bonded over music. Jon was the rare film executive with a deep knowledge of rock 'n' roll. Once, he held a party at a restaurant in Beverly Hills, and Bob Dylan actually showed up and played an entire set of new material with a brand-new band. That was unheard of. I held Jon in much higher regard after that.

Two things plagued the MTV Networks–Paramount relationship and

I never made progress resolving them with Jon. Exclusivity was the main issue. Although common in television, very few film producers were locked into exclusivity. But we were. If Paramount passed on a project we were interested in, we couldn't take that project to a rival studio. Dolgen told me repeatedly that it would be "embarrassing" for a Viacom division to have a hit that wasn't produced by Paramount's studio. That logic foreclosed our being able to partner with, for example, Summit Entertainment's five-film *Twilight* series, which we had optioned, written a script for, and which ultimately grossed $3.3 billion.

Profit splits were another. When we did make a movie, MTV Networks made very little money. Producers with less clout than MTV Networks could earn a percentage right off the top of the box office. We were only paid a small flat fee, barely worth all the effort, which usually included also doing the promo campaigns for these films. Worse, the movie drained our in-house talent pool. Everybody wanted to work on movies. My failure to correct the imbalance between MTV Networks and Paramount was one of my biggest defeats at the company. In the end Dolgen would always blame Redstone: "I'd give you a ride, man, but it ain't my train." We often felt like the prisoners of Melrose Avenue. After a while, I lost interest in the film side. We could make more from an hour or two of television than we did from a feature film.

Now, however, in 2004, Paramount was front and center in my portfolio. When Dolgen left and Paramount split in two, Sherry Lansing stepped up to run everything at the film studio. Sherry was already a Hollywood legend when I met her in 1994, charismatic, charming, and beloved. There was no pretension about Sherry. She was bright, eternally positive, and an excellent manager of talent. It was "Hi, honey" to everyone. The first woman to ever run a major film studio (Fox), she was ahead of her time. She even had a star on Hollywood Boulevard. Once upon a time in Hollywood, studio chiefs were so famous that even civilians knew their names, and film fans could list the movies made under their watch. Sherry had caught the tail end of that. She had a direct hand in some of the most iconic films of her era: *Fatal Attraction*, *Indecent Proposal*, and *Black Rain*. At Paramount, she was behind the Oscar-winning blockbusters *Braveheart* and *Titanic*.

Sherry was a creative soul who had made a career on her instincts and her wits. She significantly upped our moviemaking game. And we could be difficult. Sherry understood the back-office stuff, but it was not where she enjoyed spending time. She wanted to bow out elegantly and do something different—start a new chapter in the not-for-profit world. In early November 2004, she spoke to Sumner and then she spoke to me. "I've done this for the last thirty-five years, Tom, and often thought I'd leave to do something else when I was sixty. Well, I'm sixty." I said I fully understood. I was fifty-nine.

Sherry's contract ran through the end of 2005, and we agreed to keep her departure top secret while I looked for a replacement. The job of studio head is at the apex of Hollywood. And the few people who occupy these rarified positions tend to move from one studio to another, like musical chairs. I wanted someone with new energy and fresh ideas.

Hollywood is a peculiar town. You would be hard-pressed to find a more opaque or closed industry. It was tough to crack the code and find out where the money flowed, where the power sat, and who got charged what. If you ever tried to follow a Hollywood lawsuit, where people sue studios to get what they are really owed, you met a web of obscurity, double-talk, hidden fees, and cross-collateralizations that would baffle a Mafia accountant or the smartest auditor at the IRS. I also thought the culture at Paramount could be healthier.

I needed tutoring from a neutral party who knew the game. My hope was that perhaps Bob Daly could give me a hand. At Warner Bros., Bob had one of the longest hit streaks in the history of Hollywood. With his partner, Terry Semel, Bob had reigned for more than twenty years. Bob and Terry were co-chairmen, proof that it was possible to split the top job at a major entertainment corporation. The two even drove to work together. When Sumner made Les and me co-presidents of Viacom, we agreed to try to model ourselves on Bob and Terry, without the riding-to-work-together part.

Bob and Terry had tried to hire me to run the Warner Music Group. Now Bob was semiretired, and everyone came to him for advice. He had tables at the Grill and Mr. Chow's, where he held court. Bob loved rules. His new company was called Rulemaker. "Show business is two words, you know, 'show' and 'business,'" he'd say. "People should not forget that second one." He had a steel-trap mind for every deal, every box office number, every TV show ranking, and rating going back through his career at CBS, which he ran before coming to Warner Bros.

I took Bob to lunch and asked him something I'd never asked anyone out loud—to help me as a mentor. Up until then, I had winged it, soaking up tips through observation and osmosis. "I'm just the cable guy, Bob, suddenly dropped on top of Paramount Pictures. I need some grooming."

Bob lit up. We made a deal. On many a summer afternoon, I would head over from my office in Santa Monica to huddle with Bob at his compound, a beautiful home tucked away in a leafy corner of Bel Air. He had a curriculum. We'd go through the intricacies of film financing, P&Ls, and so forth. He'd give me homework and I would report back. I was the only student at the Bob Daly Film School.

Now I had to find a new studio head. Bob and I came up with a list of current and former studio chiefs, but no one on the list worked out. The best people, like, say, Stacey Snider at Universal Pictures, were all under contract. Then I got a tip while I was hungover in Beirut. It was like a scene from a movie.

CHAPTER THIRTY-THREE

A HOT TIP IN BEIRUT

It was not all Hollywood all the time for me in those days. I had other jobs to do. Early one Saturday afternoon in November 2004, I woke up with a massive hangover in a Beirut hotel room, staring out at the blazing sun bouncing off the Mediterranean. I had gone to Beirut to investigate starting a Middle East MTV based in Lebanon and the town had had its way with me.

I hadn't been to Beirut since the early seventies, when the city was called "the Paris of the Middle East." Pre–civil war, it was sort of a Las Vegas on the Mediterranean for the Arab world, where anything went. Beirut and Cairo were the cultural wellsprings for the Middle East. A tentative peace had returned to Beirut, and despite the hovering vibes of radical Islam, the city's crazy nightlife had come roaring back. I was thrilled to return after thirty years, although the Viacom plane flight crew did not share my enthusiasm. They dipped down to the runway, quickly dropped us off, and then bolted to Greece, citing insurance rules.

My contact was a jubilant, smooth-talking former economics professor with a contagious personality, Nadim Munla. He had married not one, but two Miss Lebanons. Nadim ran Future TV, Lebanon's coolest network, and he was excited to give my team a taste of the town before talking any business. He rolled in a big SUV with a chase car full of bodyguards behind. After dinner at Casablanca, a lively restaurant in a classic Lebanese villa, we made our foray into the Beirut club scene.

At Music Hall, a cabaret-style nightclub with an eclectic musical revue, we saw the hilarious long-bearded, dark-turbaned "Taliban Brothers," then another group sang the Bee Gees' "Stayin' Alive"—a song that took on a whole different meaning in a city emerging from years of warfare. The audience rose to its feet to chant, "Feel the city breakin' and everybody shakin', and we're stayin' alive, stayin' alive!" There were fists in the air and tears in their eyes.

I made it back to the hotel as the sun was rising. Now my BlackBerry was buzzing. David Geffen was calling from LA. David was aware of every moving piece in the entertainment business. Bono once described Geffen to me as a "brain on a stick."

David wasted no time. "I have the perfect guy to run Paramount."

I sat up in bed and said, "Hallelujah!"

"It's Brad Grey. Brad could be the guy." Everyone knew Brad. He was the Grey in Brillstein-Grey, a top talent-management company. He had been one of the moguls on our infamous Cuba trip. Brad had recently cofounded Plan B Entertainment, a production company, with Brad Pitt and Jennifer Aniston. He had producer credits on *The Larry Sanders Show*, *The Sopranos*, and *Real Time with Bill Maher*, of which I was a great fan. A few months earlier, Brad had invited me to a seated *Sopranos* cast dinner at his home in the Pacific Palisades. He held it on the lawn by his pond. The guy had a pond. David made his pitch: "Listen, Brad's a great guy. He has impeccable taste, he's savvy, wonderful with talent, and he could be just the guy to turn Paramount around. Plus, I think he'd like to do it."

A short, soft-spoken man with deep-set blue eyes, closely cropped dark hair, and a tight-lipped smile, Brad, forty-six, had a cool demeanor and worked meticulously to project a certain elegance about himself. Bronx-born, he had started his career working as a gofer for Harvey Weinstein in Buffalo when Harvey was a concert promoter. He then burrowed into the stand-up business in New York, managing comedians like Bob Saget. In Los Angeles, he partnered with the legendary Bernie Brillstein, who represented Lorne Michaels and many of the *SNL* stars.

Brillstein-Grey was ground zero for the comedy business and Brad had extended the company into a sort of mini TV studio. Brad had accomplished a lot, but working against him taking over Paramount was the small detail that he had no experience running a studio or producing feature films. There was significant precedent for that. Bob Evans was an actor when he took over Paramount in 1967 and made groundbreaking films like *The Godfather*, *Rosemary's Baby*, and *Chinatown*. David Geffen insisted that Brad could rise to the occasion. Although Brad hid it well, he had a burning ambition to be a bigger player in town.

I put Brad through the wringer. I met with him several times at the airy Craftsman home he'd built in the Pacific Palisades. He had a budding contemporary art collection and there was a spotless new blue Bentley convertible in the driveway. He said he would bring Brad Pitt and Plan B to the studio. I had Brad spend time with Daly, one-on-one. Bob was impressed and liked him. He felt that Brad could be a change agent at Paramount.

It was time for the Redstone test. On a Saturday morning, I took Brad to Beverly Park for Sumner to get a sense of him. Sumner lived in an odd house. You arrived and stepped onto a gauntlet of stones that ran through fishponds swarming with colorful koi fish. That got you to the front door. Down the hall came the great reveal: on the far side of the living room the house opened to expansive views of Franklin Canyon. Separate banks of brightly lit and cavernous fish tanks lined two other sides of the room. They were jammed with brightly colored tropical fish. When bored at meetings, I'd imagine myself trapped inside a submarine.

Brad went into full charm mode and won over Sumner. Both men shared a love for all the tradition and pageantry of Hollywood. Brad deftly dropped in his top-tier talent connections and his detailed knowledge of the great films. Then came *Sopranos* stories. Sumner loved *The Sopranos*. After Brad left, Sumner gave me the thumbs-up. Brad didn't just kiss the ring, he inhaled it.

Brad started as Chairman of Paramount Pictures in March 2005. I knew there would be many in Hollywood, especially in the snarky trade press, who would think this was insane. I was taking a big shot that could very well sink me. But I came to believe Brad could step up. Before Brad even moved into his new office, we went to work strategizing how to get Paramount out of last place. Morale was bad and there were few pictures in the pipeline. Only eleven titles were locked for 2006, far fewer than the normal sixteen to eighteen.

Brad hired John Lesher, a quirky, well-regarded agent with a sharp eye for edgy material. John represented the most prestigious film directors around, people like Martin Scorsese and Paul Thomas Anderson. Brad and

Lesher quickly established Paramount Vantage, a "specialty label" focused on the booming independent film game. These smaller films brought prestige, awards, heat, and creative buzz to a studio.

Brad made some other key changes in marketing and home entertainment, which back then meant DVDs. Paramount had a couple of big films in the pipeline that Sherry had put into motion. Both starred Tom Cruise: *Mission: Impossible III* and *War of the Worlds*. His company, Cruise/Wagner, had offices on the Paramount lot. Tom was the biggest star in Paramount's creative galaxy. Sherry had built a strong relationship with Tom and his team over the years. They had stuck with us through good and bad, and Tom's pictures were a mainstay of our library. You could not find a nicer or more accommodating actor than Tom Cruise. He was always respectful and proud of the studio.

But for Brad, running Paramount would be child's play compared to the roller coaster that lay ahead for him. In May, just before the *Mission: Impossible III* release, the *New York Times* splashed a long investigative piece on its front page accusing Brad of using the notorious private detective and fixer to the stars Anthony Pellicano. Allegedly, Brad had hired Pellicano to spy on and intimidate two former clients—comedian Garry Shandling and a screenwriter named Bo Zenga. This was a five-alarm Hollywood scandal that put the chattering class on both coasts into double overtime. Brad was completely humiliated and froze in place.

The news leaked from an ongoing federal investigation of Pellicano. The FBI had even been in to interview Brad, something we did not know. Pellicano's stunts included vandalizing a reporter's car and leaving a rotting fish on the car's front seat along with a rose and a one-word note—"Stop"—allegedly at the behest of the powerful CAA kingpin Mike Ovitz.

The *Times* piece landed next to my breakfast. I had a flashback. I remembered my negotiations with Brad two months earlier. At the very last minute, Brad took me into a separate room to mention a "small thing. There's this nuisance lawsuit against me by this guy Bo Zenga," he said softly. "It's really nothing. The guy is a pest. There is no way in hell it will ever come to anything. It's surely nothing that will ever embarrass Paramount. It's about to be put to bed, anyway, so don't worry. I give you my word."

I had taken Brad at his word. Then Bo Zenga filed another lawsuit against

Brad personally, days before the article broke. The suit charged Brad with using Pellicano to illegally wiretap Zenga's phone, as well as to conduct illegal background checks. Garry Shandling reemerged with an awful lot of nasty things to say about Brad. Suddenly talent-friendly Brad Grey was not seeming too talent-friendly.

Two weeks later, the *Times* ran a second front-page story. I drove to Paramount for an unannounced drop-in on Brad. When I got to his office, he couldn't even get up to say hello. He just sat there; I thought he might slide under his desk and disappear. He had been branded a wiretapper, a liar, a lowlife, and a cheat for all to see. He was devastated.

"Well, you're sure famous now, Brad," I said. "Front-page news."

"Can you believe this bullshit?" he said. "It's so wrong. How could this crap be a Page One story?"

"*Two* front-page stories," I corrected him. "You know, you promised me that this was nothing and would blow over. When do you think that will occur, Brad?"

"Who the fuck knows now? But there is nothing there, that's all I can say," he insisted. "It's just crap made up by some losers. None of it is correct."

"Well, maybe there is a movie here for us. We could put you into development." Maybe he thought I was there to fire him. Rumors were flying about that. Early on, I had given Brad a good tip about how to fire someone: "Always go to their office to pull the trigger. Close the door and sit down. That way you control the discussion. When it's over, you can get up and leave and not be stuck there. People often have a lot to get off their chest. If you do it in your own office, you can be trapped."

Here I was in his office. And I had sat down. Trying to put him at ease, I said, "You've been swept up into an irresistible Hollywood crime story. It's got everything. And you are the star. But, if you've been truthful, you'll win in the end."

"But when the fuck is that?" he demanded. It was clear Brad had enemies; Hollywood feasts on jealousy. A friend told me Brad was "dead meat" whether I fired him or not. He was dirtying Paramount's reputation and would forever be a pariah. But I couldn't fire Brad with no proof of wrongdoing. I stood by him and told him to get out and make his case. That's what the pros do. And to go see his new pal Sumner up in Beverly Park.

Sumner was concerned. Some face-to-face would be helpful. Brad survived the Pellicano crisis. He was ultimately exonerated in court on both lawsuits.

—

A couple of months later, Brad and I made a play to buy DreamWorks. Movies can take forever, but life in Hollywood can turn on a dime. In the fall of 2005, we heard rumblings that DreamWorks Pictures was in negotiations to be bought by NBC Universal. Word on the street was that the deal was a lock, but the negotiations had been dragging.

DreamWorks had started in 1994. It was the film studio version of a music supergroup. Three Hollywood heavyweights—David Geffen, Steven Spielberg, and former Walt Disney Studios CEO Jeffrey Katzenberg—had opened their own studio. The guys had a big vision: film, television, a record label. They were even planning to build a brand-new lot near LAX. People were rooting for them.

By 2005, DreamWorks had produced fifty-nine films including Academy Award winners like *American Beauty*, *Gladiator*, and *A Beautiful Mind*. The record label and TV production arms were up and running. But they hadn't achieved the scale of a major studio. That's why they were in talks with NBCU, but those talks had stalled. Brad and I thought that they might be ripe for partnering with Paramount. Acquiring DreamWorks would give us a pipeline of projects. Plus, we would get a valuable movie library, beef up our distribution clout, and it would move three Hollywood legends into our tent. What if we could sweep in and steal DreamWorks from under Universal's nose? Working against us was that Steven Spielberg had very long relationships with Universal. Spielberg had worked on the lot for over forty years—since before *Jaws*.

On the plus side: David and I went way back—and he had recommended Brad—and Jeffrey was a friend and one of MTV Network's biggest clients for over twenty years. Movies were our biggest advertising category and Jeffrey spent more per movie title than anyone on earth. He made sure he got his money's worth. He would come into our offices, sit down, and work with my staff on ideas. No other advertiser did that. I half expected to see Jeffrey in the halls with an ID around his neck. He'd go to MTV and Nickelodeon meetings, throw out ideas, and take producers to lunch, all to make sure he got his imprint on promotions, talent appearances, and contests to sell his movies. He also spent up to $8 million per title.

I brought the idea of buying DreamWorks to the Viacom board that October, but they demurred—too expensive. Brad and I were not willing to take no for an answer. In late November, Brad and I pitched the board again. This time, they gave us permission to take a shot.

On December 2, Brad called David. Geffen was fed up with General Electric, NBCU's parent company, for taking weeks on minor deal points and treating them like a captive entity. Brad said, "We really want to make a deal to buy you guys." David responded, "Listen, we've been through this before. Come to me with signed contracts that require only our signatures. Otherwise, forget it."

We went into overdrive and back to Sumner and the board. There were questions.

"Spielberg is not exclusively signed to DreamWorks," they pointed out.

"Yes," we conceded. "His deal with DreamWorks allows him to make pictures with other studios, but there is plenty of precedent for that." Spielberg was the most profitable director in Hollywood. And buying DreamWorks did not buy us some blockbusters, like *Indiana Jones* and *Jurassic Park.*

The deal we presented was for $1.6 billion, which included $400 million in debt. Brad's team said they could recoup $900 million of that by selling the controlling rights to the DreamWorks library, but we would keep the distribution rights to those pictures. We got board approval, and I jumped on a plane to LA.

The next morning, Brad and I headed to Spielberg's home in the Pacific Palisades to meet the three partners. We had the contracts in hand. Before he signed, Steven wanted to see us personally. David and Jeffrey were enthusiastic about the deal and moving to Paramount. For Steven, this move had significant emotional overtones. He was going to divorce Universal. He wanted to get a sense of us as people and he wanted to get some creative assurances.

We all sat down in his home office. Brad and I talked about why we thought this would be a perfect union, how great it would be for all of us. Then for about an hour, we heard Steven's thoughts about personnel and creative independence. All three of the DreamWorks trio were great businessmen, but Spielberg was also an artist. He cared most about the movies.

We passed the audition. We shook hands and signed the contracts.

This was a huge coup. DreamWorks stood for creativity and quality. Now the triumvirate that built it had chosen to join Viacom. I saw it as a game changer. I was happy for Brad.

DreamWorks Animation was another key component. Jeffrey Katzenberg was the CEO there. These were the folks behind *Shrek*, *Kung Fu Panda*, and other animated franchises. While the animation company was not included in the deal, the distribution rights for its films were. Animated family films were the top of the pile in terms of box office power. These big animated movies were called "locomotives" because they gave the distributor the muscle to drag lesser films along with them on better terms than they would otherwise get.

I liked the idea of having Jeffrey in the trenches with Paramount's marketing team. Paramount had a subpar marketing operation. A micromanager, Jeffrey would be all over them, and I thought they would benefit from having him kick their asses a bit. Jeffrey is a man of modest height on a wiry frame with animal energy. His uniform at the time was a V-neck sweater over a white T-shirt and baggy khakis. He had a lot of nicknames—"Sparky," "the Golden Retriever," and worse. All attested to his tireless work ethic. When he was at Disney, he famously told his staff, "If you don't come in Saturday, don't bother coming in Sunday." He was part man and part machine.

People in Hollywood like to make a big deal about how early they get up. Jeffrey rose at four thirty to work out on a stationary bike while reading the papers and watching the news. He'd then shower and dress and head off to his first of three scheduled back-to-back breakfasts, where he could hoover up information. He also had a system for "rolling calls," very short conversations, usually just a minute or two, with his wide network of contacts. It was another chance to inhale information, stay in every loop possible, and give the town the impression that he was everywhere.

Years later I would serve for a decade on Jeffrey's DreamWorks Animation board. He kept a plane at the ready, idling in Burbank. He'd fly off to China for a meeting and be back the next day, then head to New York and back to LA the same night. Once, he asked me to join him and reality-show producer Mark Burnett on a trip to Madagascar. I was intrigued. When Jeffrey said it was just for a weekend, I begged off.

I was naive about how Jeffrey's tough discipline would play at Paramount.

He tried to insert his own people into the Paramount structure, but many of the Paramount executives saw Jeffrey and DreamWorks as a threat and a Trojan horse—they wanted to know exactly who had acquired whom. "That's bullshit," I countered. "That's your insecurity talking. DreamWorks will only improve our game."

My greatest disappointment about my Paramount tenure came after I left. I watched the goodwill of the early days of the DreamWorks marriage fade away. Paramount did things I thought were stupid, ego-driven, and unnecessary, such as refusing to use the DreamWorks logo in movie trailers and not giving proper credit to DreamWorks executives at movie premieres, acting more like a victor than a partner. This was Brad.

There was one awful behind-the-scenes dustup at the premiere of the big-budget musical *Dreamgirls*. Geffen had spent twenty-five years shepherding *Dreamgirls* from a Broadway musical to a motion picture. He had very particular ideas as to how he wanted its premiere at Manhattan's Ziegfeld Theatre handled: a cold open with no speeches. Brad ignored David. Brad stood up at the Ziegfeld and thanked his Paramount colleagues, but not the DreamWorks executives. It was a needless slight you shouldn't do to anyone. To add insult to insult, Sumner told the press that *Dreamgirls* did not get an Oscar nomination because "everyone hates David."

Steven Spielberg soured on Brad, too. Maybe the Pellicano scandal was part of it, but mostly it was that the man who directed *Close Encounters*, *E.T.*, *Raiders of the Lost Ark*, *Schindler's List*, and *Saving Private Ryan* deserved to be treated with respect, and he got little from Viacom. Philippe Dauman even went so far as to denigrate Spielberg publicly at an investor conference in 2007, saying, if he and his creative team wanted to leave Paramount, "the financial impact to Paramount first and especially to Viacom overall would be completely immaterial." It's hard to exaggerate how many enemies a dumb statement like that can make in the film community. Things went terminal after that. Spielberg, Geffen, Katzenberg, and their company were assets for Brad and Sumner to use, not cocky subordinates to take down a peg. In 2008, DreamWorks left Viacom.

Brad did not step up, but he managed to remain there until 2017, when he died unexpectedly, at age fifty-nine. He was not the man to run Paramount. My mistake.

CHAPTER THIRTY-FOUR

THE DIGITAL WAVE

In early 2005—two years before the iPhone debuted—the stock prices of traditional media companies, including Viacom, began to drift down, while digital outfits like Google, Amazon, and Apple were seeing their stocks go through the stratosphere. The digerati were in the house and Wall Street loved them. We were the "legacy media" now. Various efforts to gin up our stock price, including buybacks, failed and Redstone began flailing, looking for answers.

How to compete in this creeping transformation? That was the billion-dollar question. You could lose everything if you answered it wrong. Ever since the disastrous merger of Time Warner with AOL in 2000, all media companies were wary about drinking the new-media Kool-Aid. MTV Networks was particularly vulnerable. Our young audiences were the canaries in the media coal mine, the first to defect to new outlets like Yahoo and YouTube.

Music videos were ideal content for outlets like YouTube and Launch .com. Now fans could see any video they wanted any time they liked—they no longer had to turn on MTV and sit through Blind Melon to get to Gwen Stefani or the Black Eyed Peas.

At first, we were hopeful that we could easily join the new digital world. We'd pack our websites with our twenty-thousand-plus library of music videos and stake out a nice streaming position in coordination with our television networks. But the record labels shut us down. All of them refused to license us the digital rights to air their videos or wanted unrealistic fees.

Our TV company ran on music videos, but we could not use them on the internet. Up until now, we had always followed our audience. But no longer would it be that easy.

The sad truth was that the record labels did not want a new online iteration of MTV. They felt we had built a huge business on their backs. That we paid them millions of dollars for the use of their videos and made hits of their acts never seemed to factor into their list of grievances. I had always implored our folks to be humble with the labels. No arrogance, be friendly and keep throwing money their way. Make it a two-way street. Do favors. But it was inevitable—the more power MTV Networks accumulated, the more the record companies resented us.

I was made keenly aware of this in late 1994 when Bob Morgado, the combative brutish new Chairman of the Warner Music Group, summoned me to his lofty office at 75 Rockefeller Center. Morgado was the new sheriff in town, an outsider from the world of hardball politics who arrived at Warner on a mission to clean up the mess the hipsters had made.

We had enjoyed our closest relationship with the Warner Music Group's three record labels: Warner/Reprise, Elektra, and Atlantic. They represented the best in rock and pop music with legacies that went from Frank Sinatra to Prince and R.E.M. They were the industry leaders. Artists loved them. When Morgado arrived, he took a buzz saw to the place. He fired Mo Ostin and Lenny Waronker, the beloved duo who built the Warner Bros. powerhouse. Then he drove out Bob Krasnow, the Chairman of Elektra Records, and alienated Doug Morris, Chairman of Atlantic Records. I loved and admired all these guys.

I sat down in his office and ordered a coffee. Perhaps the new honcho was going to thank me for the recent $250 million in retail sales from our popular *Unplugged* franchise.

Nope. He was declaring war. Without a pleasantry, he started in. "MTV is too powerful. We need control over our own promotion. I am organizing all the record companies together now into a television venture. We are going to start in Germany with a TV network called Viva, then go through Europe, then come here. I am going to take you down."

I was thinking, *Well, fuck you, too*, but I didn't say it. I told him good luck trying and headed to the elevator. On the way out the building, I was thinking, *The good old days are over.*

As the internet grew, the labels granted music video streaming rights to independent websites like Launch.com, but not to us. Our TV company ran on music videos, but couldn't use them on the internet. Not only were we not going to become an online music video hub, the websites we had built to work in tandem with our television brands, MTV.com, VH1.com, etc., were crippled. Without music the sites had little value.

We needed to hurry to figure out another way to get into the digital landscape. Historically we had been builders in a closed system. Now we needed to be buyers in a more open system. We all saw what was coming. We needed an acquisition. In 2000, I hired an ambitious, savvy young New Yorker, Jason Hirschhorn, as our head of digital—we bought his small company and tasked him with helping lead us into this new landscape. Our digital group created and acquired a portfolio of small, noteworthy websites, but nothing transforming.

In February 2005 Kevin Wall, an old friend and entrepreneur, called to see if I would be willing to meet a young man named Mark Zuckerberg at our Times Square offices. Zuckerberg was twenty and had just started a website called "The Facebook" at Harvard. I was keen to meet Mark and learn more about his social network for college students. No one knew much about social networks. There had been a site called Friendster, but it had gone out of business. Social networks would begin the greatest paradigm shift the media business had ever seen, although it sure didn't look that way at the beginning. In this new world the future would increasingly belong, not to content producers like us, but to the platforms, the platforms that gave people, particularly young people, the ability to communicate directly with each other. How were we going to get in on that?

Mark came on a rainy day in a hoodie and sandals, younger than anyone on our young staff. The Facebook had about $9 million in revenue and had not yet allowed anyone but college students onto their platform. Mark said they were considering adding high school students. We were very interested. Discussions ensued.

After a meeting at Facebook's California office, Michael Wolf, then COO at MTV Networks, called to say that he was with Mark Zuckerberg in Palo Alto, and Mark told him he was about to go home to Dobbs Ferry, New York, to see his parents. Michael asked if he could have the company plane and offer Mark a ride. That would give them an uninterrupted five hours together. I agreed. When they landed, the Zuckerbergs were there to meet their son at the airport.

In early 2006, after discussions with Owen Van Natta, Facebook's COO, we gave Mark and his board a formal offer letter to buy Facebook for $1.5 billion, a huge sum for us at the time, the most we ever contemplated spending for anything. We offered $765 million in cash and the rest as an "earn out," were Facebook to perform to plan. We had hoped that Facebook could get to $25 million in revenues that year. We were the first company to make an offer to buy Facebook, an outfit with a $875 billion market cap today.

Zuckerberg was never a seller. He didn't want his MTV. He turned us down. Later he walked away from Yahoo and Microsoft and everyone else who came to his door. He's now one of the world's richest men.

We kept looking for a transforming opportunity. There was one company that would have changed both MTV's and Viacom's fortunes forever . . . YouTube!

Chad Hurley and a couple of his PayPal pals launched YouTube in February 2005. Anyone could upload, view, comment, and share videos, from user-generated files to bootlegged TV reruns and movie clips. It built an early buzz a with stunts like putting up *Saturday Night Live's* "Lazy Sunday" and having it shared by millions. YouTube would go on to to build an ecosystem few could have imagined. YouTube was revolutionary, like MTV had once been.

We faced the Innovator's Dilemma. After all, we were already the leaders in short-form video. We saw open platforms as part of the future. But our legacy business got in the way; our eyes were bigger than our means. We had to follow legacy media rules the new digital companies didn't have.

They didn't have to worry about losses. We did not have the appetite or ability to absorb the losses required to fund the infrastructure that YouTube needed to grow. Further, our board saw YouTube as an enemy, a copyright-infringement machine. No matter how great a fit it might have been, Viacom could not absorb the losses and lawsuits.

You could make a case that with outside financing we would have been able to run YouTube smartly as a quasi-independent entity without stuffing it with advertising. YouTube could have transformed everything and Viacom would have been a leader today. But there was no appetite for that among the Viacom board. They assumed the world they knew would remain as it was.

Taking another shot at social media, we began discussions with MySpace in late 2005. The LA-based social media company was hotter than Facebook at the time and had a huge following among new independent bands and their fans. They got more traffic about our shows than we got on our own websites. We were intrigued, but had concerns that it might be a flash in the pan and follow the recently deceased Friendster out the door. We were not convinced MySpace was worth what they were asking. But we kept talking.

I'm often amused when the business press attributes moves by great moguls to keen strategies and careful chess maneuvers. In my experience, big decisions are often made based on ego and impulse. Sumner hated Rupert Murdoch, the other octogenarian media mogul, whose News Corporation was an even bigger empire than Sumner's. Much of this hatred, I think, came from envy. Unlike Sumner, Rupert was not overly worried about his stock price, often to the frustration of his investors. He played a longer game and focused intensely on strategy and operations. Constantly in orbit on his 737, he would fly all over the world dropping in on his far-flung businesses. He actually wanted to know how his companies operated and how they connected with their consumers.

Redstone was more a sedentary Scrooge, sitting in New York or LA, maniacally obsessing on stock price, the caricature of the money-hungry billionaire. We had offices scattered all over the globe, but he rarely went to any. When he flew cross-country between stock tickers, he'd spend the entire five or six hours screaming into the phone from forty-five thousand feet up at his poor broker trying to get the stock to move. We'd pretend to read magazines while he wailed. He'd revert to human form once the market closed, order a glass of wine, and feel like he put in a hard day. When we finally got off the plane, first-time Viacom flyers would be shaken.

Sumner went off his rocker when Rupert swept in on a July weekend and grabbed MySpace. With no due diligence, Rupert bought it for $565 million like he was buying a pizza. It was a big bet. Sumner had never really heard of MySpace, but when he saw Rupert had bought it and found out that we'd been kicking the tires for a while and hadn't made a quick bid, he saw us as losers.

I was on a summer holiday in Hawaii with my family when Rupert made the big score and swept into Santa Monica on what Sumner felt was the big steal. He felt I'd been asleep at the switch.

Murdoch's purchase of MySpace was the largest digital acquisition by any legacy media company since the Time Warner/AOL deal. Suddenly Rupert was on the covers of all the business magazines, the "New Media Visionary." I had no idea how much this upset Redstone. The man with the fax machine wanted to be a digital visionary, too.

In October 2006, Google bought YouTube for $1.65 billion in stock. They could afford to run it at a loss while they built it up. You could say that this was the moment that MTV began to surrender its mojo. In March 2007, Philippe Dauman—for whom YouTube had been a stone in his shoe—sued for $1 billion for copyright infringement. After ten years and tens of millions in legal fees, Viacom lost. Financial analysts say YouTube is now worth north of $550 billion.

CHAPTER THIRTY-FIVE

SUMNER SPLITS THE BABY

In early 2005 a swarm of bankers, always on the hunt for a new angle, began to talk to Viacom about a new idea. Their thesis was that Viacom was no longer a "clean story." It was too complicated a company and had too many disparate pieces. That's why the stock wasn't going up. Mind you, these were the same bankers who had made fortunes putting our large, complicated media company together.

Now they argued that investors wanted either "growth" stocks or "value" stocks, more mature businesses that threw off a lot of cash. We were too much of a mix. Conglomerates, they said, were going out of style. MTV Networks and BET were rapid growers, while on the other side CBS, Simon & Schuster, radio, and outdoor, while valuable cash generators, were not. We needed to split Viacom.

The pitch resonated and top management on both sides of Viacom—Les Moonves's team and mine—felt it was a good way to get rid of the other guys and take total control of our destinies. Sumner, having run out of stock-boosting card tricks, came around as well to the idea we would be worth more apart.

When he left his wife, Phyllis, Sumner said, "Divorce can be better than marriage." He went all in for our CBS/Viacom divorce. He felt he was a trailblazer, that other companies would follow. He decided to split us into two separate companies: Viacom Inc., the "growth" company, which I would run, and CBS Inc., the "value" company, which Les would helm. We would debut both companies on the New York Stock Exchange in January 2006.

A huge part of late 2005 was spent ripping the place in half. It was brutal—a monumental task, very expensive, full of small details. It occupied much of our collective time. The bankers, lawyers, and other advisers were hoovering up boatloads of cash to peel us apart. Every shared department—finance, HR, legal, etc.—had to be split in two and replicated. Where there was once one Investor Relations department, now there were two. Corporate people were chosen to go with one team or the other.

There was also some unfinished business I didn't fully appreciate. One task Les and I left for near the end of our split was what to do with some of Sumner's old friends and cronies who had remained on the payroll long after they had stopped contributing to the company in any way that we could see.

Carl Folta was executive vice president of Corporate Communications for Viacom. Les couldn't stand him and did not want him at CBS. He thought Carl would be a Sumner spy. I wanted to put my own person, Carole Robinson, there. We told Sumner that Carl was out. Instead, Sumner hired him as executive vice president, Office of the Chairman. He became Sumner's Minister of Propaganda. I had made an enemy close to the throne.

Mike Fricklas was EVP and general counsel for Viacom, very smart and skilled. I liked Mike. But he'd been brought into Viacom by Philippe Dauman. Mike also did a lot of work with Sumner, who always had some lawsuit cooking. Les did not want Mike as CBS's General Counsel and advised me to say the same: "Get rid of him. Mike is Philippe Dauman's soul brother. He'll spy on you for Philippe. Use your head." Philippe topped Les's enemies list. Mel Karmazin had fired Philippe from Viacom in 1999, but Sumner brought him back to join the board in 2004.

I got along with Mike, and he worked well with the creative people. He had given me a lot of good advice and he rooted for the company. Despite Les's warnings, I gave Mike the nod for our General Counsel job. (Several people later said Mike was a key to my undoing, but I never believed that.)

Bob Bakish headed up planning and business development for me. A former Booz Allen consultant, Bob was wickedly smart and was working for Viacom when I hired him. He found the comanagement situation especially frustrating and was a strong advocate for the split. In 2016, he became CEO of Viacom, put the shoe on the other foot, and reunited the companies in 2019. Bob would walk the CEO plank in 2024.

The last thing to split was the Aviation Department, the Viacom air force. We had two Bombardier Global Express jets. One was brand-new with a five-year service agreement; the other was a bit long in the tooth. In fact, it was so old that Bombardier told us it was the fourteenth one they ever made. That caused me pause whenever I got on it. Apartments never have a thirteenth floor. I wondered who had the thirteenth Global? I bet we did.

Late one afternoon, Les and I met in my office to flip a coin for plane ownership. It seemed fair as anything, a multimillion-dollar flip. One toss. I took out a quarter, called heads, and flipped the coin. It rolled all around the floor before landing heads up. "Be safe with that thirteenth plane, Les," I said. We shook and went our separate ways.

Looking back, the split of Viacom and CBS haunts the company to this day. In 2006, the industry was on the cusp of a paradigm shift ushering in the digital era where size and scale were paramount. The smarter players were expanding, growing larger than ever. Disney would gobble up iconic independent entertainment companies with strong brands, important libraries, and production capabilities like Pixar and Marvel and Lucasfilm. Comcast bought NBC Universal and took positions in various digital companies like BuzzFeed. News Corp bought DirecTV and Dow Jones along with networks to fuel their booming Asian business. Increasingly, the smaller CBS and Viacom companies were off on the sidelines, losing leverage and sliding further down the food chain of the media/entertainment complex.

But all that was in the future. On January 3, 2006, I stood on the balcony of the New York Stock Exchange, looked down at the assembled traders, reached over, and rang the bell to inaugurate trading for the year. "New Viacom" was born. The stock debuted at $41.59. I was finally in charge, a freshly minted Fortune 500 CEO. It had been a long trip from Chicken Street to Wall Street. I had been a traveler, entrepreneur, clothing smuggler, and early MTV crusader. Now I was running the only public company I could even imagine working for. I was thrilled and only wished my parents were alive to see it. My mom had passed in 1980, my dad in 1990.

We got off to a big start in January, but a letdown came in April. After seventeen years and sixty-eight straight quarters of double-digit growth under my watch, followed by the big press buildup about how the New Viacom was going to grow to the sky, our first-quarter earnings came out and we fumbled. Revenues were up 12 percent, less than usual, and earnings were up a piddling 3 percent. There could not have been a worse time to look like we were slowing down. It was as if the heavyweight champion came out for round one and tripped over his shoelaces.

The stock dropped to $39, down 5 percent. CNBC's loudmouth Jim Cramer opined that I must be spending too much time with talent having fun and not watching the business. "Growth company. Show me!" he shouted. I laughed. But Sumner was not laughing. The big buildup put a target on our back. However, all our domestic businesses were on track. Our international business was the culprit—MTV International was down 13 percent.

By 2006, we were in over 150 countries. It was complicated and we needed a better handle on their financial performance. I had trouble getting straight answers. Trying to audit monies flowing in and out of India, Brazil, South Africa, Russia, and dozens of other countries where we had a potpourri of joint ventures, licensing deals, syndication, and owned and operated networks was a challenge. But this was a bad time for the cracks to show.

Then in May Paramount's expected summer movie blockbuster *Mission: Impossible III* with Tom Cruise came out. It underperformed. Our stock faltered again. I'd arrive in the morning to a pile of faxes left by Sumner's New York secretary. As always, the stock price, not operations, was his obsession. The faxes in his handwritten scrawl shook with anger. They looked like bomb threats. "Do something, goddamnit!"

Sumner Redstone was a gambler. He had an addictive personality and was a stone-cold junkie for the stock market. He'd built a large part of his fortune playing entertainment company stocks. In the 1970s and early '80s he would attend early exhibitor screenings of movies and when he saw what looked to be a blockbuster—say, *Star Wars*—he'd walk out to a pay phone, call his broker, and order large chunks of 20th Century Fox. He made a fortune at this. He watched the stock exchange like a roulette wheel.

If I'd been more alert or just plain paranoid, I would have picked up that Philippe Dauman, whom Sumner called "the son I never had" (of course, he did have a son—one he would sue with typical Sumner sensitivity), wanted my job. I later learned that during that summer, Philippe went up to Beverly Park and presented a book to Sumner with a plan on how he could take Viacom to greater heights than Tom Freston could. A coup was in the cards. I was a little too confident to suspect this. I had overdelivered for Sumner for seventeen years. You work successfully at one place too long and your radar can dim. After fighting off so many lions and tigers, you may not notice a weasel sneaking up on you.

By August, Viacom was moving in the right direction again. *Time* magazine had just anointed me as one of the "world's most influential people" in their first edition of the "*Time* 100" list. Our second-quarter earnings came out and revenue was up 24 percent, and earnings were up 27 percent. The stock stayed flat, though. It was now at $37, down 10 percent for the year, pretty much on par for the media category.

Sumner was calling less frequently. No dinner invites. No meeting invites. I was reduced to mostly faxes and he was not even sending his usual barrage of nasty ones. I took that as a positive. He was eighty-three years old and had a new wife and a house full of tropical fish to fry in his mansion on the hill.

Then Sumner and I had our first screaming match. Over the years I had seen him scream at all kinds of people all over the world—waiters, assistants, drivers, brokers, bankers, employees—but never at me. On August 22, I should have realized I was dead meat when I had my first real fight with him.

I had just taken my seat on the company plane that morning for a short flight on a digital mission to San Jose from Van Nuys when I got a call on my cell from Carole Robinson. She said, "You must stop. You are not going to believe what just happened." I told the pilot to pull off the runway. "Sumner just had a press shit fit, up at his home in Beverly Park."

"What?"

"Yes, Carl Folta invited some reporters up to Sumner's house."

"About what?"

"Sumner wanted to make a statement. Now, prepare yourself. . . . He said he was 'firing' Tom Cruise! Firing him for the performance of *Mission Impossible III*."

"He's 'firing' Tom Cruise? Tom Cruise doesn't even work for us."

"Does not matter. It's Crazy Town."

The film had been well reviewed, some critics called it the best of the series, but the box office was less than the earlier *Mission: Impossible* movies and not enough to get the stock boost Sumner had hoped for. He decided that he needed to come off the sidelines and swing into action.

Sumner's new wife, Paula, was a voracious daytime TV viewer. She had been tracking Tom Cruise closely from her couch. In 2005, she had seen the famous episode of *Oprah* where Cruise jumped up and down proclaiming his love for Katie Holmes. Then she saw Tom go after Brooke Shields on the *Today* show for advocating antidepressants. Paula was distressed. She decided that with all his Scientology proclamations, Cruise was becoming a joke. This was why *Mission Impossible III* had not been a smash.

Sumner agreed. He was going to take back control over the empire. Bristling with resentment, he summoned *Wall Street Journal* reporters to his chateau to announce that he was firing Tom Cruise from Paramount Pictures. Cruise was making a fool of himself. He was hurting the stock price. He had to be made an example of.

I got on the phone with Sumner. "What the fuck are you doing? You can't fire Tom Cruise! First off, he doesn't work for us." Tom had a production company on the Paramount lot, but was, like every movie star, a free agent. "And you just do this out of the blue? Just fire Tom Cruise, the world's biggest movie star? Go out on your lawn and shout to the world that you're firing someone who doesn't work for you? And never tell Brad or me?" For Brad, the beleaguered head of Paramount, this was far more of a public humiliation than it was for Cruise.

Sumner cut me off: "Tom Cruise is a FUCK. He cost *Mission: Impossible* a hundred million dollars. Women EVERYWHERE hate him. Paula hates him. And men can't stand him anymore, either. I HATE him." Then he added, "We look like idiots." On that, I agreed. We certainly did look like idiots.

I pushed back hard. "Why would you humiliate Cruise this way? Take a shit on him after all he has done for us?" For the first time ever, I was screaming at Sumner Redstone. "You are shitting in your own pants!"

No one had been a more faithful supporter of Paramount than Tom

Cruise. His films were among the most valuable in our library. And the new film that Sumner considered such a disaster had already earned $150 million.

I shouted at Sumner: "You are making Brad Grey look like a fool! Forget about me. Brad runs the studio. He has to live in this town. You cut his balls off. What A-list actor will want to make a movie for a company that publicly humiliates movie stars? This is so damn wrong!"

I was getting nowhere. Sumner was screaming at me, and I was screaming back. I was furious and let him have it, then hung up and headed to San Jose. I called Brad from the plane. He was shaken. "Let me see how I can put this back together," he told me. I was shaken, too.

I could not tolerate anyone yelling at me like that. It was so raw, Sumner's rage. Where was it coming from? I should have worried more about where it was going. My fate was sealed.

Vanity Fair was putting together its annual New Establishment power rankings, which ran in September. Sumner craved this foolish stuff. Did Carl Folta get an early look and tell Sumner that his hated rival, Rupert Murdoch, had moved up to number one, while Sumner had dropped all the way from number three to number thirty? And that I had risen to number seventeen? If Sumner had not already made up his mind to can me, that would have finished me off.

Labor Day weekend rolled around two weeks after the screaming match. It was a summer holiday weekend, primo firing season for Redstone. And I had just flown to Los Angeles from New York.

I was in New York on Thursday, August 31, for our annual bacchanalia, the MTV Video Music Awards at Radio City Music Hall. The VMAs were always a who's who of what had happened in pop culture that year, part circus, part cavalcade of stars, and part award show. It was where Madonna kissed Britney Spears, where Pee-wee Herman made his comeback after jerking off in a movie theater, and where Howard Stern swung on a rope with his ass hanging out, dressed as "Fart Man." The show was our biggest franchise. That night, it brought in $75 million. No single event we did made more money or was more notorious for us than the VMAs. But the shouting match with Redstone was coloring my thoughts. How would Sumner and I ever get back to normal?

That year we had the usual potpourri of celebrities, criminals, and dignitaries: Jay-Z, Beyoncé, Justin Timberlake, Lou Reed, Missy Elliott, the cast of *Jackass*, and Mayor Bloomberg topping the bill. Pop stars, comedians, movie stars, and oddball celebrities were backstage, buzzing around with their many attendants. I took a seat next to my friend Brian Grazer and watched the red-carpet proceedings unfold. This was the twentieth VMAs for me, and for the first time, I was kind of bored. Brian and I flew back to LA after the show.

The weather that weekend was California perfection: golden sunshine, deep blue sky, no humidity, seventy-five degrees. You could see forever. On Labor Day, I drove up the coast to Malibu to play tennis with Yahoo CEO Terry Semel and Kevin Wall. Cars and vans lined the Pacific Coast Highway. I finished around 4 p.m. and got into my car to head back to Beverly Hills. I loved this drive. I'd conjure up some Beach Boy imagery from the early sixties and step on the gas, a Connecticut kid scoping out California girls. I turned off my cell phone and put in an advance CD of the new Bob Dylan album, *Modern Times*. I cranked it up and rolled my windows down. The ocean was on my right. I was counting my blessings. "The landscape is glowin,' gleamin' in the golden light of day," Dylan sang. Work was the last thing on my mind.

When I got back to my house near the top of Coldwater Canyon, my answering machine was flashing red. There were five messages from Sumner. They got progressively more animated and profane. The last one was "I can reach President Bush easier than you, goddamnit. Where the fuck are you? Call me." This did not sound good. There was also a message from Mike Fricklas, my General Counsel. He asked me to call him.

I called Mike. "I see Sumner is trying to reach me. He seems a little crazed. Could that have any connection to why you are calling me on Labor Day?"

"Yes. He really needs to speak to you. Better call him back."

I'd seen this movie before. "Is this the ultimate conversation, Mike?"

"Well, I will leave that to Sumner."

I shook my head. "What the fuck?" The jig was up, my gig was up. It was true to form, a holiday weekend, the moment when the Boston CEO Strangler was most prone to strike. I would be roadkill by dinnertime.

On death row, I needed a lawyer, not a priest. I called Allen Grubman, my attorney of twenty-five years, as he was sitting down for dinner at his summer home in East Hampton. "Allen, I am about to be fired."

He was startled, took a beat, then blurted out in his Brooklyn accent, "He's a lawyer. Just keep your mouth shut!" He admonished me not to do anything. "Just sit there, schmuck. Stare into space. There is going to be a knife, but you won't even feel it go in. Get out of there as fast as you can."

I dialed Sumner. It was sweet Sumner now on the other end. He was almost whispering. "Hi, Tom. Why don't you come over and see me in Beverly Park. Have time for me? Come now, if you can."

"Sure. I see you left quite a few messages. Been out, you know. Labor Day and all."

The grizzled old mogul was lying in wait, just a couple of miles away. I took a few deep breaths and decided I'd hot-rod it over in my old BMW. I had bought this car brand-new in 1975 for $5,800 and had it restored to mint condition. My relationship with it was the longest in my life, thirty-one years. Viacom came in second, twenty-six years. The BMW should carry me to my execution.

As I headed over to Crazy Town, I had two thoughts: How would he position this? And that the autumn would now be wide-open.

When I got to Sumner's house I parked on the street to facilitate a quick getaway. I walked up the driveway and stepped carefully, making sure not to fall in the koi pond. The butler led me through the house to Sumner's inner sanctum, a living room lined with large aquariums on three sides. It overlooked the canyon below. We always joked there was a shark tank somewhere.

Sumner was in his favorite chair. He beckoned me over like the Godfather. "Come sit." I perched on the ottoman, facing him. We were eye to eye, about two feet apart. He opened with "I have terrible news for you *and* me."

"What's that?" I said.

"Well, the board of directors wants me to fire you immediately. They aren't convinced that you are the right person to run the company. I have no choice but to go along with their request."

Replacing me would be Philippe Dauman, the colorless snob with the perfect SATs. Sumner had all the choices in the world to lead his entertainment empire into the future and he chose Philippe. He and Sumner were two litigious lawyers in love.

I didn't blow up. I did not say, "Fuck you," or "Hey, I've only been on this job for eight months and I built the bulk of this company for you for decades," or "The board making you do this is bullshit, you control the board," or, even, "Take this job and shove it." I just got up and left. No goodbye. I didn't say a word and did not look back. The whole exchange probably took less than two minutes.

As I was going out to the driveway, Carl Folta, his ever-faithful flunky, came out from behind a bush. He chased me down the walk and screamed, "Hey, Tom, do you want the press release to say that you were fired or that you quit?"

"Fuck you, Carl."

I'd been fired for the second time in my sixty years. As I peeled off, I put my arm out the window and gave the international sign of disgust. I couldn't even think about what might lie ahead. Debt-ridden from a failed venture and fresh out of India, I had joined a tiny crew with a rough idea for a new company in 1980. Now I was leaving twenty-six years later with dozens of friends, hundreds of memories, and a worldwide empire in my wake. I would miss my team and the challenge of pivoting the company into the digital age. But I was a free man again.

I couldn't say I didn't have a good time.

I had booked the corporate jet to return to New York the day after Labor Day. In a display of corporate pettiness, Philippe decreed that I would be denied any free ride. "Viacom flew me out here on business, my home is in New York, and I believe I'm owed a round trip," I told the Aviation Department. "I need to go clean out my office. Then you'll be rid of me." Philippe backed down. I took my last ride on the Global Express. The crew seemed sad to see me go. I hadn't held a boarding pass in years. The plane I would miss. We had been everywhere together. They presented me with a half gallon of Johnnie Walker Black as a goodbye present.

The next night, Sumner went on Charlie Rose's TV show to talk about why he fired me. "Was MySpace a factor?" asked Charlie.

“I was humiliated,” Sumner said. “I hate to lose to Rupert Murdoch. Freston had the prize and lost it.” That was the story he chose to tell. Rupert had paid a cool $565 million for MySpace; when it collapsed in 2011 he sold it for a mere $35 million. Not doing that deal had saved Viacom $530 million. I’m still waiting for a thank-you note.

My run as Viacom CEO was just eight short months. Philippe jacked up the stock price, spending $16 billion to buy back stock, rather than buying into the future like Bob Iger did. Bob bought Marvel and Pixar and Lucasfilm for the same $16 billion. Philippe ran the company into the ground and lined his pockets with $500 million. A failing, fragile Sumner finally canned him by email. No doubt Philippe has his own spin on the story. Wardens like to say there are no guilty people in prison. No CEO ever thinks he deserves to be fired. The day after I left 1515, my friend Bob Evans, the legendary former Paramount studio head, called to commiserate. “Remember, Tom,” he said, “there are three sides to every story: your side, his side, and the truth.”

Guess who called next to invite me to dinner? Tom Cruise.

CHAPTER THIRTY-SIX

BURMESE DAZE

News of my exit had hit the wires. At 6:30 a.m. LA time, I had my first caller. "Wake up over there! It's a brand-new day!" It was Bono, shaking me awake from Dublin.

MTV and U2 had grown up together, and Bono and I had become friends in the process. I had great respect for him and the band. In 1993, their manager, Paul McGuinness, asked if I'd like to join them on the European stadium leg of their Zoo TV tour, maybe the most elaborately staged show in rock history. I met them in Verona and was awestruck by the power of it all. Zoo TV was a multimedia extravaganza designed to wreak sensory overload on its audience, kind of like our mission at MTV. From the stage Bono would call the White House or the space station. In Rome, I watched the show standing between Pearl Jam front man Eddie Vedder and film director Federico Fellini. I had joined Zoo World, a high-spirited troop of artists, activists, writers, and supermodels. When I came home from that trip, my bond with U2 was unbreakable.

Now Bono was calling to offer me a job. "Fuck Sumner Redstone! Count your blessings, dude. I've got the perfect idea for you. . . . Come with me and run (RED). We need you. And it'll be fun." Bono had started (RED) with Bobby Shriver to engage the private sector in the HIV/AIDS fight. When Bono talks (and he loves to), he can be one of the world's most persuasive men. He was going on like I had already said yes.

"I just got fired twelve hours ago, Bono," I protested. "Gimme a moment. I'm still half asleep and wondering if it was all just a bad dream."

"Not a dream at all. It's liberation." Bono lit up his network. Steve Jobs called, then Patty Stonesifer, the CEO of the Gates Foundation, both to sell me on the role. Flattered by the heavy lobbying, I said I'd consider it. When you arrive among the newly unemployed, advice comes at you from every direction. It can be a full day's work just to listen to it all. One I remember: "Get to Starbucks before four p.m.—the tables outside begin to fill up."

Rupert Murdoch called to discuss funding a new venture. "You can count on me," he said. The main appeal of that was thinking how it would infuriate Sumner. David Geffen and Jeffrey Katzenberg checked in. All the calls and notes were a balm to my battered ego. Allen, my lawyer, told me to grab a new job while I was hot: "Schmuck, you better take a big job right away or you'll end up in that fucking dustbin with everyone else."

The best advice came from my old MTV boss, Bob Pittman. "First, say no to everybody and everything. Second, get lost. Go far away. You have nothing to prove and are in no position to make a big decision now." He went on. "Slow down. Let things come back into focus. Your humanity will return." Bob generously offered me free office space at his new venture fund, the Pilot Group, in Rockefeller Center. "But not until you go away."

I don't want to suggest that I was okay with what had happened. I was furious. Also alternately depressed, disoriented, and embarrassed. Deep down, though, there was a glimmer. Something new was going to happen. At sixty years old, I had time for another good run. But I didn't want to jump into anything new until I had time to recalibrate.

I decided to disappear and knew exactly where to go. Beautiful Burma, the crazy uncle of Southeast Asia, a country run by generals and fortune tellers, completely cut off from the rest of the world. I fell in love with Burma when I visited in 1977. It was isolated and weird back then and even weirder now. Burma had no internet, no cell phones, no newspapers. There was no more perfect place to remove myself from outside static. The world's most media-free environment awaited me. I headed off the grid like a man on the run. With my wife, Kathy, my brother, Bill, and a few friends from Shanghai and California, I went in search of contemplation and clarity. I called it the "Tom Got Fired Tour."

I had been coming to Burma with Kathy since 2003. We started our own humanitarian projects there, building a nursery school, an orphanage, and a health clinic up in the jungles of the Shan State, near the center of the country. Since 1962, the generals running the country had followed a lame ideology they called "the Burmese Road to Socialism," which pretty much ran into a ditch. This gentle Buddhist land, once the richest country in Asia, had been transformed into a pariah, a predatory state, rife with gangsters and drug lords, sealed away from the world. Its citizens were now Asia's poorest. But for all the nation's agony, you would not find kinder or more resilient people anywhere. And these folks were still happy to see a foreigner. Burma was a throwback to the old Asia I once knew before globalism transformed so much of the region.

George and Jane Soon, friends in Rangoon, were members of the small, connected Burmese-Chinese community. George was part owner of Myanmar Airways. He also sold Burmese cigarettes to North Korea, where he traveled frequently. "There's a lot of heavy smokers there," he told me cheerfully over drinks.

Jane thought it would be interesting for me to have a session with one of the country's top fortune tellers. The Burmese are famously superstitious, and a special caste of high-end soothsayers had long guided politicians and military leaders in making big decisions. Ne Win, the military strongman who overthrew the democratic government in 1962 and ruled ruthlessly for decades, kept a retinue of fortune tellers and astrologers on his staff. One told him he'd live to be ninety if he changed the currency to denominations divisible by nine, instead of ten. Overnight notes were demonetized, and 45-kyat and 90-kyat bills were issued in their place.

People's savings were wiped out, but it worked for him. He died at ninety-one. If it was good enough for the generals, I figured, it was good enough for me.

Jane had a beauty salon in an old Dutch colonial building down a dirt lane lined with banana trees in a verdant corner of Rangoon. The clientele were local elites, including a dodgy crowd of generals' wives. I met the fortune teller there late one afternoon.

Jane took me out to a small table on the veranda. The fortune teller sat under a whirring fan next to a man in Western dress, her translator. She made quick eye contact, then bowed her head. I had imagined that, as a seer for the powerful, she would be an elegant woman in stylish clothes and jewelry, rewards from her many years of predictions for the inner circle.

Instead, she had the aura of a simple peasant. She was older, with rather plain features, an almost flat face and no makeup. She wore a patterned longyi and a beige long-sleeved blouse. She remained seated. I put my hands on my stomach and bowed. She nodded in response. I was getting excited. Maybe she did know my future.

She knew nothing about me but my date of birth. The translator asked if I was married and how many children I had. Jane did not know of my recent ouster. She thought I was still the king of MTV. I sat down and the translator handed me a pad of paper and a pencil. "She is going to say things. Just write them down," he said. I could ask a few simple questions, but this would not really be a conversation. She started in, looking straight down at the table.

She didn't seem to be a Nostradamus. There were warnings about plane rides not to take and a prediction on the color of a car I was going to buy. She said I would "have a urine problem in 2008 or especially in 2010, that will require an operation." So far my urine is holding up fine.

"Someone from your company will spread rumors about you and you will need to change jobs between December 2006 and February 2007. He will make bad news around your name. He is jealous and will get at you." That was pretty good . . . but a little late on the curve.

"You will not lose money, do not worry about finance, but a company you worked on the hardest on will be the least successful." That might have been the most accurate.

Bizarrely, near the end of the session she whispered that an African American woman "will want to hire you in business to use your name and thinking. It will be okay for a short time." It meant nothing to me then, but it would very soon.

Our destination was Inle Lake, up north in the jungle, one of the most beautiful spots I knew. Here I was going to detach, get present, and cruise the lake hoping to catch an epiphany. On Nigeen Lake in Kashmir in 1972, I had one. Maybe history could repeat on another Asian lake.

Inle Lake covers one hundred sixteen square kilometers and sits three thousand feet above sea level. The air is clear in a way you rarely see in the tropics. Only a few wisps of distant smoke from burning sugar fields marred the vivid blue sky. The flat surface of the water made perfect reflections of the cloud formations. Removed in remote Burma, away from the noise of the entertainment/industrial complex, the horizon began to clear. Inner peace was on the way. I began to let go of wishing I hadn't been fired. Viacom had been an epic chapter in my life, but I had nothing left to prove there. I was lucky to have lived it and was probably getting out just in time. My experience at MTV Networks was not likely to be duplicated. We built that place from the ground up. The idea of being dropped onto the top of another entertainment company, almost any kind of company, in a full-time role had little appeal right then. The passion and the pride of authorship would not be there.

I came to see that a better option would be to try something totally different, work on different projects with people I liked and not get locked into one endeavor, one office, or one boss. I wanted a more unstructured existence with the freedom to travel. More money was not important. Get into a new flow, be more useful, follow my heart. On the trip's last day, I stepped off my boat and the man at the dock told me there was a message for me up at the hotel. Someone had called? I'd never heard of anyone who got a call there. At the front office, they handed me a paper slip that said, "Oprah Winfrey."

I headed back to New York shed of a lot of burdens and ready to begin the next chapter. Plus, I owed Oprah a call.

The Queen of all Media picked up. "Oprah, is that you? It's Tom Freston. You left me a message at my hotel in Burma."

"Yes, I would just love to meet you, Tom," she said. "Why don't you come up to Montecito? I'll make you breakfast." Now, there was a royal invitation.

Montecito is ninety minutes up the coast from LA. It's a gorgeous mile-wide slice of lush California landscape sandwiched between the Pacific Ocean and the Santa Ynez Mountains. Flattered and curious, I headed up the 101 in the early morning. I was announced at her gatehouse and was ushered onto her forty-two-acre compound, "the Promised Land." There was a large lake with a fountain in the center spraying water high in the air. I pulled up to a sizable neo-Georgian homestead. Oprah was standing outside. Meeting Oprah was like meeting an old friend. I'm stating the obvious, but there cannot be many people easier to talk to than Oprah Winfrey.

She led me into the kitchen complex. A whole spread was laid out, and she went to work at the stove. Scrambled eggs with cheese and grits and a plate of beautifully sliced fruit were served. After some get-to-know-you chatter, often hilarious, she took me on a tour of the property. We rambled through her rose garden and gazed at the islands offshore, finishing at an enormous oak tree. "This is where I read and meditate."

I pointed out a property up on a mountain in the distance. "I'm building a home up there, Oprah. We are going to be neighbors."

Oprah's empire, Harpo ("Oprah" spelled backward) Productions, was based in Chicago at that time. It was a multimedia empire built around a single personality, with a magazine, a book club, a film unit, and the centerpiece—*The Oprah Winfrey Show*, her syndicated afternoon series. Harpo's current CEO was retiring, and Oprah wanted to know if I might be interested in the job. To say I did not have an innate feel for women's programming would be an understatement. I was flattered, but begged off. "Too early for me, Oprah." She understood.

But I made a new friend that day. Oprah told me in the cone of secrecy that she was interested in starting her own cable network. That would be a first I told her, a whole network wrapped around the ethos of a single person. I gave her the lay of the cable landscape and some challenges she'd be facing.

Fifteen months later, in January 2008, I was en route to Burma again, sitting in the bar of the Metropole Hotel in Hanoi. My cell phone rang. It was Oprah. She was about to announce an agreement with Discovery Communications to form a joint venture to create OWN: the Oprah Winfrey Network. She wanted to know if I would consider coming on as a consultant.

OWN was to debut in 70 million homes in 2009. Her track record in television was perfect. It took me a while to see that those expectations might be more of a burden than a blessing. My friend David Zaslav, who then ran Discovery Communications, called next. "We need you. It'll be fun," he said. I signed up.

Like any start-up, there were challenges. Oprah was prohibited from appearing on her network until her syndicated show ended in mid-2011. Basically, the Oprah Winfrey Network would have no Oprah for a year and a half. That would be like MTV starting and not having any music. As that sank in, the launch of OWN was pushed back. The network probably had no rougher development period than, say, FX or VH1 did in their early days—FX took eight years to get traction. VH1 took more than a decade to figure itself out. The difference was that it was Oprah. There was no forgiveness. She was expected to reach the moon on her first flight. I helped mostly on the business front. The programming work was handled by the close circle of women who ran her syndicated show. I felt bad that I wasn't more help to her. I'd worked with consultants, but never been one myself. I found it to be frustrating. If you don't have official responsibility for anything, you don't have the authority to tell people what to do. You can suggest and try to help solve problems, but no one has to listen.

Oprah quickly responded to the early criticisms, rolled up her sleeves, and the network soon found its feet. I thanked Oprah for the experience and moved on. My time working for her left me with enormous respect for her unique talent, intelligence, and unassailable work ethic.

But increasingly, my heart was overseas, in Afghanistan and Africa.

CHAPTER THIRTY-SEVEN

KABUL CALLING

"Fuck Sumner Redstone" had become a regular conversation starter from friends when I answered my phone. The words sounded slightly staticky this time, traveling from Afghanistan. It was mid-October. Saad Mohseni continued: "This is the best thing that could ever happen to you, Mr. Tom. Come back home. Help us." Of all the offers coming my way, an invitation to Kabul made the least sense and was the most tempting.

I was introduced to Saad in 2005 by Sarah Takesh, who had moved to Kabul soon after the Taliban were routed in 2001. She went to manufacture clothing and had heard that "some MTV guy" had done the same things thirty years earlier and tracked me down. She told me that her Afghan boyfriend, Saad, was "the Rupert Murdoch of Afghanistan," having started the first commercial radio and TV stations. I coughed up my Pellegrino at that.

After I left in 1978 life became an unrelenting nightmare for the Afghans. The Soviets invaded in 1979 and ten years of war followed. A million people were killed. Six million fled the country. Then came years of civil war between warring mujahideen groups. In 1996, Osama bin Laden and al-Qaeda rolled in from Sudan, the Taliban took over, and things went full-on medieval. Until 9/11 the West paid little attention. Post-9/11 the United States chased the Taliban out. Excitement and optimism were in high supply. There was a gusher of American money. Democracy was coming.

The international brigade of UN and NGO types and journalists, think tankers, bounty hunters, entrepreneurs, and thrill seekers descended on Kabul. Bars and restaurants opened amid the rubble; their doormen armed with AK-47s. The Elbow Room served Tora Bora specials and gin martinis for $10. A Frenchman from Phnom Penh opened L'Atmosphere, with a DJ by the swimming pool. Chinese entrepreneurs opened brothels with names like Crazy 8. A house that had been occupied by one of Osama bin Laden's wives was transformed into the Gandamack Lodge, a favorite with journalists. Marijuana grew in its central garden. The adrenalized "Kabul Bubble" was underway.

A steady stream of Western-trained and -educated Afghans returned to flood the ministries and other new government offices. Among this diaspora was Saad Mohseni. Saad was almost forty, clean-shaven with a full head of unruly dark hair that curled out like 1965 Bob Dylan's. We first met at Manhattan's Four Seasons hotel in January 2006. He shook my hand, grinning while holding my elbow with his other hand. There was something mischievous about the guy. His eyebrows arched above the thick black-framed glasses that dominated his face. Saad seemed cool and square at the same time. We would become best friends. Saad is the greatest optimist I ever met.

Saad's father had been an Afghan diplomat. When he was twelve, his family relocated to Japan, where his father was Deputy Ambassador. After the 1978 communist coup, his entire family of six was kicked out of the embassy onto the streets of Tokyo and demoted overnight from esteemed diplomats to homeless refugees. Eventually, they reached Australia, where Saad attended college.

When he returned to Afghanistan in 2002, he heard a commercial radio license was available. "I knew absolutely nothing about radio or business," he explained. He and his brothers secured $225,000 with a USAID grant. "Americans were doling out money." They formed Moby Media.

"Arman FM" burst onto the air in 2003, playing Shakira, Michael Jackson, and Ahmad Zahir, the Afghan Elvis. "It was as if we pushed a button, and the whole country lit up." The Taliban had allowed only one radio station, which featured nothing but prayer chants and edicts from the mullahs. Arman FM was sort of a "Good Morning Afghanistan," with a DJ named Massood Sanjer as the morning-drive guy spinning records, telling jokes, and taking calls.

Saad said, "Listeners could call in to complain about having to bribe someone. Massood would immediately conference in a government minister and get him to deal with it on the air. And he would!" The population plagued by endemic corruption and traumatized by twenty-five years of war and bans on anything fun—music, television, videos, dancing, kite flying, football, even chess—was ready to rock. Emboldened, Saad and his brothers pushed on. They got a TV license. They borrowed even more money and set out to launch two networks, one for each Afghan language group: Tolo in Dari and Lemar in Pashto.

Early on, they filled the schedule with foreign programs. Since few Afghans could read, their genius was to set up a dubbing facility with Afghan voice actors. Soon Afghans were watching Turkish and Indian soaps where buxom Indian ladies flirted with Hindu shopkeepers. They produced aspirational shows on home decor, cooking, even on how to shave, something the Taliban had banned. Comedians did topical humor late-night, à la *The Daily Show*.

After our lunch, I emailed Saad. "I'd like to introduce you to a fellow Australian, the real Rupert Murdoch, the next time you are in town. He'd love your story." We had lunch at Rupert's offices on Sixth Avenue. Saad and Rupert hit it off, two media moguls of different generations who had left Australia to seek fortune and influence. News Corporation would later make a series of investments in Moby Media. I brought Saad to Hollywood and turned him loose. He met Howard Gordon, producer of *Homeland* and *24*, who would help create and coproduce *Eagle Four*, Tolo's first venture into scripted programming. The series centered on an elite police unit that fought major crime and corruption. The premise was that these policemen were honest and effective, a revolutionary idea. It was such a hit that the actors would be swarmed like the Beatles when they went out shopping. *Eagle Four* cost a mere $30,000 an episode. That killed me.

Tolo's biggest hit was *Afghan Star*, a knock-off of *American Idol*. You knew the show was hot because the government didn't turn off the electricity until it was over. People in the countryside would gather around TV sets connected to car batteries. It brought music back center stage to the ravaged country. The finalists for the show campaigned all through Afghanistan.

Viewers voted via texts. The singers got more votes than candidates in the presidential elections.

Saad and his team may have done more to transform Afghanistan than all the diplomats and soldiers combined. For the first time, the population was connected to the outside world and to each other. He built an ambitious and credible news operation, Tolo News, which morphed into a separate twenty-four-hour network and became the country's gold standard for current events and accurate information. As Saad explained, "In the US, news is a hobby. In Afghanistan, you have to watch the news to survive."

A purposeful agenda promoting social change was baked into the company's mission. Gender equality and tolerance were at the top of the list. Simple things like having female news readers sit next to males sent a powerful signal. Moby became one of the country's most successful private companies, with over one thousand employees. Free media became one of the big success stories in the new Afghanistan, helping to nurture a more tolerant and sophisticated population.

Saad developed many enemies. He regularly received death threats and began to travel with a retinue of gunmen. His reporters were continually arrested, or even murdered, and there were many court cases to fight. He was under constant pressure to ban shows like the Indian soap operas and *Afghan Star*. His response was "These poor people have been starved of any kind of entertainment and deserve some joy in their lives. Those who are offended can turn it off."

For me, going back was the perfect circle. I had ended up at MTV because I had been pushed out of Afghanistan. Now that I had been pushed out of Viacom, Afghanistan was calling me back. I thought, *This is my purpose.* There was no question in my mind. I was returning to Kabul.

After accepting Saad's invitation, I began to wonder if I had romanticized my years in Kabul to the point where returning was bound to be a disappointment. Kabul was now a crowded city of 5 million, surrounded by refugee camps. Many places were in shambles, and it was a war zone.

In 2007, Dubai was the main gateway to Afghanistan. Flights left from a small, worn-down, one-story building, quarantined in a corner of the huge airport, Terminal 2, nicknamed "the Terror Terminal." The signboard read: "Kandahar, Mogadishu, Khartoum, Karachi, Tehran, Basra, Peshawar, Mashhad, Quetta, Kabul." This was the departure lounge to the least popular places in the world. I took a seat amid tall Pashtun tribesmen lugging burlap sacks, beefy security guys, and nervous-looking Filipino guest workers. Nobody was checking for knives or guns.

My flight was on Kam Air, soon to be rated one of the "world's unsafest airlines," then blacklisted by the US for bulk opium smuggling. My seatmate was the young Iranian Ambassador, a friendly man who was fascinated by my youthful exploits in the sybaritic Iran of the 1970s. Two hours later, the spectacular vista of Kabul came into view. It was about the only thing that hadn't changed.

Saad flew with me. Right before we landed, he told me that he might be arrested by the Attorney General upon arrival. *Off to an exciting start*, I thought. At the bottom of the stairs, we were hustled into an SUV waiting on the tarmac. "Give this man your passport and luggage tag, Mr. Tom," Saad said. "You'll get them later." There would be no immigration for me. And no arrest. After we exited the airport security perimeter, the driver stopped, rolled down his window, and someone passed him two AK-47s and a pistol. Another SUV full of bodyguards followed us. My adrenaline revved up.

The main route from the airport to the city had been closed off because it ran past the new American Embassy, a grim high-rise fortress adjacent to buildings with armor plating on their balconies. But the road was opened for us. Gates were raised and lowered as we drove past sandbags, guardhouses, blast walls, and gleaming strings of concertina wire. Security was run by muscle-bound private American contractors from the Armor Group.

Inside Kabul, there were no longer carefree hippie girls in sheepskin coats giggling their way down the streets. At almost every corner, Afghan soldiers manned jeeps with .50-caliber machine guns or wielded Kalashnikovs. This was Kabul's "Ring of Steel."

Saad took me to my hotel, the Kabul Serena, on the site of the old Kabul Hotel, the former meeting spot of the elite. In 1979, the American ambassador was kidnapped by militants, brought here, and murdered. Rebuilt, the new Serena was a five-star Fort Knox. Despite the elaborate security, it would be attacked more than any hotel on the planet. The Taliban would regularly sneak in and kill everyone they could. Not fans of spas, they'd often head there first to shoot a masseuse. The joke was that rates always dropped after an attack.

My room had a minibar (no alcohol) and overlooked a garden. There was a local magazine on the table, *Afghan Scene*, a peculiar publication with pictures featuring beautiful women at local soirees. *This war zone had parties?* I wondered. Thai and Mexican restaurants ran ads. The articles had odd headlines: "Paratroopers, Parties, and Parasites" and "Love in the Land of Cholera." One advertisement warned: "Your Convoy Hits a Mine. You Develop a Chest Pain in the Middle of the Night. Who Will Respond?" It was an ad for a "we go anywhere" medevac service: sort of *ER* meets *Mad Max*.

I asked Saad to take me on a spin around the city's clogged streets. A permanent layer of smog was now settled over Kabul, blotting out the mountains. The roomy old Russian Volgas were gone. It was a Toyota town now. They had a helluva salesman. Even the Taliban drove them. Kabul was battle-scarred, but it bristled with activity. The bazaars were crowded, and there seemed to be construction everywhere. Billboards hawked cell phones, bank cards, and energy drinks. But every restaurant, hotel, and storefront I remembered was gone. The old restaurant at the Seasons Hotel was now two shops that sold toilets. Every store seemed to have its own small, gasoline-powered generator running outside. It sounded like an orchestra of lawn mowers.

The Soviets had destroyed Kabul's leafy boulevards, chopping down trees to deny sniper cover or for firewood. Trash was piled high on street corners. The Kabul River had become a garbage pit, dry and dense with refuse and plastic bags. Drug addicts, including raggedy old men, smoked heroin through straws, huddled underneath bridges. Most of the men wore Western clothes now, but many women still wore burkas. Widowed beggars with children in tow squatted by the roadsides. Children chased each other in the street with toy rifles.

I wanted to wander down Chicken Street, but Saad didn't think it was safe. A foreigner had been killed there recently in a suicide bombing. I pushed back, and he had a gunman accompany us. It looked like the exact same merchandise as thirty years ago: antique weapons, woven carpets, wooden furniture, lapis lazuli boxes. Among the few new items were Soviet military medals. I wondered if American medals would someday appear in the windows, relics of another failed invasion. New were "war rugs" featuring tanks and grenade launchers. Some bore messages in fractured English. "Terrorism Rowted 2001." Groups of small, ragged boys hawked postcards, including one with an image of a Taliban tank firing upon the Buddhas of Bamiyan.

Many beautiful old Kabul homes in the Share-Nau neighborhood were being torn down to build new monstrosities. "Narco villas," explained Saad, describing the grotesque, mirrored, candy-colored, multistoried mansions that resembled a mad baker's wedding cakes. These were the fortified castles of Afghanistan's new elite: warlords, drug lords, and corrupt government officials. In the brand-new neighborhood of Sherpur, formerly wide-open grassy plains with breathtaking mountain views where we rode horses, the government had distributed land to cabinet ministers, the mayor, militia commanders, and various warlords. Built from the proceeds of drug money and corruption, seventy-five "Poppy Palaces" sat one on top of another. Some had fifty rooms, with space for thirty vehicles within the walls. The international community, always an enabler, rented quite a few of these monstrosities as homes for news organizations, diplomatic residences, and guesthouses. You could pay up to $100,000 per month to live in a damp, dismal, moldy mansion. On one trip I toured them with a real estate agent, pretending to be a renter for an article for *Vanity Fair*. Some had pools and bars in the basement.

Back in my hotel room I collapsed in a chair, took a swig of the Johnnie Walker Black I'd smuggled in, and exhaled. Through the window I heard the muezzin, the call to prayer, and I briefly caught the sound of the city I knew forty years ago.

Other changes were exhilarating. When the Taliban fell in 2001, Afghanistan had only eleven thousand phone lines and zero TV stations. By 2007, there were 30 million cell phones and seventy-five television stations. Afghanistan's media was rated as the most independent and liberal in the region, ahead of even Turkey and India. Journalistic independence was enshrined in the new constitution. Moby Media's Tolo TV and its companion Pashto-language network, Lemar TV, were the market leaders with a combined seventy-plus market share.

Tolo had almost zero interaction with the US government or military. It was managed and run almost entirely by Afghans. I'd walk through the offices and studios and see Afghan men and women, twenty- and thirtysomethings, working easily together, joking, just like their counterparts in other countries. I thought I was watching the future of the nation. Saad asked me if I wanted to help as a mentor, come on as a consultant, and join the board for Moby Media. It was an easy yes. I had the skills. I felt this was my purpose. This is what I knew. "Just cover my airfare." I was a Rip van Winkle, thrilled to be back. When I told my wife, Kathy, that I was getting four free round-trip tickets to Kabul a year, she asked if second prize was five free trips.

I quickly learned that expat life in Kabul was a life in the fast lane. People were always on edge, full of adrenaline. The drinking was heavy. The Gandamack Lodge dinner special was "three courses and five drinks." Almost everyone seemed to smoke cigarettes, and despite a dispiriting male-female ratio, everyone was hooking up. Women would admit, "A five is a ten in Kabul." Hashish was everywhere. I imagined this Kabul as the 2000s version of 1960s Saigon, thunderheads slowly closing in.

I pitched Saad's story to Ken Auletta at the *New Yorker*. He went to Kabul and in 2010 he wrote "The Networker," an article that won the prestigious Mirror Award. Auletta described Saad as "a gregarious man with a politician's habits." He would become one of Afghanistan's most articulate champions. He frequented the White House, the State Department, and was a regular at the Halifax International Security Forum, various Aspen conferences, and Hollywood parties.

CHAPTER THIRTY-EIGHT

ADVENTURES IN VICELAND

After Viacom, I wasn't always abroad. In December 2010 I was in Brooklyn. Shane Smith waved his hand, motioning me to his table in the Hotel Delmano, a low-lit hipster saloon in Williamsburg. Three shots of tequila were arranged in front of an empty seat. "Say hello to your three little friends," Shane announced. "Drink those, and we'll talk."

Shane, the forty-one-year-old cofounder and CEO of VICE, wanted to rekindle our relationship. A bear-sized man with extensive tattoos across his torso and up and down his legs, a salt-and-pepper beard, and stringy long dark hair swept back over his red Irish face, Shane was complicated . . . a punk, a showman, a shaman, a sweetheart, a blowhard, an intellectual of weird shit, and a family man. He was also a man of large appetites, which sometimes got the best of him.

Invariably charismatic, he had assembled a small cult of bearded young men around him, who wore the coveted twenty-four-karat VICE gold ring on their fingers. They had convinced each other that they were going to turn VICE into the next big media player. One of these men was Eddy Moretti, Shane's "creative director." Like Shane, Eddy was Canadian, a sweet, wiry hipster who looked like Vladimir Lenin with a black fedora cocked on his head.

I met these two characters in April 2006, when I was still CEO of Viacom. Spike Jonze, the film director, had arranged the meeting. Spike had a great eye for odd talent. Years earlier, he introduced Johnny Knoxville to MTV. Johnny became the nucleus of MTV's *Jackass* crew, a very successful physical comedy series that spawned several hit movies.

Shane and Eddy ran *VICE* magazine, an edgy cultural monthly that originated in Montreal and gave away a million-plus free copies every month in boutiques, head shops, and skateboard stores in more than twenty countries. VICE began as VOICE—"The Voice of Montreal"—and mostly covered the Canadian music scene. Soon, they dropped the "O" and pivoted to articles like "The VICE Guide to Shagging Muslims" and hired prostitutes to write sex-advice columns. They moved to New York in the late nineties, a boom time for edgy media. (One of their original Canadian partners, Gavin McInnes, would soon part ways and descend into some far-right rabbit holes, eventually starting the neo-fascist Proud Boys in 2016.)

Shane and Eddy wanted to start a digital project with MTV, but had the impression that MTV was "scared of them." Spike thought a meeting with me could break the logjam. Shane and Eddy strolled into my fifty-second-floor office smiling and looking nervous. I had them sit on the couch. Spike described Shane as a "poor man's Hemingway," a curious and audacious adventurer. VICE, he said, was going everywhere in search of new and unusual stuff . . . smart and stupid. They were "the truffle pig of cool." Shane would turn out to be one of the greatest salespeople I'd ever meet, maybe the greatest bullshitter, too, but bullshit and all, he was charming.

From the edge of the couch, Shane pitched me: they were proven storytellers, the world was in turmoil, they were in all the hot spots, and they could produce quality video inexpensively. Eddy pulled out a DVD and flipped it on my coffee table like it was the ace of spades: *The VICE Guide to Travel.* The cover was a photo of a completely tricked-out jingle truck from Afghanistan. Maybe they had studied my history and knew about my days in Kabul. Maybe it was serendipity. Either way, it worked. I popped the disc into my DVD player.

There were three or four segments. First was a silly but mesmerizing report on Shane hunting down "radioactive wild boars" with an automatic rifle in the "forbidden zone" around Chernobyl, the doomed nuclear reactor in Ukraine. He seemed inebriated, shooting while holding a drink in the irradiated landscape. Between drinking and shooting, he also seemed to be hitting on his rifle-toting female companion, who, he said, worked with him. Next came a segment featuring pygmies in the Congo. The elevator pitch might have been "programming by drunks to amuse stoners."

The next segment featured Shane's partner Suroosh Alvi in Darra, an infamous little burg on the lawless Afghan-Pakistan border. I'd been to Darra decades earlier. Back then, bricks of hashish with gold stamps on them and baggies of opium, as well as an arsenal of guns sat in shop windows. Darra's claim to fame was "bespoke firearms," made by Pashtun gunsmiths who could duplicate any gun: AK-47s, German Lugers, and old British rifles. Need a grenade launcher? Darra was the place. On the screen Suroosh, wearing a flat Afghan pakol hat and a flak jacket, popped up and started firing an AK-47, looking like an al-Qaeda jihadi.

I was impressed. Odd for sure, but each segment was framed with a wry, comic presentation. Edited in a lo-fi way with a reportorial voice and style, they had a wacko authenticity. Nobody was doing anything like this, making gonzo stories in faraway places on low budgets. VICE presented itself as a daring guerrilla operation with a sense of humor—the bastard sons of Hunter S. Thompson. "I want to be the next MTV," said Shane. "I want to conquer the world." The scent of bullshit was rolling in, but no one else was coming into my office saying that.

MTV folks seemed incapable of producing anything for low prices anymore. Some of them had agents. They were making shows like *My Super Sweet 16* and *Laguna Beach*. It was no wonder they had resisted these wild bozos. Maybe I needed to bring in an outside rebel unit. YouTube had just launched. Shane saw that as the opportunity of a lifetime. Someone had to make good content for it. He insisted that internet video would transform VICE into a global powerhouse. VICE would move the young international audience that already loved the magazine onto digital platforms and would expand their numbers by multiples.

"What else have you got?" I asked.

"Nothing," said Shane. "That's the only video we've done."

"One video? That's it?"

"Yeah, but we're onto something big and we want to make more. MTV and VICE would be a perfect fit."

Shane was hitting a nerve. MTV had come up against multiple brick walls in our attempts to join the digital world. Perhaps these guys could be a good low-cost online video source. We ultimately agreed to a joint venture, VICE Broadcast Services, or VBS.tv, separate from VICE's magazine business. We'd be fifty-fifty partners. Five months later I got fired and took off for Burma, Oprah, and Afghanistan. Four years after that I got an email out of the blue from Shane: "My beautiful baby boy. When are we loving again. Drinkie??" Curious, I headed to Brooklyn.

After I guzzled down my "three little friends," we got to business. "Philippe Dauman is a nasty stiff," said Shane. "He didn't get us, so I just bought the fucker out."

"How'd you pull that off?"

"I made myself out to be more trouble than I was worth to him," Shane replied.

"Ahh, the *Fish Called Wanda* strategy we call that. It can be effective."

Shane had bought back MTV's half of VBS for a mere $3 million and he was now a free man in Brooklyn. By the time we met in Williamsburg, Shane had more than delivered on his vision. VICE had evolved into accomplished video storytellers. They had a hot website, a growing library of videos, and a suite of YouTube channels that racked up millions of views with the weirdest shit you could imagine. Shane had become the face of VICE, a tattooed hipster Walter Cronkite. Eddy chimed in, "We made a movie, too, *Heavy Metal in Baghdad*, about the music scene in wartime Iraq. It premiered at the Toronto Film Festival. We have other films in development, too, dude."

We went to dinner at another neighborhood haunt, where Shane and Eddy were greeted like heroes. VICE, they told me, was the largest employer in Williamsburg. Shane immediately ordered extremely expensive wine, a recurring theme when he dined. Then he made his new pitch: "Join us, Tommy boy. Get richer! How about making millions? We are hot and need some heft. Got to raise some money and take this thing to outer space." I was skeptical, but Shane plowed on. "You know everyone. You can help introduce us and connect us. You could help us raise money. You can be a consultant. I'm setting up a board. You can be on it. I'll give you a piece of the company. It's all right up your alley."

He wasn't wrong. I had once run a very hungry, very young creative company full of hustlers. These VICE guys were talented, but I was wary of being an adviser or consultant. I could also see that Shane was a mercurial dude. VICE might just explode.

"Are you ready for the big show now, Tommy Gun?" Shane asked. They pushed me into a black car and we rocketed over the Manhattan Bridge to the Box, an infamous downtown club known for wild, sexy burlesque shows. When we arrived, you would have thought the president of the United States had pulled up. Shane and Eddy were underground celebrities. Doormen came out to meet us, then strong-armed us through the scrum to a ringside table just below the stage. A three-foot-tall bottle of Grey Goose and an ice bucket awaited us. A naked man in a dog collar was being led around by a dominatrix. She rammed a plug up his butt with a poodle tail attached. He wagged it. The crowd went wild. I leaned over and told them, "I love show business."

That was the opening night of my ten-year journey with VICE. I did my due diligence. They were shaky, a bit mad, and poorly organized, but they were fun and were filling a gap in the market with something new and brash. There was a bit of the early MTV mayhem, the sky's-the-limit feeling with a crusader energy about them. I signed up, invested some money, and VICE entered my post-Viacom hodgepodge of a portfolio.

When I joined up with VICE, they were one of the largest and fastest-growing digital publishers in the world. BuzzFeed, Refinery29, and Vox couldn't compare; VICE would more than double their revenues every year. They had about 750 employees, thousands of contributors, and thirty-four offices all over the place. Blue-chip players like Dell, Coke, Intel, and Anheuser-Busch wanted in. One day, Shane brought in a $45 million piece of business with Intel. They were going to sponsor a traveling exhibit called *The Creators Project*, which Shane had dreamed up. Truly money for nothing.

They built a suite of specialized channels resembling the MTV Networks model: "Motherboard," a respected tech news source, "Noisey" a music site deep into the new music scene with acts like the Yeah Yeah Yeahs and Florence & the Machine, and "Munchies," a food channel for hipsters. Their hit show, *Fuck, That's Delicious*, was hosted by an obese, raucous rapper named Action Bronson, who looked like a holy man with type 2 diabetes.

A separate brand strategy and creative services agency called "Virtue" sold "millennial expertise" and directed new clients to VICE's ad-supported channels. Virtue became a talent magnet attracting respected next-gen marketing professionals.

VICE was located inside a series of converted warehouses in low-rise Williamsburg. Hundreds of tattooed, flannel-clad twentysomethings milled around, giving it a bit of an ant farm vibe. People crammed at long tables across from each other, cheek to bearded jowl, peering into laptops. In the parlance of the day, this was a "content farm." I'd fantasize it was a nineteenth-century factory, the laptops morphing into sewing machines.

In 2011, I introduced Shane to Raine, a new-media merchant bank run by my friends Joe Ravitch and Jeff Sine. Raine invested $25 million and brought in WPP, the British advertising and PR company, for another $25 million. VICE formed a partnership with William Morris Endeavor. VICE's valuation was set at $200 million; I negotiated a deal for 2 percent of the company in options. Full disclosure: I went on to become a senior adviser at Raine. It was raining gigs for me.

Shane, Eddy, and Suroosh had brilliantly positioned themselves as the gatekeepers to the Williamsburg hipster aesthetic, a demo advertisers and established media companies coveted, but did not understand. The VICE crew sold the promise of connecting old brands to a youth population in trucker hats. It was as if the Fabulous Furry Freak Brothers had set up a media company in Haight-Ashbury in 1967 and invited all the squares on Madison Avenue to pay them to translate hippie into English.

VICE's calling card was VICE News. It was Shane's passion and he was good at smelling a story and piecing it together. I brought Shane and his crew to see Richard Plepler, president of HBO. Would he be interested in a series? I asked. Richard jumped at the idea. He enlisted veteran journalist Fareed Zakaria and comedian Bill Maher as executive producers, then recommended the very bright Josh Tyrangiel to show-run. Josh had cut his teeth working for me at MTV. They would attract a cadre of very talented young journalists.

VICE News on HBO went on air in 2013. It was a weekly half-hour series that covered provocative stories that had gone unreported. HBO called it "groundbreaking news from the edge." The HBO team really upped VICE's production skills. It was a big hit out of the box. Suddenly, Shane was famous almost everywhere. Shane worked his ass off making these shows, bouncing from Afghanistan to Antarctica and winning Emmys and Peabody Awards. *VICE News on HBO* documented neo-Nazis in Charlottesville, Dennis Rodman on a romp with Kim Jong Un in North Korea, collapsing glaciers in Greenland, floating garbage islands in the Pacific, crackheads living in the sewers of Bogotá, teenage suicide bombers. Shane interviewed President Obama about America's criminal justice system—from inside a prison. VICE had the media elite chattering. The HBO series went on for six high-profile years. Two years in, they added a daily *VICE News Tonight*.

Shane had started out wanting to be the next Hunter S. Thompson. TV stardom made him the new John Belushi. At one Christmas party at an Armenian club in Brooklyn, he dressed up as Santa, got on the stage, and rolled out a trash barrel. "I've got one million dollars in cash in this garbage can," he announced to the lit-up crowd. Dollar bills were flowing over the top. "We've got a party to start. It's bonus time! Line up! Let's see who of you has been naughty and who's been nice."

He called out names. People would walk onstage, and he'd hand over a fat wad of cash and pat them on the back. He'd repeat on the microphone, "Now, I don't want any of you going outside and calling your drug dealer with this cash. We got our eyes on you." I thought I had run an insane asylum in *my* day.

Shane would call me his mentor and I did try, but he was a difficult protégé. He always said he wanted advice, but he didn't really. Like Napoleon attacking Russia, one day in 2015, Shane announced that VICE would launch its own cable network, VICELAND. I advised him against it. "Linear cable networks are all in decline now, Shane." He did it anyway. It would have been easier to find a moon rock on a Brooklyn sidewalk than to talk him out of it. "TV is where the money is, Tommy Boy." The man who hated the establishment and dissed television as passé now wanted a cable network, just as they were going out of style. I also told him he was hiring inept leaders. He didn't listen.

Nonetheless, Shane was always entertaining. Sometimes we'd travel together, and other times our paths intersected. I'd be in Turkey, and suddenly, he'd be there on a boat on the Bosporus. We went through the Panama Canal together and swam in a huge dolphin pod eighty kilometers off the coast of Costa Rica.

He could not stop hunting for bigger and bigger deals. A steady caravan of black cars from Manhattan rolled into Williamsburg disgorging media executives. They'd march into the ant farm slack-jawed, then upstairs to the "Bear Room," the conference room with a stuffed grizzly bear in the corner. After soaking up the local color, seeing Shane perform, and watching one blistering tape after another, they'd retreat across the Brooklyn Bridge.

Jeff Bewkes came. Barry Diller, David Zaslav, and Bob Iger, too. And Rupert Murdoch. "Global success," Rupert tweeted, then invested $90 million. Rupert's son James became a good friend of Shane's and a solid addition to the board. TCV, a Silicon Valley venture firm, invested $250 million. A&E Networks invested another $250 million. Nancy Dubuc, A&E's CEO, joined the board. Kevin Mayer, VICE's champion at Disney, invested $400 million and went on the board, too. It was starting to feel like the musical *The Producers*. Where exactly was all this money going?

Shane moved to a new $23 million mansion, "Villa Ruchello," in Santa Monica, three thousand miles from a company based in New York. The trophy home was featured in the *Wall Street Journal Magazine*. They chronicled his wine cellar and "onyx-walled" separate "drinking room." The piece touted his net worth as "estimated at $1 billion." A photo showed Shane floating on a huge pink flamingo in a pool with his two beautiful daughters. The article received a venomous reaction from his cohort of lowly paid content farmers in Brooklyn. And nothing but derision from the Hollywood establishment. There's an old adage that "Hollywood always wins." That perfect record would continue.

Stepping up to run the shop in his absence, Shane brought in a vastly under-equipped executive, James Schwab, to be co-president next to Andrew Creighton, a long-time VICE veteran who was sole president. The demotion of Creighton was demoralizing and became destructive. James was a respected white-shoe corporate attorney from Paul, Weiss, Rifkind. He was smart but had no experience in running any part of a media company. The senior team was mystified. I was shocked. His expertise was employment contracts, and he negotiated a great one for himself. He escaped with a $45 million payout, the only VICE executive to get anything when the boat sank.

Every January, VICE held a board meeting at the Bellagio Hotel in Vegas during the big Consumer Electronics Show. Shane loved Vegas and was a high roller. Casinos would send private jets to bring him to the tables. I had watched him repeatedly commandeer an entire blackjack table playing every spot for $250,000 a hand and casually flip the waitress a $1,000 chip for bringing him a double vodka ("special water," he called it). A few times I saw him win millions. . . . Impressive, but probably not a good habit for a CEO. In retrospect, I ignored many a warning sign.

At the CES, VICE rented huge suites to make presentations to its biggest clients. Afterward, Shane hosted a joyful, wine-soaked board dinner in the private room at the Bellagio's Prime Steakhouse. The wines he chose included Domaine de la Romanée-Conti (DRC), the most coveted burgundy of all. It was $25,000 a bottle. "I'm trying to corner the market," he once told me. Shane financed these dinners with his gambling winnings.

It was a hot dinner to crash. People like David Zaslav and Martin Sorrell, CEO of WPP, would pop in to join the action. Revelers packed the room to swill down Shane's no-expense-spared vino. Waiters would simply ask, "Red or white?" In 2015, the *New York Post* and the *New York Times* reported that "VICE CEO Shane Smith splurged on a $300,000 dinner in Las Vegas." Shane whispered to me, "It actually cost five hundred eighty thousand dollars."

In September 2015, at the peak of this frenzy, VICE missed its moment. Disney was already an investor and Kevin Mayer, VICE's champion at Disney, convinced Bob Iger to offer to buy VICE outright for $3.5 billion with a small earn-out. They were ready to take it to their board. It was an astronomical sum. Shane, though, demurred. He wanted something closer to $4.0 billion which, with his shares, would make him a billionaire. Disney balked. "Let's revisit in a year and see if you make your 2016 numbers."

Ben Sherwood, then president of ABC News, came in for a "kick the tires" dinner and got a bit spooked. Next came Iger. He was invited for a "get-to-know-you" lunch at VICE's Brooklyn headquarters. Rather than getting a couple of turkey sandwiches and shooting the shit, Shane brought over Michael White, the celebrity chef from Marea, a Michelin-starred Manhattan restaurant, to prepare the meal. Expensive wines were offered. Bob is neither a high roller nor a day drinker. He got cold feet. *What the hell kind of underground hipster outfit offers pricey French burgundies at lunch?* he wondered. "VICE is in my rearview mirror," he told me. An offer never materialized. Bob dodged a bullet, although VICE might well have prospered in a larger media company.

Investors, employees, and option holders (like me) were aghast. This was to be payday. Now there was nothing. Without the deal, VICE needed to raise about $450 million in working capital. Shane tasked his bankers at Raine to shake the bushes. Multiple offers surfaced at valuations in the $4.6 to $4.8 billion range, but Shane and Schwab demanded a valuation over $5.0 billion. There were two reasons for that: Shane wanted Iger to feel he missed some kind of boat and, of course, he'd walk away a billionaire, at least on paper.

In 2017, they finally managed to wrangle the $450 million from TPG, a tough-as-nails Texas-based private equity firm at a staggering $5.2 billion valuation. The catch was that this huge new tranche of loot was essentially a loan that compounded at a sky-high rate of 12 percent. The deal became a ticking time bomb that put the company in a death spiral ultimately dooming it. Much of the money was squandered on nonsensical ventures like a direct-to-consumer business. Not that the VICE crew noticed. There's a country song from the movie *Crazy Heart* that says, "Funny how fallin' feels like flyin', for a little while."

The shame of all this was that VICE had attracted a sizable and dedicated creative cadre of spirited young men and women who were fearless and anxious to do good work. But they were aboard a ship with no one at the captain's wheel. Just before Christmas 2017, at the height of the #MeToo era, the *New York Times* stuffed VICE's stocking full of coal with a front-page piece, "At Vice, Cutting-Edge Media and Allegations of Old-School Sexual Harassment." Bang.

VICE's bad-boy culture had finally caught up with them just as they were trying to become more earnest and legitimate. The improprieties were not as pervasive as the story claimed, but it wasn't good. Some execs got fired and many large clients ran for cover. Morale hit rock bottom. Shane remained untouched, but moved himself further upstairs to "Executive Chairman." He formed a Diversity and Inclusion Advisory Board and smartly had both Gloria Steinem and famed lawyer Roberta Kaplan join it.

Nancy Dubuc, a widely admired executive and board member, someone I had once tried to get Oprah to hire, became the new VICE CEO in 2018. VICE became healthier and more diverse and employees were better compensated. I left the board in 2019, just before the ever-fickle media winds began changing direction again. The legacy linear cable networks were melting icebergs. Now it was the digital publishers turn. BuzzFeed, Vox, and VICE had all cleverly dominated the chaos of the internet for a decade, but they were beginning to wilt.

Although the digital advertising pie was gigantic, bigger than television's, by 2018 most of it went to two companies, Google and Facebook. These two behemoths grabbed 85 to 95 percent of the money. They offered advertisers home-by-home targeting. No one could compete. In spring 2023, BuzzFeed News shut down. A few weeks later VICE filed for bankruptcy protection.

The VICE story is a lesson for young start-ups. They captured a cultural moment perfectly with a new and authentic voice. Few youth brands endure. Hipness evaporates without regular reinvention. Coming out of bankruptcy, a chastened VICE, now owned by Fortress, a private equity outfit, is trying to reemerge in a much smaller configuration focusing on their studio business, a production company selling shows and series to the streamers.

VICE's collapse left many lost dreams and fortunes between the founders, the journalists, and the investors. I still feel affection for Shane Smith and continue to root for him. It sure was fun for a while. Shane had good intentions. He really did want to inform and empower young people. Rodney Dangerfield once said, "You can wait so long for your ship to come in that your pier collapses."

CHAPTER THIRTY-NINE

LIFE DURING WARTIME

Saad never lost faith in the new Afghanistan till the end. The ultimate insider, he had the special ability to move seamlessly among generals, diplomats, producers, warlords, journalists, businessmen, artists, and everyone up and down the Afghan political ladder. People wanted his information, advice, and perspective. Text him, and you'd hear right back. His brashness created no shortage of enemies. He was a marked man from Pakistan's ISI to the Iranians, the Taliban, and many Afghan ministers. "Who have you yet to piss off?" I'd ask. He'd shrug.

Being at Saad's side, I met virtually every mover and shaker in the country and heard firsthand snatches of what people thought was really going on, starting with the American ambassador William Wood, known as "Chemical Bill" for his burning desire to defoliate the Afghan opium fields (he had Columbia's coca crop poisoned when he was ambassador there). I introduced myself to Wood at a dinner party saying how I was excited to reconnect with the country. He took a sip of his scotch, sucked on his cigarette, then sneered, "There's nothing good here," and walked off. The next US ambassador, Karl Eikenberry, who arrived in 2009, loved the country, but I could see he was worried. He solicited Saad's perspective and listened closely. He craved outside information. Unlike other countries, most of our diplomats were rarely allowed to leave the embassy grounds. They were stationed in a country they couldn't see.

In 2008, General Dan McNeill, then head of the NATO-led coalition, was happy to tell me that "the Taliban were on the run." In 2014, General

Joseph Dunford told me over drinks at Saad's house (where he arrived in a heavily armed convoy) that he was especially "optimistic" about the future. The newly trained Afghan National Security Forces "meant business."

Afghan leaders often had different perspectives. In 2015, I went on a hiking trip in the mountains surrounding the Panjshir Valley with Amrullah Saleh, the former head of the notorious NDS, Afghanistan's FBI/CIA. Winding up narrow mountain trails with his heavily armed security detail, I fantasized I was on the hunt for bin Laden. Saleh told me the situation was "hopeless" and that "Karzai was a fifth columnist."

Zamarai Kamgar, the US-blacklisted owner of Kam Air, would invite us to down chilled Grey Goose shots with him in the basement of his narcovilla. He had a bar and a swimming pool there. He'd regale us with stories of hunting rare game speeding along in his Land Rover, standing up through his sun roof with an AK-47. Meanwhile, his airplanes were busy nonstop ferrying suitcases of currency and opium out of the country.

Moby's revenue increased every year, as did its profits. By 2021, Moby had built up a healthy roster of 225 advertisers just in Afghanistan. We expanded operations into Pakistan, Yemen, India, Iraq, and Ethiopia. I fell heavily for Yemen and travelled deeply there, even camping amongst the otherworldly landscapes of Socotra Island. Ethiopia was a wonderful surprise. There was no war there, and in Addis Ababa there was music every night. We partnered with a creative group of young Ethiopians to create Kana TV, the first private Amharic language network. Since there weren't any Amharic shows on satellite, we saw our opening. We hired sixty Ethiopian voice actors, sent them to Kabul for training, then bought rights to the most popular Arab shows and voiced them into Amharic. When Kana launched, it lit up the nation. If you told someone you worked at Kana, they went ballistic with joy. It was the same sensation I'd experienced with MTV in the early '80s. In 2019, we sold the network to Canal+.

For a while we operated a satellite network that beamed into Iran called "Farsi 1." Its biggest hit was a dubbed Colombian soap opera featuring busty women in sexy outfits. It became so popular that viewers named their children after the characters. The Iranian government was horrified. This was a "foreign invasion" meant to "destroy the chastity and morals of young Iranians to have sex and drink alcohol." MTV redux. To protect his citizens, Iran's President Ahmadinejad announced he'd blacklist any company that dared advertise on Farsi1, which included the Singapore Tourism Board and local ski resorts in the Alborz Mountains. They all pulled out. So did we.

But Moby was primarily a mini-Afghan conglomerate, its offices and studios squeezed into a narrow lane in Wazir Akbar Khan near the presidential palace and many embassies. Moby eventually took over every building on both sides of the lane. The atmosphere reminded me of MTV's start-up offices in Mumbai and Shanghai. With its success, Moby became a target. The Taliban lobbed in missiles and the place started to resemble Fort Apache. Sandbagged gun positions equipped with grenade launchers flanked Moby's entrance. Beefy South Africans manned the gates. Saad put together a contingent of uniformed gunmen from the Panjshir Valley for his personal security detail. "They are the most loyal," he told me. No one knew Saad's movements in advance.

I brought in two MTV alums I loved to help mentor and create systems for Tolo, Cyrus Oshidar from India and Cristian Jofre from Chile. I funded a scholarship program to send several Tolo producers to LA every summer for a ten-week program at USC's School of Cinematic Arts to improve their skills.

After thirty-five years of war, Afghanistan's only heroes were mujahideen fighters. There were no film stars, no pop stars, no sports stars. So in 2022, Tolo set out to create Afghanistan's first professional sports stars with the Afghan Premier League (APL), a football (soccer) league with eight teams. It was no easy endeavor.

At this point, eleven years in, the United States had spent hundreds of billions of dollars on the military. You had to wonder why someone in Washington didn't think to invest in more things like a sports league that would give people pleasure, make them feel that life was improving, and offer them something to talk about other than who's killing whom. Popular culture and entrepreneurship are skills Americans know a lot about.

The league was financed by Moby, along with some cell phone sponsorship and a smidge from the US embassy. Saad and I visited the State Department in Washington to plead for more. "It cost one-point-four million dollars just to keep *one* Marine on the ground for a year," we pleaded. "Just two hundred fifty thousand dollars of that could get you a lot for your money." No dice. It was all guns, little butter.

Nevertheless, football fever took off. Sixty percent of Afghans had access to television and the players became new heroes—buff, polite young men in bright uniforms with gelled hair. The TV production was state-of-the-art: ten cameras, slo-mo, instant replay, sharp graphics with stats, and lively announcers. A control room was rigged up in a shipping container outside a new stadium, where five thousand fans could comfortably watch.

I loved going to the games. Kabul was always tense, clogged with blast walls, soldiers at most intersections, and endless sirens. Here security was sound and Afghans were free in a new stadium. There was happiness and normality. I thought this was an irreversible turning point. The simple joys of a football match were hard to deny. Would the people allow the Taliban to just walk back in and wipe it out? I did not think so. I was wrong.

I felt a jolt in 2008 when I checked into room 250 at the Serena Hotel. The second I dropped my bag to the floor a huge explosion rocked the building. A suicide car bomber had just blown up inside the gates of the Indian embassy a block away, killing fifty-eight and blowing out the Interior Ministry windows next door. My ears were ringing. Frightened, I went down to the breakfast buffet to see what was going on. The dining room was a madhouse. Muscular security contractors with brush cuts were running out the door holding phones to their ears. I sat at a vacated table and a waiter came over to ask if I wanted coffee or chai.

By 2013, the night skies over Kabul began filling with the window-rattling, deep thump-thump of twin Black Hawk helicopters coming and going from lethal night raids. About the same time, the Taliban decided to begin targeting foreign civilians. Supermarkets were bombed. Americans were kidnapped. Packs of suicide bombers would periodically stream into guesthouses, hotels, small shopping centers, and cafés. Everyone would be shocked, then things would quiet down for a bit and life would resume.

Everything changed in January 2014 when a band of Taliban fighters attacked the foreigners' most beloved restaurant, the Taverna du Liban. The standard security routine for places like Liban was a peephole in a metal door, sometimes two doors separated by a corridor, with armed guards to pat you down and a "gun room" to check your weapon. But if a suicide bomber blew himself up at the entrance, all bets were off. That's what happened. In the chaos after the bomber blasted himself and the guards to pieces, several fighters ran in and went table to table, killing everyone. No one had a weapon to fight back.

The resident representative of the International Monetary Fund in Afghanistan, Wabel Abdallah, was murdered along with two Americans and nineteen others. This marked the end of Kabul's quasi-normalcy. The Gandamack, the journalist watering hole of choice, stayed open, but most everything else shut down.

Saad invited me to stay with him at his family's home in Share-Nau, a classic upper-class, low-rise Afghan home on a quiet street with a well-tended garden full of roses. The house could not have been more secure. The Minister of Finance lived next door, and Saad piggybacked on his extensive security arrangements. The minister had a machine-gun nest on his roof. One day, a tank appeared in front of the garage.

Saad stepped up to fill the social void. His dinners and parties were a mix of diplomats, UN folks, journalists, aid workers, Afghan luminaries, and whomever interesting was passing through town. Whenever an American general would come (and they didn't mind having a drink and a cigar and shooting the shit in the garden), the house would have an extra level of protection. American soldiers lined the street.

Ironically, Moby's profits grew as the country fell into increasing chaos. The programming became more ambitious, ratings remained high, and advertisers continued to line up. The foreign aid–fueled economy was booming and Moby evolved into a sophisticated television operation. As things became more dangerous outside, people were more locked down inside. Might as well watch television. There wasn't much else to do. Television became the window into the world.

Saad remained certain that the Taliban would never take over. "They still haven't taken even one regional capital. Our special forces are on a par with the Navy SEALs," he'd tell me. "Afghans have plenty of experience fighting." So did the Taliban, I'd say.

I would often travel around in Saad's three-car convoy. Like most foreigners, I was increasingly reduced to just peering through the windows of an SUV at the passing parade of people adjusting to permanent war conditions. Outside, where I wanted to be, was dust and crushing poverty and men with weapons, but also perfectly arranged fruit stands, schoolgirls in uniforms, and whiffs of hot naan and spices. Inside the car there was filtered air-conditioning and gunmen. People would stare at the privileged SUVs and sneer. They felt occupied by unseen foreigners and a wealthy elite who never emerged from their vehicles. Who could blame them?

Late at night our little convoy would race in complete darkness through the streets at a hair-raising one hundred kilometers an hour to avoid kidnapping. I'd feel my adrenaline flowing, hoping I was getting away with something. I never felt more alive than in Afghanistan.

CHAPTER FORTY

THE GRAVEYARD OF EMPIRES

"The main instructor of Saad Mohseni is the former head of MTV, Tom Freston." So spoke the Taliban narrator in a diabolical video in 2016. By then I'd been helping Tolo TV for nine years. The hairy insurgents, part religious fanatics, part motorcycle gang, posted the video on their website and Twitter feed. In the 1990s, they banned television. Then they discovered that online video and Twitter were great new ways to terrorize the population. Unfortunately my connection to Saad had captured their attention. "Freston first came to Afghanistan in the seventies as a CIA operative."

There I was in the Taliban production wearing a tuxedo and standing next to Saad and CNN host Fareed Zakaria at the "*Time* 100" dinner in New York City. Next came a clip of me talking about how television could accelerate social change, promoting bad things like "gender equality" and schools for girls. Someone dug deep to find that footage tucked away in a three-hour-long interview from the Academy of Television Arts & Sciences, made when I was inducted into the TV Hall of Fame. Finally, they posted a family snippet, including photos of me with my two sons, Andrew and Gil, and my brother, Bill.

I was just a sidebar in that video, a minor supporting infidel. Its primary evil purpose was to celebrate the Taliban's recent "brave operation," a car bombing that killed seven innocent Tolo employees in a commuter bus. I'd mentored one of them. The video, terror porn essentially, showcased the burning bodies. Zabihullah Mujahid, the Taliban spokesperson, proclaimed that Tolo TV was a "legitimate military target" because its mission was "obscenity, irreligiousness, foreign culture, and nudity. . . . Tolo is an intelligence network opposing our religious and national values." For good measure, he improbably added, it was "a prostitution center."

The Taliban never built anything. But they were canny enough to understand that, while they might wait out the Western presence and regain power, it would be hard to restore their medieval culture if the population got used to entertainment, fun, and freedom. Modernity.

Saad, to whom death threats were a dime a dozen, was all over the video. He wore a suit, led staff meetings, and appeared with "the Jew" Rupert Murdoch. The Taliban claimed Saad had recently become a Jew to get closer to Rupert and promulgate "dirty Jewish culture." The tape was a wanted poster and a death warrant for Tolo. Everyone at Tolo was now under an "execution order." Many parents of the employees began to have second thoughts about their children's careers. My visits to Afghanistan slowed down. Our board meetings moved to the safety of nearby Dubai.

But to the employees the suicide attack had the opposite of its intended effect. Saad told the staff: "They murdered you to silence us, but they will never achieve this evil goal. The voices of those we have lost will not be forgotten, and the voice of Afghanistan will not be silenced by this incident." Morale skyrocketed. The news department was more determined than ever.

Despite massive corruption and failed American policies, good things did happen in those twenty years. Minds were opened, lives were extended, a consumer economy began. Girls went to schools and universities. They became lawyers, parliamentarians, and ambassadors. One cannot overestimate how impactful this new media landscape was in moving Afghanistan into the modern age.

The Taliban were never popular. Study after study showed their support was never higher than 15 to 20 percent, and mostly in the south. But the Afghan government that we supported rated about the same. Citizens saw it as a predatory regime and people were exhausted.

Early on a Sunday morning in August 2021, my girlfriend, Carey Lowell, called me from downstairs at her house in Northern Westchester. "Tom, Tom, get down here right away. Kabul is falling to the Taliban."

I raced downstairs and stared in disbelief at CNN and BBC World News for hours. The Taliban in all their ragged, scowling glory were jammed into a fleet of white Hiluxes and mounted on a swarm of idling motorcycles waiting for orders to enter Afghanistan's capital city. I was heartbroken. My hopes for the country, built on a fifty-year love affair, were evaporating. In New York, the weatherman called it a "Top 10 Day of the Year"—mid-seventies, a brilliant sun, a perfectly clear blue sky, with a slight snap of autumn in the air. Just like 9/11. Our Afghan war would be bookended with perfect New York weather days and two of the most frightening series of images of the twenty-first century: the falling Twin Towers and now hordes of desperate people hanging on to the outside of planes as they raced down the Kabul runway. It was hard for Westerners to comprehend how this lightly armed band of Pashtuns in sandals could take down the best-equipped, most powerful military force in the world. Yes, the British and Soviets had limped out of Afghanistan. But America? With twenty-five NATO allies in tow? The war was fought to a stalemate until Donald Trump basically surrendered the country to the Taliban during his last year in office and set a date for US withdrawal.

Trump didn't even make the US leaving conditional on the Taliban denouncing al-Qaeda, which was why we went there in the first place. After that, it was all logistics. Trump went out and Biden came in, but the policy did not change. America left the Bagram air base in the middle of the night without even a goodbye note. We left behind over a hundred thousand Afghans who had helped us. Then the Afghan government and its extravagantly funded army rolled over.

Afghanistan fell one month short of the twentieth anniversary of 9/11. Once the US committed to pulling out, Taliban emissaries spread across the country to tell civilian and military leaders that the war was lost. "You have been abandoned by the Americans," they said. "No one cares for you any longer; your corrupt government is not worth fighting for and after the Americans leave, we are coming around, so you'd be better off to join us." It was a compelling argument. Biden had claimed that the Afghans did not want to fight for their country. Nothing could've been further from the truth. An unimaginable seventy thousand soldiers and police had been killed. We helped lose the war for them.

I'm no analyst, but I have my own thoughts as someone who was there. We joined forces with the wrong people from the start, the old warlords. At the Bonn Conference in 2004, we strong-armed for an over-centralized government structure in the new constitution. It ignored the reality that this was a country where kinship was more important than anything else. We hired and empowered thugs, criminals, and brutal warlords who were less popular than the Taliban. People assumed they were our representatives. With the hubris and naivete we demonstrated in Vietnam, we flooded the country with soldiers and cash and turned a blind eye to the massive corruption that would delegitimize the government. Let's face it, Americans are not very good at this. In the end, the American way of war, something we model so much of our identity around, begins with blind optimism followed by betrayal. We abandoned thousands who helped us in Vietnam. We abandoned the courageous Kurds twice. Hundreds of thousands of Afghans and their families believed in us and put their lives in danger on our behalf—not just military translators but the larger pool of activists, female judges, NGO workers, teachers, and journalists. They were the brave members of a new civil society, good people who worked hard to bring a sense of justice and order to their country.

I remained speechless that Sunday, shaken to my core. Afghanistan was not my country by birth or residence. But it was the nation of my heart, a place that had never escaped my fascination.

A month earlier, Carey and I had invited Saad to stay with us on Antiparos, a Greek island where we rent a house. He arrived directly from Kabul, never imagining he had just left his country for the last time. He spent much of his days Skyping with news outlets from a room we set up in the basement. When President Ghani would later flee on a helicopter to Uzbekistan with bags of cash, outrunning the Taliban, Saad tweeted he was the "Benedict Arnold of Afghanistan."

On Monday a group of Taliban fighters made it to Tolo's Kabul headquarters. Tolo had been making contingency plans for months, wondering how to keep going. We looked at perhaps transforming into an exile satellite operation from outside the country. Thousands of hours of the programming library had been uploaded to the cloud, away from the Taliban's clutches.

Tolo News remained on the air, bravely reporting on the Taliban takeover. Now the Taliban was at the gate. Ten soldiers were dressed in ripped and dirty clothing. All wielding automatic weapons. The terrified Tolo staff wondered if these were their executioners. But the Talibs said they just wanted to "look around," then asked if Tolo might need any protection, as if they were trying to drum up some business. "No thanks, we can handle it" was the reply. The Taliban emissaries asked for the return of any weapons that had been issued by the government. These were handed over. Strangely, Tolo was told it could keep the rest, a sizable arsenal.

Soon, another Taliban group arrived asking, "Would you please put our official on the air right now?" Khpalwak Sapai led the entourage into the news studio. He sat the official behind the news desk, affixed a microphone, and then brought in an unveiled Beheshta Arghand, Tolo's leading female newscaster, to interview him. The Talib's spine stiffened seeing a woman. He hesitated, but then said to go ahead. Tolo interrupted its programming and cut to the bearded man in a turban. He sat there stone-faced, barely looking at Beheshta. Her hands shook, and she tried to conceal them under the desk.

The Taliban leader said he had a message for the people of Afghanistan. Everything "was going to be okay," he said. Our female newscaster was not impressed. She and eleven other professional women escaped to Albania the next day. Albania turned out to be one of the few heroic actors in the fall of Kabul. The small nation accepted 2,400 Afghan refugees, primarily high-target women—parliamentarians, human rights advocates, political activists—and their families.

Watching the Taliban reassert themselves was deeply painful. There were reprisal killings. People were hung high on cranes with their bodies left to blow in the wind for days. Women, now forbidden to work, were shot at and beaten at protests. Amputations and stonings made a comeback. Thousands of musical instruments were destroyed. Girls over sixth grade were forbidden to go to school. Women were erased from public life.

I worked with several private networks to help evacuate Afghans in peril, keeping people in safe houses and trying to secure visas and transport in the brief window after Kabul fell, but before the entire country completely shut its exits. This unlikely rescue alliance included former military and CIA operatives, entrepreneurs, church groups, private foundations, journalists, and generous philanthropists like Eric Schmidt, Jared Cohen, and Bobby Kotick. They funded charter flights and helped with relocation efforts. Good people did whatever they could. Not surprisingly the US State Department was of zero help. However, Hillary Clinton, the former secretary of state, got her private rescue network going and brought hundreds to safety.

I buttonholed her that August for an hour at a party on Long Island to make the case to evacuate female students at the American University of Afghanistan, a university that had bestowed me with an honorary doctorate in 2021. I had been told they were not on the White House's "final list," the official roster of people to be evacuated in the last days of our airlift. These girls attended the American University; many with scholarships from the American embassy. The Taliban was already targeting them, calling them "wolves." The school had told them to burn all their books and correspondence. But the Biden administration said, "Others had priority." I was out of my mind as I pleaded with Hillary. She understood, but even she had no influence. Biden had turned his back on all things Afghanistan.

Thanks to Hillary Clinton, her top aide, Huma Abedin, and a lot of good-hearted people in and close to Afghanistan, many Afghans whose names were on Taliban kill lists did escape. Including some from AUAF. I hope their heroic secret stories can one day be told in a free Afghanistan.

In May 2023, Saad and I traveled to Albania to personally thank Prime Minister Edi Rama for providing visas to Tolo employees and others on Taliban kill lists. A gracious six-foot-seven giant of a man, he put us up in his guesthouse and told us that the whole thing was easy for him. "These were people in trouble." He then recounted a conversation he had with a high-ranking member of the United Arab Emirates royal family in the wake of America's humiliating Afghan retreat: "To a be a friend of the Americans can be fatal."

CHAPTER FORTY-ONE

BONO THE DIPLOMAT

In early summer 2007, I was in my New York office when I got a call from Paul McGuinness, U2's manager, inviting me to visit him and his wife, Kathy, on the French Riviera. Then he gave me a weather report on U2. "Bono's started up three 'do-gooder' organizations, you know, but they're beginning to run off the rails. It's causing big problems for me and the other three members of the band." I sensed that my invitation might not be entirely social.

U2 always had a strong social bent. Their first hit MTV video was 1983's "Sunday Bloody Sunday," about a civilian massacre by UK security forces in Northern Ireland. After the band's breakout performance at Live Aid in 1985, Bono and his wife, Ali, went to Africa and worked as volunteers in an Ethiopian refugee camp. A million people died from that famine, one of the worst humanitarian disasters of the twentieth century. Bono returned determined to use U2's public platform to support social justice. "At that moment," he once said, "I became the worst thing of all—a rock star with a cause."

In 1997, Bono engaged with the Jubilee 2000 coalition, a movement supported by Pope John Paul II that advocated for debt relief for poor countries at the millennium. Bono studied the issues as if he were a doctoral student, engaged professors and economists as mentors, and became an expert on the issues around debt relief. He lobbied Clinton Treasury Secretary Larry Summers, Republican Senators Jesse Helms and John Kasich, and President Bill Clinton, among many others on the left and right. He could argue his position from economic theories. He could also quote the words of Jesus to Bible Belt conservatives. The showman turned out to be a terrific salesman. He had wit, charm, and sincerity. President George Bush's chief of staff, Josh Bolton, would later tell me, "Bono was the most effective lobbyist I ever met."

The "Drop the Debt" campaign worked. Billions of dollars in old loans from Western powers to African nations were forgiven, freeing up capital to be reinvested locally. Finding success in this first entry into the corridors of power was a bit intoxicating for Bono. In 2002, he cofounded the nongovernment organization DATA—for "Debt, Aid, Trade, Africa." It would address the AIDS crisis and extreme poverty. Bono secured funding from Bill Gates and George Soros, the first in what would become a long line of billionaire benefactors.

"Two and a half million Africans are going to die next year," Bono would say. "All because they have no access to the two little pills a day that could save their lives."

In July 2004, Bono and Bobby Shriver asked me if MTV Networks could run public service announcements about their new ONE Campaign, a bipartisan advocacy organization. ONE's mission was to "fight for a more just world demanding the investments needed to create economic opportunities and healthier lives in Africa." Since ONE formed twenty years ago, the world's poor has been halved, but 60 percent of the remainder live in sub-Saharan Africa.

"We are the NRA for the world's poorest citizens," Bono always says. "Everyone has a lobby but the poor." ONE picked up a million members in just a couple weeks with our PSA support.

Two years later, Bono and Bobby hatched another idea in the AIDS fight, Product (RED). (RED) was ONE's outreach to the private sector offering consumers an opportunity to do good by buying items that contributed to getting antiretroviral drugs into medical clinics in Africa. It partnered with iconic companies like Apple and Starbucks and Bank of America. (RED) funneled the money to the Global Fund to Fight AIDS, Tuberculosis, and Malaria, which ran state-of-the-art clinics that dispensed the coveted pills that kept HIV at bay. The (RED) model is now cited in business schools as a first mover in "social entrepreneurship." Bono enlisted a bevy of big names from George Clooney to Oprah to support it.

Bono was an intrepid lobbyist. He convinced Jesse Helms, the right-wing senator who once decried AIDS as "the gay disease," to change course and vote for President Bush's PEPFAR (President's Emergency Plan for AIDS Relief) legislation, the greatest legacy of that controversial administration. Bono and Helms knelt and prayed together. PEPFAR became the largest health intervention for a single disease in human history. Bono told Bush he should make the pills red, white, and blue so everybody knew they were coming from America. PEPFAR, the Global Fund, and other efforts would save the lives of over 25 million people, the equivalent of the population of Canada.

Bono's activism was extraordinary and U2 supported it, but some of the side effects raised concerns among his bandmates. They were not enthusiastic about seeing pictures of Bono smiling with architects of the Iraq War. They did not appreciate finding Jesse Helms on U2's guest list. Most of all, they wanted their singer to be available at their recording sessions. Bono was exhausted, but didn't want to slow down. He had another idea. Me! His first request, made the morning after I got fired from Viacom, had fallen flat. Now a new seduction was about to begin.

Eze is a picturesque hilltop village between Nice and Monaco. Eze-sur-Mer, its seaside outpost, is right out of Graham Greene. Rock royalty had colonized this coast in the years since the Rolling Stones recorded *Exile on Main St.* there. I walked down the hill to Bono's seaside compound with Paul and Kathy McGuinness. We'd been invited for Saturday lunch. Cicadas droned in the heat. A large table was set out. I saw magnums of rosé on ice. The blues grooves of Ali Farka Touré wafted in the breeze. *Geez*, I thought, *Bono is playing my favorite African music*. It felt like a pitch was coming.

Bono greeted us in shorts, sandals, a wrinkled short-sleeved linen shirt, and a porkpie hat. He extended his arms in greeting. "Come on!" There would be no talk of ONE or (RED) that day. This would be a relaxing, wine-filled Riviera afternoon. We riffed about Afghanistan and what I'd been doing there and he regaled me with tales of his oddball neighbors.

The record producer turned mogul Jimmy Iovine joined us at lunch. So did Bono's Dublin pal Simon Carmody. An unexpected guest, Timbaland, the hip-hop producer and rapper, glided into the Bay of Eze on a two-hundred-foot yacht. Bono, Iovine, Carmody, and I joined him on board with Bono's houseguest, Queen Rania, the glamorous wife of King Abdullah of Jordan. This was turning out to be a hell of an afternoon. We sailed to Cannes and watched Timbaland rock the Riviera in a dance club.

Afterward Bono dragged Simon and me to a low-end, jam-packed disco. "I love Eurotrash," he kept shouting in my ear. Soon, it was 5 a.m. We had been drinking since lunch and I was starting to fade. My shoes were sticking to the floor. It was closing time. Simon, Bono, and I were standing around with a ragged bunch of dishwashers, busboys, and one remaining server who clearly wanted to go home. She took Bono's wineglass and a bouncer came over to politely usher us out. On our way we passed a microphone connected to a karaoke machine. The stadium singer could not resist. "Pick a U2 song," Bono announced. "Any one!" The server chose "I Still Haven't Found What I'm Looking For," a perfect coda for 5 a.m.

The wine-eyed Bono cradled the microphone in a Frank Sinatra pose, tilted his head, and stared at the floor as he launched into a brooding, crooner version of the U2 classic. When he finished, the waitress was the only one clapping. We stumbled into the dawn in hysterics and fell into a waiting car. Simon wanted breakfast, so we went for pancakes and eggs and got back to Eze at 7:30 a.m. People in athletic gear were jogging by as I stumbled my way back up the hill from Bono's house to the McGuinness's. Kathy McGuinness took one look at me, pointed to the stairs, and said, "It's all right, Tom. You're only old once."

At one o'clock that afternoon, Bono was all business. We were back on the patio, me feeling ragged, Bono apparently no worse for wear, Paul McGuinness smooth and composed. Bono went into his pitch about ONE and (RED). *My God*, I thought, *was that entire all-night bacchanal designed to soften me up for this?* I considered that if Bono offered me two aspirin and let me go back to bed, I might say yes to anything.

Bono explained why he wanted me. "Every job you've ever had, everything you've ever done, Tom, has been fun. You are drawn to stuff you really enjoy.

You love Africa, I know. I know anti-poverty work doesn't sound like a lot of laughs, but trust me—you, especially you, will have fun saving the world, and these organizations need a little law and order." Hearing out my host, a friend who had been so generous over the years, I offered what I thought was the best compromise. I agreed to do a three-month review of his entire empire and come back with recommendations as to how to better organize it for success. "I'll take it!" shouted Bono, pounding the table. He wasted no time in setting up a game plan. "For starters, you should go see Condi and Josh right away. Then Pat. Get their sense of what we need to do."

"Who are Condi, Josh, and Pat?"

"I beg your pardon. The US Secretary of State, Condoleezza Rice, and the White House Chief of Staff, Josh Bolton. Pat is Pat Leahy, the senior senator from Vermont, head of the Judiciary Committee."

A child of the sixties, I had always avoided politicians. They had wanted to send me to Vietnam in the sixties and had shut down my business in the late seventies. Next thing I knew, I was dishing with Secretary of State Condoleezza Rice over coffee in her office on the top floor of the State Department. Like everyone I would meet in government, the secretary took Bono and his work seriously and had nothing but compliments for him. She believed that ONE could become a formidable movement. Josh Bolton turned out to be a wonderfully gracious man. His office shelves had Harley-Davidson gas tanks on them, which I found odd but reassuring. Josh was the man who masterfully orchestrated the introduction and interplay between Bono and George W. Bush, a relationship that became essential to the historic PEPFAR legislation. Josh gave me some boxes of White House M&M's, which I still have. Senator Leahy was another good soul and Bono admirer. We were also fellow alumni of Vermont's St. Michael's College. If Rice, Bolton, and Leahy were examples of public servants, I had been writing off a lot of good people for years.

Next came a deep immersion into the ONE, DATA, and (RED) staffs. They were activists, high-minded idealists, a much different breed from their young entertainment business counterparts. They were on a tear to cure injustice and worked harder for less money. Ultimately I made several recommendations including combining ONE and DATA, to make it both a policy shop and a public campaigning organization, and bringing in a DC insider, David Lane, as CEO. Bono accepted my recommendations. He was only hesitant on one recommendation, firing anyone. I overruled, but could see why U2 had maintained its original lineup since high school. He is an exceptionally loyal man.

Mission accomplished, my foot out the door, Bono stopped me with a request. "Be our board chair, Tom." It is very hard to say no to Bono—ONE was a respected, highly effective organization, founded by a man I deeply admired. I said yes. Loyalty is a two-way street.

I'd been enormously affected by the horrifying poverty and suffering I'd seen in my 1970s Asian years and my later work in Burma and war-weary Afghanistan. Some of it was nightmare stuff that haunted me. It opened my heart. I did what I could, but now with ONE I figured I'd have a platform to do something much more impactful. I had a lot to learn about helping move the levers of government and private sector power to address their issues, but the passionate, plugged-in, young activists who had joined Bono on his mission helped me along.

As of this writing, I've been board chair for eighteen years. We've always had a high-voltage, influential board of all political stripes, from former prime ministers and senators to African business leaders.

"We don't want your money, we only want your voice" is what we tell the public. Our funding has come a generous bipartisan array of philanthropists: Bill Gates, Susie Buffett, Howie Buffett, Jeff Skoll, Michael Bloomberg, George Soros, John Doerr, Mellody Hobson, and Sheryl Sandberg among them. Bono and the members of U2 have also been huge contributors.

Sustained social change requires movements, not just a charismatic individual. ONE has worked long and hard to build and motivate an army of activists to ask for justice . . . in person and online. We set up the "ONE Academy" to train activists in North America, Europe, and Africa on how to best apply pressure on governments. We engage with credible, influential African leaders to understand the types of financing needed to achieve healthy lives and economic transformation. We use our Rolodexes to find storytellers to make public-facing campaigns to amplify those messages. We have won countless awards with these campaigns.

I found the best way to get influential people to care about Africa is take them there. They never forget, their hearts open, and they become advocates for life. I've made countless trips—not the Africa of safari parks but the real Africa of health clinics, slums, digital start-ups, brothels, parliaments, government offices, refugee camps, regular farms and solar farms, stock exchanges, coffee plantations, and more.

These would be jam-packed, seven- to ten-day trips. We'd meet a wide range of people—from heads of state to entrepreneurs, local activists, and artists. I've been to half of Africa's fifty-four countries with ONE and (RED). The trips got me closer to our work, made me smarter, and took me to a lot of places I'd dreamed about as a young stamp collector.

They were my first chance to really get to know politicians and, to my surprise, I enjoyed it very much. With men like Bill Frist and Tom Daschle, there was much to admire. John Kasich was intensely curious and most amusing. Sitting next to Mike Huckabee in a van for hours in Rwanda, I discovered that not only was he a decent man but, surprisingly, also a big Kinks fan. One Labor Day in Liberia, we crossed paths with several US senators, including Lindsey Graham and John Thune. I was impressed they were spending their holiday weekend doing the hard work of transversing some of Africa's poorest nations. We threw them a barbecue overlooking Monrovia, Liberia's capital. The next day we all went to meet Ellen Johnson Sirleaf, Liberia's president.

At this event, I saw what made Bono the irreplaceable man. He swept into a large conference room filled with political, business, and military leaders as well as the president. The attention of the whole room shifted toward him, like the listing ballroom of a great ship. He seemed to engage with everyone as he moved through the room, delighted to be there and equipped with all sorts of statistics and knowledge. When the reception ended he took his time moving out to the car that was waiting for him, smiled and waved, and then as the car pulled away, his face changed. He was exhausted and in pain. He fell back on two pillows his staff had borrowed from their hotel to ease the pressure from a back injury that would soon require surgery. He fell asleep for the half hour it took to get to the next stop on the itinerary, where he bounced out of the car smiling like there was nowhere in the world he would rather be.

"If you don't have a seat at the table, you're probably on the menu," Bono said. "In 2050 Africa will constitute one-third of the world's population, but still has no voice." We work hard to get the continent better agency, smarter financing, and improved governance. We advocated successfully to get the Africa Union (AU) a seat at the G20.

Since 2004, ONE has helped secure $1 trillion in new investments for economic opportunities and healthy lives that build a safer, more prosperous Africa. Our activists have taken 25 million actions to create more economic opportunities and support programs that have saved millions of lives from preventable diseases like HIV/AIDS. And we have successfully pushed for Africa's fair seat at the global decision-making table.

We seek to bring together grassroots activists, cutting-edge data analysis, and decades of expertise to build political capital and empower citizens to hold their governments accountable.

(RED), now approaching its twentieth year, has contributed $800 million from sales of (RED) products to The Global Fund.

ONE is now more than twenty years old. Going forward, we face a much less benevolent, more populist world, increasingly ravaged by climate change and conflict. Our job is getting harder. We needed a reinvention. In 2023, I led an eight-month process with McKinsey to reimagine, modernize, and reinvigorate the entire organization. Bono used to whisper to me, "We aren't really ONE, we're just HALF. We're northerners, 'white saviors' trying to fix Africa. That era is over. We need an African takeover." In 2024, I hired our first African CEO, a dynamic, uber-connected social entrepreneur from Lagos, Ndidi Nwuneli. She would take us into new territory as we keep trying to improve the lot of the poor.

For more than sixty years the bipartisan efforts of the American government have made the US the linchpin of the global health and development mission that has driven down poverty levels. The US consistently funded 30 percent of all spending, the largest funder by far. A key to the US effort is USAID, a program that has saved millions of lives in the developing world while strengthening alliances, building political capital, and helping keep expansionist China in check. Though not perfect, USAID was America's leading instrument of soft power.

All of this good work was imperiled in early 2025 when a vengeful Donald Trump returned to the presidency and empowered Elon Musk, the eccentric South African billionaire and world's richest man, to "put USAID in the wood chipper." The new administration set out to destroy America's foreign aid programs—along with many other fundamental federal services. As I write this in the winter of 2025, it is unclear whether the courts and Congress will be able to stop much of the dismantling of the government of the United States. By the time this book is published, the good work of ONE, (RED), and a thousand other organizations may be gutted. If that comes to pass, take this as testimony that there was a time when politicians of different parties and philosophies came together to help the most vulnerable citizens of the planet and, in doing so, served and preserved the highest values of America.

Leading ONE, along with my return to work in Afghanistan, have been my life's most rewarding work. It's a far cry from *Beavis and Butt-Head*, but for me it all fits together. I felt useful and was challenged. Everything I learned along the way from India to Hollywood prepared me to be able to make a significant contribution in the third act of a jam-packed life.

"Pursue what makes you happy, without fear, and don't let it go." Another gem from Joseph Campbell.

CHAPTER FORTY-TWO

CODA

In the summer of 2016, I got a call from Shari Redstone, Sumner's daughter. Shari and I had always remained on good terms. She had finally wrested control of Viacom from Philippe Dauman and had installed herself at the top of her father's empire. She was asking me to return as part of a new slate of directors. "It will be fun," she told me, adding that my firing had been one of Sumner's greatest mistakes.

I thanked her for the kind offer, but declined. So much had changed in ten years that it would be hubris to think I could help fix what was broken. Viacom was like a long-lost girlfriend; after a wonderful first day back, I would remember all too well why we broke up. It was good to be asked, but my only motive for returning would have been vanity. Vanity is the worst reason to do anything.

In April 2024, Shari fired the next CEO, Bob Bakish, and I got another call. "We'd love to have the Godfather back," Charles Phillips, Paramount Global's lead director, told me. "Investors and the creative people would love it." Talk about irony. I said no thanks, again. The past is best left in the past.

I have watched brands, bands, businesses, fads, and even countries rise and fall on the tides of technology, fashion, and politics. Success comes in cycles. It's fleeting. It's almost impossible to stay at the top, no matter how hard you try to prolong it. Life moves on. Things happen to you. It can be humbling. But, like most of us, I tried to roll with the punches and reinvent. I never had a career plan. I was always attracted to creative work.

I never really focused on money. I wanted to be rich in experience, lead an interesting and useful life without compromise, see faraway places I read about as a boy, and leave some good behind. My early bohemian exposure and experiences were invaluable in helping me find my lane and follow my heart. My path has been mostly exhilarating and joyful.

I know a big part of my success was random and had much to do with timing. I was gifted in the birth lottery, born white, male, and in the USA in the middle of the twentieth century, when America was ascendant. Early boomers had the freedom to fail without huge consequences. I could get a master's degree and tend bar in resort towns, then get and quit a job on Madison Avenue to roam across the world at a time when most countries were wide-open. I could raise money for a risky import business and live very well in Asia for years. I could talk my way into a television start-up with zero TV experience and go on to conquer the world. For a third act, I could return to Asia and Africa to use my skills for greater good.

I have mostly had a good life. It has been the interesting and improvised life I had hoped for. I got to do a lot of things with people I liked. I always had intention, and I was tenacious. If you are flexible and curious and have a sense of humor, you can do well in this world and create your own destiny. I give gratitude every day. I have two loving sons, Andrew and Gil; and a wide-ranging circle of friends all over the world.

I have also had my share of failures and heartbreak. My marriages to Margaret, mother of my two sons, and Kathy, both once loving relationships, ended in painful divorces. My parents left Bill and me way too early. And my beloved brother, Bill, died unexpectedly after a traumatic fall in the Caribbean. It has not all been a steady upward road; more a crooked, winding path with missteps and a lot of vigorous work. I have seen many people I loved die early, unexpected deaths that would remind me to take nothing for granted—especially time.

At the end of the summer of 2023, I spent days at the bedside of my dear friend and fellow buccaneer Jimmy Buffett. He asked his wife, Jane, to keep the "party going," and she carefully invited his closest friends to a series of farewell lunches and dinners at their Sag Harbor home. I reassembled our original Timbuktu expedition crew to see him off from this world. Chris Blackwell flew up from Jamaica. Bono sent a poetic tribute taped in the Matisse chapel in France. Paul McCartney sat on the balcony outside Jimmy's bedroom and sang "Blackbird" to him—"Take these broken wings and learn to fly." Jimmy said he loved us.

Nothing made by humans lasts forever. Nothing good and nothing bad.

To anyone of my generation reading this: Congratulations, you were born at the right time. I hope you made the best of it. I hope you were able to realize some good fortune and help others less fortunate than yourself. To anyone younger: You, too, can invent your own life. Don't let anybody tell you otherwise. The circumstances may be different, but you can prosper, revel in the excitement of living fully, and learn from failures.

It won't be until you get close to the end that you'll know how lucky you were.

ACKNOWLEDGMENTS

I owe much gratitude to the many people who helped make this book possible.

First up is my friend and fellow traveler, Graydon Carter, who gave me my initial writing assignment twenty years ago for *Vanity Fair*, followed by others. His regular hectoring—"not a business book . . . make it something more amusing"— finally got me over the line to commit to write this.

I owe an enormous debt to my longtime friend and former colleague Bill Flanagan. Bill is a man of many talents: television producer, journalist, novelist, musicologist, and disc jockey extraordinaire. He has also been my long-suffering editor who has worked on all kinds of assignments with me. As I worked intermittently on this manuscript, Bill patiently and faithfully gave me wise counsel and made things a lot better than they might have been.

My good friend, literary agent Binky Urban, was another who pushed me over the starting line. Without her persistence, encouragement, and insights, I never would've finished this. Binky also had the good sense to introduce me to Lyric Winik, who helped tighten my manuscript into a more flowing narrative.

I am especially indebted to Aimée Bell, the brilliant Editorial Director at Gallery Books. Aimee sensed a better story beyond the bold names of my MTV Networks and Viacom career. Her enthusiasm, grasp of detail, and wisdom made this a pleasure. She works in great company with the Gallery Books team of professionals including Jen Bergstrom, Sally Marvin, Jill Siegel, John Paul Jones, Caroline Pallotta, and Sierra Fang-Horvath.

Thank you, Jill Lumpkin, Mike Dolan, Amy Stofsky, and the rest of the gang at Hindu Kush for all those years. Blessings to Joe Potter, my longtime friend and business partner who passed years ago, way before his time. Nothing at Hindu Kush would have worked without our deep friendship and his continual optimism and determination.

I owe a great debt to the late Khub Chand Sawhney, my Indian partner, guiding light, and guru of sorts in the very foreign India of the 1970s. Also, to his ever-capable nephew, Chander Sawhney, maybe India's hardest working man. Thanks for all those years of hustle . . . for all the laughs and for getting us out of so many jams.

To Aquil and Khial Mohammad, my delightfully entertaining Afghan partners. I looked and looked for you when I returned in 2007, but there was not a trace. I hope you are out there somewhere and have had good lives.

I mixed with a constant parade of curious and creative souls from all over the world in my twenty-six years at MTV Networks and Viacom. Many remain in my closest circle of friends: Judy McGrath, John Sykes, Bob Pittman, Mark Rosenthal, Bill Flanagan, Doug Herzog, Van Toffler, Sara Levinson, Fab 5 Freddie, Matt Stone, Mark Booth, Gerry Laybourne, Bob Friedman, Jason Hirschhorn, Cyrus Oshidar, Nusrat Durrani, Alex Kuruvilla, Carole Robinson . . . I could go on and on. What a ride we all had.

I am ever grateful to Oprah Winfrey and Shane Smith, two names you'll rarely see in the same sentence. Thank you for bringing me on board to help guide your groundbreaking media ventures. The same for my old friends Joe Ravitch and Jeff Sine, who started The Raine Group merchant bank and brought me on as a Senior Advisor.

To my good friend and fellow traveler Saad Mohseni . . . thanks for bringing me back to my beloved Afghanistan. You and your team really did bring light to the darkness, and your impact lingers. May the curse of the Taliban be lifted once again from your country.

Thanks for the ride, Bono. Besides all the music and poetry, you have done so much good in this world. Your friendship, generosity, and inspiration have been constant. You are tireless and always keeep pushing. You make do-gooding fun. Thank you, too, to Ndidi Nwuneli, and all the ONE-sters and board members who continue to push ONE's mission forward.

U Ohn Maung and Misuu Borit . . . we were fated to meet. Thanks for letting me dig deeper into your beautiful country. May you both be well and may the continuing nightmare of Burma soon be over.

Peter and Dennis from 1972 . . . wherever the hell you are and whatever your full names may be, thanks for the lifts and the laughs. I hope your lives have turned out well.

Thank you, Phil Stutz, for the clarity and encouragement.

To Diane Cassara, my ever-faithful assistant for decades, thank you for running the show so smoothly, protecting me, and keeping my worst instincts at bay.

Thank you, Jimmy and Jane Buffett, for your close friendship and incredible generosity all these years.

To my loving mom and dad, who started it all, and to my hilarious and beloved younger brother, Bill, our family historian. I cannot believe you are gone. I miss you every day.

To my sons, Andrew and Gil, you have my complete love and respect for whom you have become. It has been a joy to watch you grow and find your place, becoming, among other things, accomplished travelers and kind citizens of the world.

Last, to Carey Lowell, my girlfriend and partner of many years. You have brightened my world in so many ways. A more loving and capable person I have yet to meet. No one makes me laugh like you.

Music has been such a powerful force in my life. I would be remiss not to thank all the musicians out there for all the joy and inspiration I enjoy every day.